Earthen Vessels

--- True Adventures Obscured By Time ---

Allen James Gourley

By:

Allen James Gourley

Rain Falling On Bells

"EARTHEN VESSELS"
[Author's Manuscript] February 1, 2020

Original RFOB Copyright © 2013 by Allen James Gourley.

Registration Number: TXu 1-861-147
Effective Date: April 1, 2013

All rights reserved. No part of this publication may be reproduced, distributed or transmitted in any form or by any means, including photocopying, recording, or other electronic or mechanical methods, without the prior written permission of the publisher, except in the case of brief quotations embodied in critical reviews and certain other noncommercial uses permitted by copyright law. For permission requests, write to "Attention: AUTHOR," at the web address: **www.rainfallingonbells@gmail.com**

To Order: WWW.AMAZON BOOKS.COM

Special discounts may be available on quantity purchases.

Publisher's Note: Some names, characters, places, and conversations are a product of the author's imagination. Locales and public names are sometimes used for atmospheric purposes. Any resemblance to actual people, living or dead, or to businesses, companies, events, institutions, or locales may be completely coincidental, or, obscured by time.

All Biblical Verses Used Are From The King James Version [KJV] of the Bible.

"Earthen Vessels" / *Allen James Gourley, Author*

Special Heartfelt Thanks:
Overview: Mrs. Rose Magness, Mrs. Erin Joyce
1st Edit: Mrs. Faith Gourley, Mr. Larry Gourley
2nd Edit: Mrs. Tiffany Gourley Carter, Esq., Mrs. Domino Kimiko Cohn, CFII
Proof Edit: Mrs. Tiffany Gourley Carter, Esq.
Final Edit:

Author's Manuscript Version

ISBN: 9781729509104

IV

Dedication

God Almighty has blessed me with the most wonderful family -- my parents, brothers and sisters -- on both sides of the water. Without them all would surely have been lost.

My beautiful wife has loved me without regard to my quirkiness and foibles, and through many cold winters and delayed springs, she has graced me with her unwavering love. Her gift of three loving, energetic and brilliant children keep both of us alive and dancing into the future.

And dance we shall, into our blessed and joyful future as
Children of Light.

DISCLAIMER

It is vitally important to clarify that some of these stories have been condensed for brevity. Some people's names have been changed or obscured so as to keep them protected from past indiscretions and or future mistakes.

It is not now, nor has it ever been, my place or intention to hurt or cause harm to anyone. If for any reason some of these stories appear to do so, I apologize and beg forgiveness. Back-in-the-day things were accepted as common that are considered foul, wrong, or mean in this current day and age. I only ask you to accept this apology in advance and give me – and time – the benefit of the doubt.

I know this at times reads as some form of an autobiography. With so many years having passed, events must have the allowance of obscured dialogues, timelines, places, names of people, locales, companies, and other events, which - to be honest - have gone astray and sometimes are jumbled and intermingled as memories often are. To call this a true autobiography would be an injustice to that specific category of writing. Instead, let's kindly refer to this work as "nonfiction".

Places and timelines have been allowed the margin of error that time itself causes. Memories fade and order of events are lost in the shuffle of a lifetime of interactions with loved ones, acquaintances and friends. Conversations -- although having the intent of creating the scenario of forming an accurate picture -- are not verbatim or true quotes of those involved. My wish is to help paint a mosaic of what was going on at that point along the way.

I am simply telling some of the profoundly odd and eclectic events that have found their way into my life. Adventures that often read like an "American Odyssey Gone Wondrously Astray".

From my birth in the late 1950's to Present, I have enjoyed true intentions of doing no harm. Yet, I would be remiss in claiming any such thing. All humans make mistakes, some for pure reasons and others by careless interactions with others. I am no exception. Forgive me for my frailties and my carelessness, for my inattentiveness and lack of decorum.

This ink on paper journey honestly omits the raging craziness so endemic to the late 1970's and through the 1980's. If you wish to see, read, or hear what that era was like feel free to listen to any of a thousand Rock 'n' Roll songs of those "lost years". They give a profound truth of the goings on more authentic and accurate than I can ever transcribe or put forth. I have purposely left that era to others for I wish not to participate or promote such foolish shenanigans any longer. Maybe age allows for a touch of wisdom to appear even in the most wayward of souls after all.

Please enjoy walking a few miles in my shoes...

God Bless,

The Author

CONTENTS:

Prologue: *"Time allows a perspective previously unknown"*

- 1: Bandit Warriors
- 2: The Valley
- 3: New Eden
- 4: Higher Learning
- 5: 1956 Kilauea Avenue
- 6: Sport Of Kings
- 7: Changes
- 8: What Happened To Fifi?
- 9: Brothers And Sister
- 10: My Sansei Princess
- 11: The Incredible Quest For Surf
- 12: Umi-Gumi-Ungawa
- 13: Santa Has A Balloon
- 14: First Time Dead
- 15: Jan Ken Po
- 16: Two Worlds
- 17: Trillion Little Things
- 18: A Mean Squeegee
- 19: Pathways In The Sky
- 20: Buying Eden
- 21: Second Time Dead
- 22: The Liberators
- 23: Spirit Of Adventure
- 24: Distant Shores
- 25: Earthen Vessels

Epilogue: *"Searching for Paradise can be such an adventure ... "*

Prologue

* * * * * * *

"Time allows a perspective previously unknown."

AJG 2019

* * * * * * *

I've had people of all ages sit in stunned silence after telling them a single episodic event, just one tiny snippet of a portion of a day in my life. Little did they know that not only had I left out the most intimate details, the oddly strange mitigating factors and the true motivations behind the characters captured within that very same story. But, in fact, I'd left out two critical elements as well: how outrageous the situation had truly been, and even more audacious, how the story had a life of its own, and how it would eventually play out during the course of time.

Time is barbaric in its cruelty when it comes to time and the human condition. It tends to slowly, violently consume all you love. Yet, time allows for two redeeming joys – the benefits of acquiring a true and deep lasting love while also obtaining an absolute touch of divine wisdom never before experienced.

In these stories of souls I've encountered, being both friends and family, I will do my best to stay true to a course of factual indifference. Enhancement is rarely needed because these tales are told downstream far enough to have decades skewer some of the pertinent details and jumble the facts. Please allow me the grace of choosing in favor of love and kindness over angst and pain. This journey may be a bit off-kilter. And, at times, will appear as an odyssey far beyond normalcy along rarely traveled byways.

With this rambling introduction imperfectly transcribed, I'll attempt to tell this epic tale as best I can with total disregard for standard operating procedure or accomplished pen. It is only honorable to keep some people, companies, and locales private, so I've taken the liberty of changing certain names and places which is only fitting and proper. They most certainly would want such courtesy.

First I'll introduce an event, person or circumstance thrust into my world by GOD ALMIGHTY'S outstretched providence and how that situation impacted my own personal adventure called life. Then, at some point in time I'll give you, "the rest of the story," to quote one of my all-time favorite radio personalities, Mr. Paul Harvey.

Should you care to go on this joyful journey with me, please allow me to start our travels by telling you about growing up on a rather unique farm captured within the misty hills of Western Pennsylvania. And, how from those humble beginnings, I took a non-lineal pathway into this crazy sojourn I've chosen to embrace, which at times became rather rugged. However, more often than not, the path shimmered pristine with joys abounding!

*Yet, in every instance, these are **true adventures obscured by time** ...*

1

Bandit Warriors

Saturday morning. February 1st, 1969. Cold. Grey. Dull. Frozen. No snow on the ground - but flurries coming and going all morning.

Like every other Saturday, chores were expected to be completed without any snot-nosed-back-lip or waver. We lived on a rural farm in Western Pennsylvania, and as such, work was both obvious and endless.

* * * * * * *

Long before Gortex, Thermal Insulate© and waterproof everything, all of us "farmers" had learned to cope by donning gumboots, two pairs of cotton socks, double-layered gloves, a hooded parka under a heavy coat, and little else. Wind-burned nose and cheeks only accentuated the country naiveté that was so easily displayed in everything we spoke or did on a daily basis.

Being the youngest of five, my chores were the leftover remnants of items too menial for my older brothers to concern themselves with. They'd send me to feed the cattle six to eight bales of hay. I'd check the water in the trough, often breaking the frozen ice to allow the inflow. The cows needed twenty shovel-fulls of chop, spread so they all got some -- not just the mean and nasty ones often snorting, prancing about and seemingly perpetually ticked off. The pigs got two bags of corn, but we couldn't get too attached. They would become bacon and sausage by Tuesday morning.

The biting wind chill would immediately change the feel of being outdoors from almost bearable to absolutely brutal. The old bank barn had many a slot to allow the cold to penetrate deeply, but the slats kept the wind at bay just enough not to destroy you. It was hard not to notice that the semi-frozen muck in the stalls needed some straw. A few bales of last year's wheat stubble needed to be spread about as well, but that meant unhitching the gate and braving the herd...

It seemed like we always had the cattle no other farms wanted -- the ornery critters sent to slaughter at my father's meat packing company. Sold for a corporate check, the wretched beasts were quickly rendered into burger and steaks for the local communities' general stores and Mom & Pop Shops that dotted the map along the back roads. In every tiny village, if there were more than six houses, one of them surely contained an enterprise of one type or another. All of them sold meat off a square oak butcher block in the back behind a smeared glass case showing off that day's offerings. The cash register was always overseen by a weathered soul willing to discuss all topics with claims of infinite wisdom devoid of need for facts or banter.

Spreading straw for bedding often became a life-threatening event. Unfamiliar cattle distrusted any type of interloper. Snorting with frosted breath, they looked at any human as an immediate threat. I, me, all 65 pounds – maybe 70 -- of me with manure stuck to my boots and extra clothing, just simply doing my best to survive the chore assigned, was Public Enemy Number 1. I'd learned never to corner any animal larger than myself. That's when they felt most threatened. It was the surest way to trigger a violent response like getting yourself stomped to death by a half-ton monster hell-bent on self-preservation with nowhere to go.

If there was ever a lesson that needed to be followed, it was my father's sage counseling: "Son, you need to be smarter than the cow."

This very day I had tremendous incentive to follow those wise words. It was not just any nasty winter's morning frozen in the outskirts of civilization on the fringe of the Appalachian Mountains.

No!

It was special, for today I turned 11. For my birthday I had talked Dad into something awesome for achieving such a ripe-old-age. If I'd be willing to spend a "bit" of my savings, he'd put up the rest of the funds needed to buy what I really wanted. Not a bicycle, even though I'd outgrown mine. Or a Red Wagon Radio Flyer. Heck, I'd gotten one of those back when I was just a kid. And, as every *real boy* knew, action figures like G.I. Joe were "boy-dolls" for "city-sissies". My older brothers made sure I knew this; after all, they did not want to be known for having a sissy younger brother.

No!

I wanted what every male child with a single ounce of Mario Andretti in them longed for -- a go-cart with a 5hp *Briggs & Stratton* engine! Something that would go at such speeds that time itself would cease to function! I wanted speed that flung gravel on every corner, with the sound of burning hydrocarbons.

We unloaded the go-cart off the back of the pickup later in the day. Dad showed me how to get it started. Then, smiling immensely, he allowed his 11-year-old son to grasp the wheel and blast down the driveway at speeds never before achieved in mankind's existence. That singular act made me feel two feet taller, and in and of itself, would change the course of my trajectory forever!

Yet, there are some things that are even more dangerous than four wheels and readily available horsepower. That very year my older brother, Keith… well… he got a stopwatch. And, when we put the two together, well, let's just say years of vehicular mayhem and toys gone rogue ensued.

* * * * * * *

Seems like being behind the wheel for me was as natural as flight for a bird.

I don't remember learning how to drive. I've been told that as a youngster I was often stood up on the seat of the old narrow front end Farmall H tractor. Dad would put my hands at ten and two on the steering wheel, idling through a freshly baled field. The older fellows would toss bales onto the wagon while the tractor put-putted between the rows. Upon reaching the end of the field, Dad would get up on the back, put his arm around me, swing the wheel, and start the next run. Tossing bales into the tractor was brutal work and required real stamina of the farm hands, but I must've been having a ball. I don't remember those times. After all, I was probably all of four years of age.

Having learned to do four-wheel drifts behind the wheel of the go-cart years earlier, a progression to ever-faster toys naturally occurred. My older brother Keith, wholeheartedly embracing noise, speed, and power, picked up a heavy metal beast of a bike known as a Kawasaki 500 street racer. It had an uncanny ability to loosen your shoulder sockets with wicked-fast acceleration. Following a mechanic's suggestion, Keith lowered the teeth count on the front sprocket so he could dominate in his class at the local drag strip.

Good old Nu Be Drag Strip was a mixture of mayhem and beer that unceremoniously announced the weekend with thundering blasts of real smoke and false glory. Bravado and minimal attention to rules or decorum orchestrated the day's events. Church-skipping and smoking the tires resulted in cancerous clouds of blue dust, perfect on any summer Sunday morning, with the coveted winner's t-shirt given out at the end of the day to the fastest racer to wear for bragging rights

Even though I was far too young to race, I did run after run. When the owner found out I was somewhere around fourteen, he excluded me from competing. But he allowed me to continue doing burnouts and trial runs. I guess he didn't want me flaunting a class winning t-shirt amongst my underage friends in the event I actually won. I was not exactly sure how this was allowed under the umbrella of his insurance, but it was certainly a compromise I could embrace.

After the hundredth run, I learned that I could sit on the gas tank and drop the clutch precisely as the drag racing Christmas Tree of lights lit green. Feathering the clutch, I was able to punch-flight a wheelie to the very edge of oblivion!

Although I didn't have enough weight to keep the back tire fully engaged, I was a sight to behold and one of the rowdy crowd's favorites. Keith always had a few thousandths of a second shaved off of his time. It was his bike, so it was to be expected.

Keith was also four years older, and he let me know routinely lest I ever forget. He got the t-shirt I so coveted.

I'd 'borrow' Keith's bike to drive myself the seven miles to school. He was putting in long days at work while his bike sat there taunting me with its power. Age meant little in our neck of the woods. To go unnoticed by local law enforcement I'd park up on Penn Street, in the 'more affluent' part of our small town. After a hard day of learnin' next-to-nothin' and goofing off with my hoodlum friends, the race to setting a new record home was on.

Racing home was an in-house right-of-passage. Or, to be more exact, we felt it as a divine calling, our natural heritage, for growing up in the rolling forested hills of Western Pennsylvania. It was a spiritual practice to embrace the reality in which we lived.

Old Route 839 was a broken paved road with loose gravel and dust-covered corners and even a few off-kilter reverse-banked turns along the way. In the 70's, the entire route of asphalt was beaten to smithereens by coal trucks and heavy farm equipment. Usual time on a normal day: 10 to 12 minutes, give-or-take. As a means of comparison, top speed in Keith's Chevy Camaro was a hair over 6. Being an aspiring road warrior and wishing to declare myself the fastest human being who'd ever braved our local back roads on a tri-cylinder Kawasaki 500, I fixed Keith's stopwatch on the gas tank with some black electrical tape.

Anytime you get 105 mph before you leave the Borough (a 25 mph zone), you know things are on a trajectory that precludes common sense and normalized outcomes! That day, after flaunting the rules of both law enforcement and angular momentum, I arrived in our driveway at the infamous Milk House Turn. Upon reaching my singular goal, I stopped and sat up straight with hands quivering from a particularly well-focused death grip on the handlebars- surprisingly alive and sweating self-induced bullets. I punched the stop button and delaminated the watch from the tank -- I had made it home in just a shade over 4 minutes!

As Keith would say, "You just used one of your nine lives!"

Growing up with speed-driven brothers -- finely tuned driving exhibitionists that they were -- created a dynamic of constant challenges of brother vs. brother. That very same dynamic often forced me to use nine lives daily, especially growing up where speed limits were for fools and the laws of physics were stretched to Newtonian extremes on a moment-by-screeching-moment basis. Upon a not-so-rare occasion, I'd burn through the proverbial allotment in an outrageous burst of intense speed, along Pennsylvania's broken roads with clouds of dust blowing skywards into the tree canopy far above.

I arrived home alive. My parents seemed happy to see me in one piece and ready to embrace the evening's chores. As for me, I was happy that I had a few extra minutes to get all of the chores done before *The Addams Family* came on. Mum set the table with large glasses of Carson's raw milk with the cream stirred in. Her finest roast, last summer's frozen sweet corn, and freshly bought potatoes placed on the well-used table for us youngsters, aspiring *bandit warriors*, a reality we embraced oh-too-easily.

* * * * * * * *

How we ever survived to become "productive" members of society I shall never know. I presume it was because of the prolific prayers our parents cast towards heaven that we would quit being the people they'd warned us about. They begged for us to embrace a future that included living to a ripe old age by acquiring the desire to live beyond the next hell-bent blast down a highway to nowhere.

*Obviously, G*od *had a plan in place from the very beginning, or these stories would never be told.*

2

The Valley

"Eventually we'll probably get shot for this..."

AJG / 1971-1976

* * * * * * *

Mr. Rantjowlski emerged from his locker room office dressed in an RVHS track red and white t-shirt, complete with pressed shorts and whistle. Everyone called him Rant Man, except to his face. If you did that, he'd have you by the neck and slam you against the gymnasium's wall. Then he'd send you off to the office with terse instructions for ten swats and three detentions.

Rant Man was carrying a clipboard with that period's roll call and corresponding check boxes to be filled in with bright red zeroes or ones. His presence was overwhelming and his methods legendary. A natural born drill sergeant, he used his whistle like a battering ram and his mouth like a weapon of warfare screaming barbaric insults likened to sustained cannon fire.

Tenth grade gym class was awesome, unless you weren't a superior athlete known as a Gold Shirt. Then it was brutal and rather sadistic. Rant Man had everyone labeled, categorized, and separated by genetic disposition, intelligence, and ability to perform whatever he demanded instantly without waver or back-lip.

I was a Gold Shirt, and I had great empathy for anyone who wasn't.

"OK, Sawdust-in-Hamburger, you're a captain today." He had started calling me Sawdust-in-Hamburger back in eighth grade as an off-the-wall homage to my Dad owning a meat packing company, claiming I'd gotten my athletic prowess by shoveling sawdust into our hamburger products. He thought it was funny. Me, not-so-much. "Armpit-of-Italy, you're the other captain," referring to another one of the Gold Shirts. Joey hailed from Putneyville, located on the Mahoning Creek, tucked in below Seminole, and was populated by generations of Italians who worked the deep underground coal mines that set just above it on the ridgeline. Putneyville would forever be known as Seminole's Armpit. Seminole would forever be known as an extended version of the *Godfather's* organized crime family. Although, the Seminolians, were never able to be organized for much of anything, other than bonfires and keggers.

He blew the whistle loud enough to make our ears sing "Hallelujah." We all instantly lined up, not risking setting him off, and began the usual drill: calisthenics of thirty jumping-jacks, twenty full body stretches of toes to sky, ten pushups and twenty sit ups. Good form or we'd be sent on laps around the half-gym (the girls controlled the other side of the full-wall divider). Three sets, then we faced whatever "activity" he thought we should be playing; one never knew exactly what type of highly modified sport Rant Man would devise to make us sweat, and on a regular basis, cuss and bleed red to match the bulldog on the side of the gym.

Taking an interest in two of the kids jostling for position, "Give me twenty-five you jokers!" He proceeded to count them out. The rest of us never missed a beat. As we did our exercise routine, Rant Man walked past us and checked the boxes on his clipboard. Even after years of being victims of his class, not one of us had an inkling how he graded.

"Sawdust, you start. Make your first pick." I chose Mikey and Joey moved on to make his pick as Rant Man continued, "Today we'll be playing Commando Basketball. Nothing's out of bounds; walls and ceiling are in play. No fouls will be called. No kicking the ball or punching the other side's players. Keep your elbows in or you'll be benched and accordingly docked." Then Rant Man got his trademark wicked-drill-sergeant-smile on as he added, "Dribbling is optional and there will be zero tolerance of tackling, intentional tripping or tearing shirts off of your opponents.

"Sawdust you'll be the 'Intellos'; Armpit you'll be the 'Tards'." He thought he was being so clever shortening my team name from the 'Intellectuals' and the Joey's team as the 'Retards'. It was in many ways crazy inappropriate. "Winners go straight to the locker room early, losers do twenty laps.

"Everybody showers! I've been getting a lot of crap from the teachers about sending stinky students back into the general population. Use soap you pack of pig farmers. Nobody likes foul smelling deadbeats emanating body odors like a barnyard stall sitting amongst them.

"Tards are on the wrestling room side. Intellos you've got the doors."

Grabbing a basketball, we took our opening jump ball positions. Rant Man blew his whistle to make it official and threw the ball straight into the air. The game began!

Armpit immediately fouled me on the jump and fed the ball to his best player, who promptly sprinted towards our hoop. Dribbling was optional, so he just bulldozed his way to the basket. Then, while going for the layup, he got pulverized by his best friend. Well, that is, best friend everywhere except on this court at this exact moment in time. After all, rules were rules, even if there weren't any.

"Come on you frozen amoebas, hustle like the Nazis are shooting at your elderly grandmothers!" Rant Man screamed directly at a couple of the fat kids. Then he lifted his clipboard and made marks beside their names.

Rant Man, looked over at Smythe sitting on the bench waiting to get his chance on the Tard team and barked, "What happened to your intellectually challenged cohort in crime? Saw him limping to the nurse's office. What do you know, Klepto?" Smythe's forever nickname, short for Kleptomaniac, had been earned back in 9th grade after being caught sneaking out of the equipment room with a stopwatch hidden in his mouth.

"He climbed the rope, sir."

"And? Then what happened you hairy-backed moron?" Rant Man referred to Smythe's fur covered back that hadn't allowed a t-shirt to touch his skin for years. "Two plus two equals four. I want the rest of the equation, Klepto. You don't go to the nurse because you climbed the rope." Rant Man demanded a better answer from a kid that just generally pissed him off.

"Well, he got to the top, didn't know what to do. So he shouted down and asked, 'what's next? How do I get down?' And Nutz yelled out, 'LET GO!', so he did, Mr. Rantjowlski, sir. Bounced pretty high too." Klepto giggled as he said it. "During his fall, he tried to grab the rope on the way down and burned his hands pretty good, sir. That and his black and blue butt sent him to the nurse, sir."

The whistle fell right out of Rant Man's mouth and his jaw went slack as he once again stood stunned-amazed at how flamingly stupid his current batch of students were. He looked Klepto square in the eyes and offered his impolite observation of his batch of hoodlum friends.

"That's why you'll forever be a Tard. All of your friends are Tards, and you infantile batch of juvenile delinquents will probably have your future class reunions in some federal prison facility! Now get in there and show me what you've got!"

He traded him in mid-game for one of the other players on Armpit's team, who came out foaming at the mouth and gasping for air.

"Twenty-five, baby!" Rant Man barked after seeing how out-of-shape he was, not letting up a single ounce on any of his tortured subjects.

We got our collective butts kicked by the opponent's brutal assaults, losing by a hefty margin. Once again, Joey's team reinforced the reality that brawn beats brains when it comes to heavy lifting and Commando Basketball. He had, after all, picked most of the front line of the football team as his starting lineup. I think half of the Tards owned t-shirts -- their claim to fame -- that summed it all up:

+++ CAPABLE OF LIFTING HEAVY OBJECTS +++

Twenty laps later we had exactly three and a half minutes to shower (with soap) and sprint to our next classes. As for Rant Man and his barbaric practices -- racist, crude, foul, obscene, wicked, off-color humor wrapped in torture and bizarre nicknames that haunted kids into their older years -- it was still the most fun class I may have endured in my entire life, bar none.

We all loved Rant Man's outlandish gym class and really looked forward to it twice a week: pure adrenaline-pumping, politically incorrect warfare, with instantaneous insults evenly distributed to every soul present. Fifty minutes of disturbed mayhem and orchestrated chaos, sadistic to the bones. For us teenage boys, it was flat out awesome!

* * * * * * *

"Eventually we'll probably get shot for this..." Cheekz deadpanned over his shoulder as we hid out in the darkened auditorium waiting for the announcements to end. Automatically, even in the dark by ourselves, we stood and recited the Pledge of Allegiance with the rest of the school as the young lady got to that portion of the morning's routine. We were perpetually late our senior year, so we snuck in the side door, intercepted the 9th Grader with the 'Absentee Students List,' crossed off our names, and waited it out for the first bell to ring in the back row of the auditorium.

It was a simple and elegant plan that worked perfectly day after day.

Officially, we never missed a day, or were tardy.

Zero repercussions.

Stealth on stealth.

"So, where are you going to college?" Cheekz made conversation.

"Keep a secret?" I answered as we sat in the dark. The cracks of the main doors allowed vertical slivers of brilliant light into the vast vacant space, giving a strangeness of lint being illuminated and slowly falling through the darkness.

"I've been accepted to the University of Hawaii, but only my parents know."

"And they're OK with that?!" Cheekz spit out. He was in shock.

"Dad is. Mum... not so much..." I allowed my response to trail off into the vapid dark expanse all around. "Did you get into Grove City?"

"Yea. Sounds feeble after what you just told me." Cheekz, an only child, couldn't believe what I'd just told him. As he continued processing the wildly different trajectories we were on, he proceeded, "Going to take business and finance. Dad wants me to run the office after I get out. Mom wants me to find a wife. They both think a Christian college will save me from myself... Doubt it."

"Ought to make you a pile of money, Cheekz. That's cool."

"Not as cool as Hawaii. Man, I'll have to come see you after you get settled in." Cheekz saw the bright side once the possibilities became apparent.

Suddenly all of the lights came on and the doors flew open! Unbeknownst to us, it was sixth orientation field trip day. And, by default, we were caught directly in its pathway. Fortunately the first ones into the auditorium were the highly animated munchkins flowing into the space. As we let ourselves out the backstage door, we saw a few of our senior classmates climbing the ladder to get above the stage and onto the catwalk system. That interwoven network went all the way across the auditorium, suspended out of sight and above the ceiling. It provided maintenance for the heating, sound, cooling, electrical and other needed conduits.

Going up there was a right-of-passage for anyone 'in-the-know'. A whole lot of shenanigans occurred up there - from partying to making out with an adventuresome babe. It was a place nobody ever checked on. Cheekz and I laughed when we saw who it was -- a couple of yip-yips who would be on Armpit's team of Tards if this were gym class. Cheekz and I expertly slid back into the general population of RVHS as the bell rang and our first period study hall began.

So far, our morning schedule of hiding-in-plain-sight was in perfect harmony with our lack of desire to do anything but exactly what we wanted to do.

We were seniors, and this was our world. Known to us as "The Valley".

One of the main reasons Cheekz and I were hanging out so much was that we'd both ended up with the same absurd schedule: back-to-back study halls, first two periods of the day. It gave us almost two hours of uninterrupted doing-nothingness. So, being innovative and bored we maximized our unique skill sets as well as our pleasure. With total contempt for the system, and being from The Valley, we simply went and got breakfast.

Brazen disregard for policy, we'd saunter out the most obvious door in the dead center of the school, cross the road, take the alley to Cheekz' house - since both of his parents worked - and cook some eggs, bacon and toast. We'd eat an awesome hot meal and tune into *Sesame Street* on TV, which was broadcast smack dab in the middle of our allotted timeline.

Perfect.

Afterwards, we'd saunter right back along the exact same path we'd taken, cruise right into school during the chaos of class change between bells and reenter our world of getting through our final year of high school.

Most times the school lunches sucked, but since we had a big home cooked breakfast, they were way more survivable on full stomachs. Yet, this particular day, our lunch was rife with wild conversation of what had occurred mere minutes after we'd exited the premises to do our thing.

"Hey! Do you think he's dead?" quipped my adversary and friend, Armpit.

"What in the world are you talking about?" I asked.

"Beatz. Do you think he's dead? They hustled him out of here fast. Everybody said he hit really hard."

"Start over, what did I miss?" I had to interrupt. Sometimes Armpit got wildly animated with his conversations, having all of the hallmarks of being on amphetamines even when he wasn't. Armpit was permanently wound tight.

Tyggar, sitting down a few seats, saw my dilemma with Armpit, and in the lead for being valedictorian, interjected her knowledge into the conversation. "During this morning's sixth grade orientation, right when Mr. Jack was giving his warning of '...*and when you're here in high school, within the hallowed halls of RVHS, we will not only expect you to be well behaved, but we will demand it...*' speech. Which he does every year." She rolled her eyes and we all lost it laughing. "Right at that exact moment, Beatz fell through the ceiling and landed directly in front of him!"

"NO!" Cheekz blurted out, spitting his tuna noodle casserole all over the place. "And we were right there! We should have waited long enough to see that!"

"We missed that for *Sesame Street*..." I lamented.

"I love the *Muppets* on *Sesame Street*." Tyggar sighed.

Half the table chimed in to share their adoration as well. Everyone tried to outdo each other by doing their best impressions of their favorite characters. Armpit did an excellent *Oscar the Grouch*, which it appeared he was born for.

"Well, so then what?" I asked, getting back to the subject at hand.

"Got some air. Bounced three feet eye witnesses claim," came a voice from the next table over, which sounded like a Seminolian.

"Heard two kids barfed all over the floor and one mini-munchkin pissed herself laughing." Another Seminolian offered from two seats over.

"Apparently half of them started crying, while the other half thought it was hysterical. They thought it was some type of stunt to start a skit we were putting on for them." Tyggar finished her dissertation with a strange grin.

"Do you think he's dead?" Armpit asked again.

"Hope not. I've known him since we were in the nursery at the Leatherwood Church, playing Hot Wheels cars under the pews. His parents have always been really nice to me." I answered, hoping for a better outcome than some of my buddies who could have cared less about anything (or anyone).

It was our senior year and apathy permeated every aspect of our confined existence.

Our days in The Valley were numbered, quickly winding down to graduation. Then we were all off to points unknown, places unknowable...

* * * * * * *

I do believe that the Gold Shirt Program was started by JFK as a means to encourage health, fitness and physical preparedness all across America.

Rant Man twisted it into a whole new paradigm.

* * * * * * *

Beatz lived! And, it appeared that he had no lingering injuries. Even though he had to sit on a pillow for a few weeks (which he carried with him at all times).

It seems he didn't get the memo about only staying on the catwalk. He'd decided to do a side tour and stepped right out onto a ceiling tile. Beatz immediately disappeared and plummeted through space to land directly in front of Mr. Jack, who really was, at the exact moment in his speech when he would declare how important it was to obey each and every one of the numerous rules listed in the handout sheet whilst attending the hallowed halls of Redbank Valley High School.

For years to come, Beatz's infamous fall-of-shame would be used by my oldest brother Larry, the school's Physics teacher, as a basis for some off-the-wall test questions:

<u>TEST:</u>

If a student takes one step off the catwalk, breaks through the ceiling tiles, and then plummets exactly 18 1/2 feet until splattering between the seats and the stage:

1: At what velocity does he impact the cement (in feet per second)?

2: And, weighing 127 pounds, with what amount of force (in feet per pound)?

<u>BONUS ESSAY QUESTION:</u>

Does he bounce? Please elaborate using as many adjectives as necessary.

>>> Many of the essay answers were borderline legendary! <<<

3

New Eden

I can still remember it as if it happened moments ago. It's very strange for me; I often forget everything and anything. Decades cascade by. Yet, some memories remain burned hard into the fiber of your being. Simply put, they stay with you forever.

Such were those serendipitous series of epic decisions that led to this profound life I so gratefully embrace as my current reality… even now, 40-plus years later.

Some choices are so much larger in scope than others. And, even when knowing that singular fact, when you make them it can be hard to tell how profound they truly are and the world that those very same decisions will thrust you towards.

Where should I go to college?

Well, it was monumental in my world and is still etched into my psyche in multi-dimensional ways.

Deep within me I knew this particular choice of pathway, this obvious fork in the road, would be profoundly momentous, so I forged ahead with a simple plan on a bitter cold February morn…

AJG / 1976

* * * * * * *

It was wicked cold outside, minus teens at least, and so cold as to freeze the tears in your eyes should you be foolish enough to linger outside one moment too long. The brutal cold was hard to describe to those not initiated into the reality of what an Arctic air blast can do. On this day, such a weather system sat lingering over the Redbank Valley, a tiny sliver of villages and hardwood forests with barren coal-mined ridgelines in Western Pennsylvania. Huge snowflakes fell softly; wafting in three dimensions and stuck at strange angles to the single pane glass of the guidance counselor's office at RVHS.

I sat alone.

It was my graduation year, 1976, and I was 18 years old, but only by a few days. I sat trying my best to figure out what my guidance counselor called a "computer", some new-fangled device I'd neither seen, or even heard of, to this point in time.

In actuality, it was a primitive type of search engine for all things collegiate. A simple light box sat accompanied by a huge file of punch-hole cards, that when inserted, created a key by light-dots. Out spate specific page numbers within two massive book volumes of every college - both public and private - in the country. My instructions - given to me by the disengaged school secretary twirling her hair and tapping her fingers - were vague at best.

"Here, Allen, put in a card like this. Choose one that is in the region you are looking for, another card for the criteria: public, private or *other*. Two years or four. Major if you are looking for something specific. Accredited or non-accredited."

I wasn't even sure what 'accredited' meant, so I just nodded, smiled and allowed her to finish.

"Once you get the cards set, look at the X-Y coordinates that the light-dot makes, kinda' like geometry, and write the number down so you can look it up in the books. Near as I can tell, low numbers are east of the Mississippi and the higher numbers aren't."

She feigned a smile and went back to put together the lunch order for the rest of the secretarial staff at the local hoagie shop. It seemed that none of the staff ever ate our school lunches. I always wondered if they knew something we didn't?

I'd already 'checked out' the local colleges with most of my fellow 'party warriors,' who were a few years older. None of the usual colleges intrigued me in any way. Penn State was overrated. Pitt was in Pittsburgh, which, at the time was suspended in smog and wallowed in crud by the outrageous fallout from the local steel industries.

Clarion College was the local, next-town-over, fall back choice when all other institutions of higher learning declined having you. Or, rarely discussed, if you couldn't afford any other version of higher education, it was the place to go. All you needed was a pulse (and a check) to get in at Clarion, or so it seemed. All things considered, lackluster grades and low SAT scores got pre-approved. Indiana University of Pennsylvania (IUP) was Clarion on steroids at its very best day. Besides, my older brother went there. It was forever to be his alma mater, and never to be mine.

Outside screamingly proclaimed in a stark declaration, "Winter is here! And it shall last forever! Until the very day you die!"

With that morbid thought rattling my cortex, I chose a few punch cards, wrote down some coordinates, and proceeded to look them up in the massive volumes.

First up was Kentucky. To be precise, the University of Kentucky was in Lexington and appeared to be a much nicer Penn State. Maybe worth a look, I thought. But then my mind wondered farther afield, so I dug out a new batch of punch cards and expanded my reach at the possibilities of it all.

I organized a fresh stack with new coordinates from my punch card choices: Colleges of the South East. Four Years. Accredited. Public University.

Out jumped the University of Florida in Miami! Heck, now we're getting somewhere!

Florida could be, over all, somewhat nice. We'd been going down to Florida my whole life to visit with my father's stepmother and aunts and uncles that lived on the outskirts of Orlando, so it actually wasn't that intriguing. Plus, it's flat terrain and rather bland atmosphere of retirees and slow-motion lifestyle made it uninviting to me in many ways. And - the true kiss of death - it was not in any way a new adventure.

Ahhhh - adventure! Is that not what leaving home for college is all about?!

I desired more. I yearned for much more. Upon glancing at the snow adhering to the glass once more, while the winds picked up and winter declared its dominance upon all things within my current reality, my need for warmth superseded all things Pennsylvanian.

I had few desires other than flight from winter coupled with adventure beyond the boundaries known as Western Pennsylvania. I was so done with school. I think I'd made that determination in 8th grade, but it was starting to really sink in that I needed to flee! If I didn't flee immediately after graduation, I would most certainly get trapped forever in what I considered a living graveyard of deferred dreams and shattered follies.

Putting together another stack of cards, this time I chose: Colleges of the South West. Four Year Public Universities. Minimal criteria.

Every college I'd looked at had two to three pages of tightly written information concerning their credentials: hosts of disciplines available, Nobel laureates, other distinguished professors of note, and why they had such a profound academic stature. Dry foreboding information only the unenlightened academic could love filled the pages. From this new stack of southwestern universities I *discovered* USC, Pepperdine, Phoenix, San Diego State and more.

Fortunately -- and serendipitous to the max -- we'd just had a family vacation in San Diego not too long prior. My brothers and I looked at the overtly tempting ocean, stripped down to our cut-offs and sprinted into the waves, throwing our bodies with great relish into the blue Pacific with wild abandon! It was ice-cold-frozen-nasty and sucked the breath right out of us. What a total let down. How could something look so inviting and be so disgustingly disappointing?! Obviously San Diego State would not do. The others seemed equally unappealing. To this day I'm not sure why.

Maybe it had everything to do with the next page number on my list...

There it was! My answer in glaring black and white imagery, in all of its glory! It is said that a picture speaks a thousand words. In this case it shouted "ADVENTURE" into my weary frozen soul. For on that page wasn't a host of majors offered or a network of illustrious professors and their credentials of higher educational skill sets.

NO! It held a picture of a fine young, gloriously beautiful sweetheart, invitingly holding a flower lei outwards, sporting an exotically perfect smile. She beckoningly stood between two palm trees under crystal clear skies with a simple caption screaming at me:

>>>>> *COME TO THE UNIVERSITY OF HAWAII* <<<<<

* * * * * * *

I sat at the supper table with my parents. Dad only liked beef and pork, so Mum always served some version of meat with potatoes. Dad often said, "I've been asked why I never became a pastor? I tell people that to be a pastor you have to like two things, women and chicken. And I don't like chicken!" Dad had a great sense of humor, but an even greater sense of adventure as would be evident shortly.

"I see you got a letter from the University of Hawaii today." Mum offered, somewhat tentative with a slightly quivering voice.

I answered very excitedly, "What was that?!"

"Well, I think you know what it is..." Mum passed me the letter while sitting beside Dad at the far end of the table.

Being the youngest of five and separated by four years from my closest sibling, Keith, I was the lone child at home these days. Despite this, my older siblings had declared the supper table's well-defined pecking order, so I still found myself sitting in my *given spot* at the far end. It made passing things a bit awkward to say the least, but the pecking order of all things family had been beaten into me too many times to renounce simply because they had all left.

I opened the envelope, and it declared: "Welcome to the University of Hawaii! You have been accepted!"

I'm sure it said a bunch of other things as well, but they mattered not for I had been accepted to the land of sparkling warm waters, tropical adventures, and breathless possibilities. It was my very own vision of the *Land of Milk and Honey!*

That was enough for me!

That letter from far distant shores I held with bated breath and trembling hands, for within its matrix of ink on paper lie my future - adventures untold and unknowable. It exclaimed excitement into my very soul!

Mum broke the silent showing inside my head.

"What are you going to do?" She asked it quietly and with obvious concern; a voice I knew. A voice that should have given me instant pause.

Yet, being too young to adhere to less enthusiasm than should have been on such obvious display and being in this awkwardly transitional phase of my rather young life, I answered with glee, "I am going to Hawaii for college!"

Mum's countenance fell and she immediately broke down and wept.

Dad saw things differently. Without a word, he got up, walked around the table to my side, put out his hand, shook mine, and uttered the words I will never forget.

"If we can help in any way possible, we will."

His sense of adventure was on full display. Mum's sense of *losing her baby boy to the world* was as well.

After some food and contemplation over an unusually quiet dining experience, Dad had a deep thought. He'd taken Mum to Hawaii not-so-long-ago for their anniversary.

With a smile he boldly declared, "Hawaii may not be for everyone. After all, it is far. Maybe you should get on out there and check it out prior to committing for a full four years."

Dad cast that statement before me with a real twinkle of mischievous joy in his eyes accompanied with a hearty laugh. Mum looked at him with her jaw hanging down in a state of stunned disbelief!

I immediately nodded yes!

All that was tearing through my racing mind was FIELD TRIP!

* * * * * * *

Two of my older brothers immediately decided I needed to be 'chaperoned' on my journey westward. Mum thought that was a good idea. Little did she know the ramifications of having those two *crazies* accompany me anywhere, let alone to the land of aloha, sand, and beer. I was 18, brother Keith was 22 and Bob was 23. For the record, Hawaii's drinking age in 1976 was 18. Even that was loosely enforced.

Your Man Tours provided all we could ever desire. For $578 you got a roundtrip and a hotel room (triple occupancy) for 15 nights and 16 days at the Outrigger East

Hotel. It was two streets back from the Pacific Ocean in some place on the map called Waikiki. Upon arrival we opened the curtains in the room. All we saw was a block wall gong twenty-plus stories heavenwards. Being a less-than-desirable room with various types of non-identifiable lingering odors and stains, our abode had zero ambiance of any kind. Obviously, the room had been in high demand by many a wayward tourist who desired *cheap* over all other factors.

All factors considered, we were thrilled to be in this wildly exotic place under any conditions that we immediately christened "WakEE WakEE"!

The quality of hotel room, or lack thereof, meant nothing. We had an agenda that did not include signing up for any of the *Your Man Tours* day bus excursions populated by old geezers with walkers, canes, and oxygen bottles. After the fifth day *Your Man Tours'* rep quit asking and left us to our own wayward devices.

On the fourteenth day of living on ocean, sunburn, pizza, and beer, I lost some type of poorly designed bet (which I still think was rigged). The result was that I was forced to do everybody's withered-disgusting-encrusted laundry while Keith and Bob ditched me. And then, a bit too late, I found out that all our whites would be forever a funky shade of pink due to my serious lack of knowledge concerning white versus red laundry dynamics, for which I was eviscerated by both brothers when they picked up their tighty whities and gazed at them disgusted.

I was summarily chastised, prior to them leaving for the day without me, that I had yet to attend to checking out the university, as had been promised to my loving parents. In my own defense, I do not ever remember promising any such thing. But, it appeared that my older brother Bob had made that exact promise. By fiat, his promise included me performing at a minimal due diligence level to assuage my parents.

Whether I liked it or not.

The family dynamic pecking order was still very much intact even a quarter of the way around the world.

When looking for information on how to get to the university and the best method thereof, one must turn to the go-to-sweetheart, who was knowledgeable in all things Hawaiian. Who else, but the blonde that worked at the pool bar? She was relatively my age, 19ish, from Southern California, and working her summer gig while having more than a bit of fun. Blonde hair blue-eyed babe with a propensity to think I was a bit entertaining while simultaneously displaying a whole lot of backwoods-hickish-naivety. We got along wonderfully. I trusted her. After all, she is the one that informed us that cut-off blue jean shorts would cause a rash where no man should ever wish to obtain one. She was famously correct with her information as we quickly discovered that abrasive North Shore sand forced us to acknowledge how immensely wise and all-knowing she truly was!

"How do I get to the University of Hawaii at 'High-Low'?"

She stared back puzzled.

"Seems that I missed the main campus' deadline with my application by one day, and the Admissions Office automatically enrolled me at their branch campus in this place called 'High-Low'. Can I catch a bus? Get a cab? Or is it within walking distance?"

Setting down the glass she was polishing, she leaned her perfectly tanned frame across the bar, crinkled her too cute freckled nose with stunned delight, and then had a real moment before completely losing it laughing while turning 16 shades of pink-on-freckle. Getting her composure back, she declared, "It is on a different island!" She leveled at me, stunned by my brazen cluelessness. "And, you pronounce it 'Hee-Low'! Not 'High-Low'! You really might want to work on that! How on earth do you not know this?"

"OK. So how do I get to 'Heeee-Low'?" I responded, undeterred. After very improperly waxing the bottom of our rented surfboards in front of the WakEE WakEE Beach Boys, I knew I had a bit of learnin' to do. So casting all embarrassments aside I asked, "Is there a boat?"

Once again she smiled while shaking her head, and very politely answered, "No." With the clear expression of dealing with a level of moronic tourist she hadn't seen yet that morning, she continued, "You take a jet. There's usually one leaving every hour or so from the airport you flew into." Then she looked directly at me with lightning flashing in the depths of her eyes, and asked me incredulously, "Are you really going to go to Hilo for college?!"

"Yeppers! You betcha! I LOVE HAWAII!" With that, I was off to scout out my college as per brotherly promise and parental demand. I couldn't think of a single reason not to attend. After all, why on earth would anyone *not* go here for school? Fabulous weather! Warm water! Gorgeous babes everywhere! Fun in all tropical dimensions! Waves, sand, food, beer, pizza - endless possibilities!

Seemed like a completely different planet!

What could possibly go sideways?

Little did I understand the question she so surprisingly blurted out, or the light years away in every possible dimension that Hilo's reality was to the Waikiki my brothers and I had become enthralled with.

I tipped my Pool Bar Angel a buck - big tippers us Pennsylvanians - gave her a huge cheeky sun-burnt-peeling-skin-smile while yelling a hearty thank you over my shoulder and sprinted to find a cab. I didn't pack a single thing. After all, I had money in my wallet, and I was wearing my favorite George of the Jungle t-shirt. To me, I was good to go. It never dawned on me why she had such a stunned disbelief look in her eyes or that she just might know something that couldn't be explained. It was to be discovered only through personal experience.

It wasn't until I was on the plane that I realized that for the very first time in my entire life, that this new journey, this wild new adventure I was so eagerly embracing, included only me. I was suddenly very much alone on a jet eastward bound in the middle of the vast Pacific Ocean to place I'd never seen. I was off to a place I knew nothing about -- couldn't find on a map. Until seconds prior, I didn't even know how to pronounce the name of it or that it was on a separate island.

I guess, somehow, someway, I was looking for a home I'd never been. Until asking a few hopelessly naive questions to the smoking hot blonde babe, my Pool Bar Angel with the stunned aghast expression, I hadn't known my heart was longing to discover my new world that I never even knew existed!

Hilo, such an obscure dot on our blue planet, was set worlds apart from my upbringing on a farm in rural Pennsylvania. Welcome to a place strangely calling me homewards as a mythological vision of my New Eden.

* * * * * * *

Looking back, I should have noticed the flash of lightning that went through my Pool Bar Angel's eyes when I mentioned I was going to Hilo for college. For that brilliant-momentary-flash-of-epiphany spoke volumes I knew not how to grasp or process. It was a forewarning that the outer islands were not Oahu.

Hilo, and the entire Big Island, was the domain where locals ruled. They owned all, saw all. Colloquial to the extreme. Highly motivated and beyond formidable in all things. They had a distinct disdain for interlopers and those who would come to occupy their land, plunder their natural resources, or attempt any type of conquest.

I did not know it yet, for the thought hadn't even crossed my mind, but I wasn't searching for just a bit of tropical adventure. For the true course of adventure I set my course upon, the Eden I so desperately sought, was my own singular quest to advance my personal agenda of conquest, plunder, and gain.

All this as I wore a George of the Jungle t-shirt that I'd gotten from a cereal box-top bargain offer flashing a grin that could melt the sky. The wheels came down, we landed into the wind, and I emerged anew to the overwhelming fragrance of being a neophyte in a very exotic foreign land.

* * * * * * *

Something I find astounding as a human, a truth which is a glimpse of the truly divine, is that being hopelessly naive allows for GOD to have the joy of orchestrating our footsteps far into our distant future, even for generations to come. It's an invaluable observation only available from a much older perspective with a touch of wisdom developed by a deep-seated knowledge of how...

"... all things work together for good to them that love GOD, to them who are called according to HIS purpose." [KJV Romans 8:28]

4

Higher Learning

"Loneliness is a yearning of the heart gone torturously astray."

AJG / 1976

* * * * * * *

Casting all fears aside, I had indeed chosen to fly 4,572 miles to attend the University of Hawaii in Hilo.

I wasn't just lonely. I was lonely in a crowd, which was infinitely worse. It seemed to be a state of reality where everything was right there but simply out of reach. Watching others laughing, chatting and interacting while I braved my first exposure into the world of college was painful to the extreme. People warned of the difficulty of the trifecta of adjustments: new place, new school, and braving the minefield of discovering new friends. The combination – and being lonely in the campus crowd of souls -- really crushed me.

* * * * * * *

I found myself with lots of time to look back, since looking ahead was truly impossible without anyone coming along to share the journey with me.

After braving the short flight over on that last day of our vacation Field Trip, I booked a room and took a nap at the Naniloa Hotel near campus. We'd been living on beer, pizza, sun, and surf, and I was simply exhausted from too much of all of the above. The sweethearts at the front desk thought I was nuts -- might as well keep the streak going -- every local I'd encountered at this stage all had the exact same opinion.

Although, I think they greatly admired my lack of luggage while sporting my ever-coveted George of the Jungle t-shirt!

After giving myself a self-guided tour of the campus - it appeared that there wasn't a soul around, not even janitorial staff - I was heading back to the airport when I experienced my very first serendipitous encounter. Some longhaired dude in a rusty Triumph TR3 ragtop convertible came whipping into the parking lot and made a beeline directly to the Administration Building. I sprinted and managed to get my proverbial foot-in-the-door -- literally -- prior to it slamming shut. I shouted down the hallway to the gent disappearing around a corner, "Do you by chance work here?"

He turned, shocked somewhat by my being there.

"Yes, I do. I am the Dean of Housing. Can I help you?"

Breathless, I answered, "Perfect."

He waved me to follow him to his office where he promptly sat himself down and gave me the look of 'who is this confused soul'?

"I think I need a dorm room."

He leaned forward while admiring my grit and, I think, my choice of fashion.

"For this semester?"

"Yes, I'll be back in a few weeks to start. You call it Fall Semester, I suppose."

He actually burst out with a fairly hearty laugh! Then he gave me a response that still resonates with me today, which is universal for anyone traveling far from home for school.

"You do know that being out here, in the middle of the Pacific Ocean, simply is not for everyone? Many fail. Others flee."

All of a sudden this cool fellow appeared to be way wiser than first blush; his roadster and ponytail appeared to be some type of facade for a brilliant soul with benevolent intentions.

"Our dorms are spoken for up to three years in advance. This is the University of Hawaii and we get students from everywhere -- all across the Pacific Basin, even on a global basis. You'll have classmates from Australia to Sweden. Some don't speak English." He shook his head at that one. It still perplexed him.

He'd obviously been in Hilo well past his due date is what flashed through my mind.

"I'm coming here for school. Do you have any suggestions for me since I will obviously be off-campus?" I declared stalwart in my purpose, while sporting my trademark smile and adjusting to my brand-new plan for housing.

This time he really connected with me, as he looked me straight in the eye.

"I have a place you can stay, it's a boutique hotel on Hilo Bay. If you are still a student here after 10 days, I'll find you a place near campus. A substantial amount of my off-island students drop out in the first week or two. If you want, I can call ahead and get you the kama'aina rate. The school has a deal with them for students such as yourself who are, you know, our 'unannounced' late arrivals."

And that is how I found myself alone - while herds of tourists came and went - staying at the Seaside Hotel for $14.50 a night. Every square inch of it needed painting. Yet, it came with room service and an uninviting pool - now that's ambiance!

I bought a bicycle at the local Sears store for a few bucks and peddled, all uphill, to school. Getting back to the hotel, after wandering the halls of academia, was an easy downhill run. Funny how going back was actually the hard part, even if it was a coast the whole way, for there was exactly nothing to look forward to at the Seaside Hotel for me.

Zero friends.

Nineteen credit hours.

And, the school meal plan.

* * * * * * *

Those first two weeks at UHH included nothing but loneliness, mosquitoes and funky sheets (changed daily). For years to come I thought 'boutique' was a euphemism for 'crappy'.

I had so much yet to learn.

* * * * * * *

When you are eighteen and perpetually hungry, eventually you discover every little thing on the menu in the college cafeteria. One main item that I could never get a handle on was this funky grey chicken that the cooks - who spoke minimal English - would serve. They served it all of the time, seemed it was a big hit with everyone but me.

I even tried it every which way -- even with ketchup. To me, I couldn't believe that anyone on Earth could cook chicken that poorly. It looked nasty and tasted like anything but chicken.

Finally, sometime during my second semester, I asked one of my fellow students, "What the heck! What are the cooks doing wrong with this stupid chicken?"

I was exasperated and needed to know, pointing at my plate.

She looked at me, looked at my plate - where I'd tried one more time of putting ketchup on the ugly grey chicken - and completely came unglued laughing. In between breaths she got out a few words, "That is ahi tuna! It's the finest ahi steaks on Earth! How do you not know this?"

Immediately I felt like I was right back at Outrigger East, being lectured by my Pool Bar Angel.

5

1956 Kilauea Avenue

"Calling it the Animal House of the Pacific would greatly diminish the daily chicanery and outright bizarre shenanigans that proceeded forth from the premises."

AJG / 1976

* * * * * * *

"Found a place for you. It's not much but you can use it to get through the semester," smiled the Dean of Housing when I stopped to check in on progress, which I did every few days.

He quickly returned to the older hippie dude already in his office and to wrap up their conversation. .

"Everything good so far this semester? How're your projects…?"

"Some of my 'trips' are over six feet tall! Gonna' be epic!"

"Great! Keep it up!"

The long-haired-shaggy-in-every-dimension-much-older student sauntered past me with a strange glint in his eyes to points unknown.

"What was that about?" I asked, naive as ever.

"Nothing. Found your spot. It's a boarding house, pay-by-the-month. They want $60 for it. Got a communal shower for the rooms on the lower floor. Not much, but it's much closer to campus. Plus, you'll meet some people that aren't tourists." He looked at me with a strangeness previously unseen. His wicked smile of playful joy dripped with tinges of 'this-ought-a-be-good'.

"Where is it?" I asked, unperturbed.

"1956 Kilauea Avenue. See Buddy Silva. He's the owner." Then, with a touch of knowledge flashing through his eyes, he added, "You might want to give a little leeway to his kids...they aren't all there."

As I thanked him and walked towards the door, he called out one final warning.

"Allen, think of this as temporary..."

* * * * * * *

With a backpack full of all of my earthly possessions, I arrived on my bicycle to find Mr. Silva in the backyard of the designated address. Yard in disarray, huge mango tree droppings of rotten fruit littered all about, fruit flies like a cloud of locusts swarming everywhere welcomed me and were only obscured by the stench from the task at hand that Mr. Silva and his drinking buddy were completing on the picnic table. They'd just finished butchering the largest fish I'd ever seen up close. A two hundred pound plus tuna carcass hung from a low branch, with guts, blood and scales scattered in a thirty-foot circle. What must have been the better cuts were lumped into a cooler, without ice, and unceremoniously set aside for latter consumption.

It appeared that the real work had been in consuming the second case of Primo Beer (also known as the worst beer on earth) while hacking the fish into submission. Both Buddy Silva and his fishing partner were hammered, and it was only 9:45 am Hawaiian Standard Time.

"What? You da' new haole?" Mr. Silva declared referring to me as all of the locals called us mainlanders, without reaching out to shake hands. That was okay with me since he had blood and guts ground into his t-shirt and hair. 'Haole' means white and/or non-local and could be either used as a vile foul-mouthed put-down or simply to denote your designated ethnicity - Caucasian - without any type of salacious innuendo attached. The outcome, being all in the inflection of the user.

"Sir. That would be me. The Dean of Housing sent me over. He said you have a room for rent." I desired greatly to be around other humans. Otherwise I would have fled. The yard reeked, the house tilted left, and the crumbling facade spoke of better times - a hundred years prior.

"Here's the room. There's the shower. Bathroom's upstairs. Everyone brings his own food. Sixty bucks, in advance - got it with you?" He pointed at a corner room under the house with six-foot ceilings, one stark naked light bulb dangling, a broken lock, and tiny bed. The shower was cement-patina-green with fungi on every possible surface, except from the foot scuff marks, which kept the green scum at bay on a small portion of the floor. With the hordes of cockroaches and clouds of mosquitoes, it was well on its own path to falling in upon itself from the ongoing assault of the embedded termites boring deep into every wooden component of the dilapidated structure.

"I'll take it!" I said as I forked over the money with glee. I had my own place. And it was glorious!

As I was moving in, a rather tall lanky kid my age showed up looking for the room right beside mine. Oddly, the place had a high turnover rate. He smiled ear-to-ear, much as myself, and paid Mr. Silva just as I had. His mother, coifed, elegant, obviously well educated, and completely aghast, started to cry. He hugged her and shooed her back to her Cadillac sitting in the driveway. He lit a cigarette and walked back to the house.

"Hi, I'm Eddie." As he reached out his hand, his eyes said 'FREE AT LAST!'

"'Appears we're going to have an epic time here!" Then he laughed so hard it made me lose it too.

Eddie and I hit it off immediately. I've never been sure of exactly how many people lived in the house. There were at least seven rooms rented out. But, at any given time, there were at least a dozen interlopers flying high and rampaging throughout our realm, including St. Joseph High School's classes of 1976 and 1977, who freely intermingled at will. Eddie and his fellow *Catholic Party Warriors* came and went from his new found digs at 1956 Kilauea Avenue, which is how I met Wade, Matt and Jeff, friends of Eddie's and members of the ever-rotation making their way through. Wade and Jeff were world-class watermen: surfing, fishing, diving, you name it. Anything to do with the ocean they were awesome. Matt was a natural when it came to body surfing the local shore pounds.

And, I wasn't any of the above - yet.

It wasn't until a moment at Wade's grandmother's house months later that I had an epiphany of biblical proportions.

"You mean Wade lets you live here?" I asked Jeff flat out shocked when he came sauntering out of Wade's grandmother's ranch style home down in the AG lots on the Puna side of Hilo.

Immediately, Jeff took great offense and countered, "Let's me? I'm his older brother!"

"There is no way on earth you're brothers!" I said exasperated at the thought that Wade and Jeff could even be related. Wade looked Samoan and Jeff looked Viking - red hair and all.

"Don't forget me. I'm their brother too." Matt piped in as we continued our game of MONGOOSE in the backyard, taking turns shooting at the bent rusty hoop in the driveway.

"No way! You're acting as if I'm stupid - or worse."

"Dad was Hawaiian and Chinese. Mom's Scottish-Irish-German-Swedish-Norwegian-Haole," Wade admonished as he won the match via flagrantly wild shot from the middle of Lama Street, which none of us could hit. "I got the Hawaiian, Jeff got the Viking and Matt got the whole tall-white-boy thing going on. That's exactly what makes us modern day Hawaiians." Wade declared with factual indifference to my look of astonishment.

"I got the German-Scottish-Appalachian-Hillbilly-thing -- anybody want to wrestle?" I was exasperated. "Basketball! I really dislike playing sports I'm not very good at."

They all knew better.

But I, not knowing when to quit asking questions, asked the worst possible one: "What happened to your Dad?"

"Cancer. Two years now." It got real sullen, real fast, and the day's fun was immediately over. Wade, Jeff, and I went back to classes; Jeff and I to UHH, Wade to St. Joe, and Matt to parts unknown. I think he was 'taking a day off'.

* * * * * * *

Not all sets of brothers are created equal; couldn't be truer than the various sets of brothers I've come to know and call family. Jeff, Matt, and Wade were one set. I'll come back to them, as their friendships have endured the tests of time and trials.

But at the *Animal House of the Pacific,* there was a set of three wayward brothers that still leaves me in stunned amazement: Buddy Silva's three sons Sterling, Hi Ho, and Quick.

That is weirdly correct. Buddy Silva had the outright audacity to name his three sons Sterling Silva, Hi Ho Silva and Quick Silva! Upon birth, they instantly became famous statewide and even had articles referencing them (other than the police reports) on how *awesomely unique* their GOD given names were. As for us, the actual paying residents of the boarding house that their father provided for our destruction and lodging, they were at best a "plague upon our house".

Sterling Silva was basically operating without a full case (of anything) and was perfectly harmless, since his world was even a mystery to him. Hi Ho Silva had a wife and graced our presence less frequently because of her demands upon his time. He appeared to have at least a semblance of morals. Maybe Hi Ho was the only one with even one ounce of honesty in the entire clan. But Quick Silva... Well, he had a completely different usage for his father's rental property: to pilfer it, and us, for everything he could abscond with that wasn't nailed down.

Although, in Silva's [weak] defense, he once took me for a ride to a place called Kalapana Beach on a late Tuesday morning after my day's classes had ended. It appeared that Quick no longer went to high school and hadn't for a long time based on his vocabulary, skill sets, and attention span. We fled in his father's hammered pickup truck (which probably wasn't licensed or insured) without permission or care.

Quick drove us down to a crystalline blue bay under deep blue skies with turquoise waves exploding onto a black-as-midnight sand beach known as Kalapana. The waves thrust themselves foaming amongst the huge palm tree trunks, then they pulled back down the beach rumbling as they went. It was surreal, mesmerizing, and fantastically exotic. Kalapana was idyllic in so many ways that I will never be able to properly communicate all of its attributes with mortal words.

That single event, going deep into Lower Puna, to this wildly exotic place forever lost in time known as Kalapana, hooked me forevermore on all things Big Island. It gave me a stupendous love for the Big Island I'd never known until that exact moment in time

Having Quick Silva and his brothers thrust into our world, well that is a far different story...

* * * * * * *

Until that excursion to the southeastern shoreline, to that hidden beach lost in time, black sand in a crescent bay captured in a myriad of blues and electric colors not available except on God's own palette, I couldn't even imagine that such a place could possibly exist anywhere on our planet. Such a profound truth and a wondrous volcanic phenomena - tumbled lava rock softened by the kiss of the ocean to a warmth and wonder that embraced humans into its own exotic reality. A perfect pureness too awesome to describe, black sand beaches create their own version of perfection along the shores of time.

I was so far from my previous Pennsylvanian reality. Everything around me seemed to be the stuff of myths and legends, of dreams and storybook fables fabricated by weavers of imagination gone far astray.

Seeing that black sand on my hands, held up against crystal blue skies, I had a flashback of a buried memory from my youth. I was prone to ear infections when I was little and during a particularly long night's struggle with soaring fever and stabbing pains, I had a wildly strange vision. I was playing in the sand at the ocean's edge, probably around five years old, with this effervescent joyous girl. She had long raven hair and huge brown eyes with flecks of gold dancing within them to a melody not of this world. She was so much fun! We played along the water's edge building and losing sandcastles to the surf as it came and went with mini-waves. Such perfectly warm waters, pleasant under the palms, and safe from all harm.

At the end of the dream the lovely young lady stood to go, just as I took a firm look at my hands. On them was the blackest of sand! It was so strange, as I'd never even heard of such a thing, and didn't know it was possible.

Then I looked up. There was the same young girl, but now she was grown and had become the most beautiful creature I'd ever seen!

Kind.

Loving.

Brilliant.

Stunning.

She was all I would ever desire...

She flashed me a knowing smile and then she evaporated into the mists of longings deferred in a faraway land. At that precise moment I sat bold upright in my bed. My fever had broken, and I was mystified by the vision of the golden-brown eyed girl of my otherworldly vision that had been firmly etched into the furthest recesses of my mind.

Little did I realize it at the time, but my ongoing quest was simply my deepest heartfelt longing to rediscover that gorgeous sweetheart in my long-lost vision of the night.

Along with it was life's ultimate treasure: love.

6

Sport of Kings

"Just because everyone is doing it does not mean you are qualified."

AJG / 1976

* * * * * * *

The Sport of Kings required a skill-set honed by both nuances and attention to details I fundamentally lacked. As a gremmy, an amateur in the Sport of Kings, I knew not the danger, nor methods needed to survive such an environment of liquid chaos. I knew not the systemic rhythm of the ebb and flow of the ocean -- waters alive with their own calling of mysterious micro-currents and deep channels. Liquid tempests of rolling horizontal tornadoes were hell-bent on separating bone from marrow, the skilled from the wayward soul who thought blue skies and warm waters were devoid of feelings, of and longings to turn all things back to the primordial elements of salt, hydrogen and oxygen. Determined basic molecules, they also yearned to add to their numbers, to crush then consume anything, or anyone, that dared to swim amongst them.

Or, in this case, surf amongst them.

Yet, I leapt with wild abandon off the small beach of black lava rocks tumbling and rolling along the shoreline of Honoli'i Beach Park, eager to join the fray.

I paddled out regardless of my naiveté and complete lack of wisdom. Put plainly, I saw others and joined them in my total arrogance as a lamb to slaughter goes silently to the holder of a knife, blood stained and waiting for its next meal. My strokes on my board were mistimed and fluid-less, somewhat sporadic in their lack of natural flow. It did not take long for me to sense the first grasps of turmoil, a faint tugging of my psyche allowing me a touch of an image of what was to come. Hair rising on the back of my neck, I paddled slightly off-balance into my first true encounter of what was set before me. A small blowback from the previous set of waves, ricocheting off the shoreline I'd just launched from – it tore me momentarily from my fiberglass vessel and deposited me a few feet below the surface. Unceremoniously, it pushed me under where humans live in small increments of time prior to panic and certain death.

The welcome embrace of air hit my lungs as I found my board, furiously clawing back upon its freshly waxed surface to avoid being picked off by the real waves advancing relentlessly towards me. How I got into the small channel was not skill or effort or knowledge; I simply received a reprieve from the ocean itself that took me with it to deeper waters when it breathed out. Sitting up, I conjured myself victorious, yet I wasn't any such thing. I was simply extremely fortunate in this singular moment in time. I knew not the difference -- such items were as foreign as the land is to the sea.

Being far too clueless to watch others, too foolish to observe the timing they employed in micro-bursts of swift strokes. Allowing them to dance to the tune of hard learned lessons and acquired advanced abilities; abilities handed down from past generations that gave the freedom to perform as the waves demanded. They exemplified ease of being born here. Having been raised amongst the tumult of sand and sea, wave and chaos, the locals embraced the calmness of their inner-selves caught within blue thundering waters exploding on this distant shore. In ones and twos the locals walked upon the waters, making this unforgiving Sport of Kings a sacred encounter between man and GOD.

Yet today, this distant shoreline stood stalwart to oppose these very sets of waves who had the tenacity to advance so far, ferocious waves assaulting this pinnacle island with greater zeal than I could ever imagine.

Certainly, more than I should have ever ignored.

Once again, fundamental errors on vivid display, I crawled my way into the lineup of the next group of marching swells. They cared not for my foolishness, as they cared not for the skilled, they simply allowed me to be swept into their path of impending doom and crushed me in doing so.

Grasping for air, I fought my leash. Its supposed purpose was to keep me close to my surfboard so as not to lose it. For a touch of needed safety, it was to keep me within a few yards of my bit of fiberglass and foam at all times. Instead, it wrapped tight, latching hold of my left arm in an entanglement of delay. While peeling it off, I lost precious seconds, and in those seconds the following wave utterly consumed me. Pressing me down, it kept me from the breath I needed to clear my mind, to allow me the briefest of opportunity to be human in an air-breathing world. Devoid of oxygen, I panicked for the tiniest period of time. Then, once again, the ocean relaxed its grip and allowed me, such a simple and frail creature, one moment's pause. A reset if you will -- it gave me a chance to change course and find a way back out of this wicked game I had so willingly embraced just a few minutes prior.

As a *gremmy*, I knew not the opportunity allotted, nor did I take stock of my frailty as a mortal being caught up in unfeeling waters. I did not allow for the reality of the situation to inform me of its real intent and purpose. I did not know that all I was to its inherent nature was hydrogen, oxygen, salt, and chaos. I did not grasp such fundamentals. To me, this was fun and games.

Surfing: such a simple sport to be conquered by direct action, not by adhering to long-proven methods earned from generations past.

For me, surfing was certainly not done by working towards earning one small step at a time. Small waves were for children, and I was no child! I was a young man in my prime and not to be underestimated by anyone or anything.

Especially today!

I would not be defeated in the warm waters of a crystal-clear ocean on a blue-sky morning with gentle white clouds that reached that endless horizon.

What could possibly go wrong?

I was stronger than most and determined to perform and be brave in all things. But, this was not land, my natural habitat; this was the mighty Pacific. The ocean has zero remorse when it comes biting at its shorelines with tumultuous waves with forces unfathomable and relentless in its pursuits.

I took off on the next wave despite it being the first of eight. Falling forward on my feet, gravity pulled me off-balance the slightest bit. It was enough to equal disaster. Pushing through the climbing face of the wave I had attempted to conquer, I found myself once again under the ocean's surface. This time it raged in all dimensions, held me firmly in its swarming molecular structure, and beat me like the fool I was. Upon being spit out, I pulled on my leash to retrieve my board. Dazed, confused, and completely out of control, I threw myself crosswise onto my board, gasping for air. Exhausted like never before, I wafted, spooked in the foam and currents.

Waves are a silent thunder unleashed. Silence kills. The second wave arrived with no forewarning or even the slightest hint of fangs bared. Pitching directly over me, with wicked hydraulics thrust outwards, it pile-drove me under. Landing upon me with such force I was s violently bashed upon my board as it crushed the air from my lungs, which escaped in one gasp of doom. All the while I was totally enveloped in whitewater exploding all around and getting wrapped and tugged by my board-gone-rogue. I was still attached to the leash that ripped me rapidly along a path of undesired currents and shallow waters.

More waves rushed to enjoin the consumption of my failed mission. I was firmly caught in their rolling thunder! Hunger to engulf this tidbit, a morsel really, of fuel for the fire known as sea and waves, ocean and current, deeps and shallows. Nary a sound was made, as I found myself once again caught in fast running waters I could not escape. The swirling elements engulfed me as part of the same vast ocean complex, which spanned the globe.

I cut loose my leash with one deft pull and found a touch of freedom as I scrambled for the atmosphere above. I was in less than two feet of water, but two feet or twenty or two hundred, it didn't matter...

Below the surface was death.

Above the surface: life.

Even I, the gremmy, was in full realization of that -- especially now with my lungs on fire and my chest horrendously bruised from being crushed against my board. Everything past seemed like eons ago, yet was really mere seconds to this newfound frailty I'd never expected to encounter.

I looked around to finally take a true stock of my profoundly blunt reality. I was alone in my distress. Somehow everyone else had vanished. I had been swept like unwanted debris far from all of the other surfers.

I was no longer alone in a crowd.

Now, I was simply alone.

Drifting in mortal danger, once again unaware of my position or forces I was captured within. The side shore current mercilessly pulled me along a wild coastline of sea cliffs and exposed boulders. I bit hard on each singular inhaled breath. Every gasp an extraordinary effort in and of itself. I tugged at the water to keep my head above it. Even if for a moment, I desperately needed the air to assuage my hunger for oxygen.

I had never been so exhausted in such a short period of time.

My singular desire was to exit the angry ocean, to claw back onto land. Oh! How I prayed to be a terrestrial being on dry earth! Yet, this ravenous current would not be denied. I looked forlornly at the rapidly receding shoreline and yearned for its embrace. Not knowing the danger of my dreams, my longings quickly became reality as the following wave boiled me along its destructive path. I was pushed, once again, downwards onto jagged reef. Barnacles hard and cruel slit open both of my heels, tearing both of my feet open.

How could such a day even exist! Such a beautiful morning with blue skies, clear water, my very first surfboard. I'd zigzagged a lightning bolt motif on it to proclaim it as my own -- my finest wax pattern. Turns out, it was the cheapest board and leash money could buy.

In this moment, I wished I could buy my way to the shore, no matter the cost.

I wished I could buy new feet.

Pushed by the turning inside waves, I tried to exit to the barren shelf. It was *just right there*. But, alas, I couldn't get a foothold or claw my way past the boulders. I tumbled and rolled, attempting to shield my head while doing so. I found a small rip current away from the obvious, immediate danger that was currently in front of me. I quickly became human flotsam in deeper water once again - all as the immense Pacific Ocean pulsed, breathed, and snaked along the spectacular windswept shoreline.

Every breath became labored and quick. Every swim stroke was torture to create. I longed for home, yet I knew not how to achieve such a simple yearning. As dolphins played not so far away, I knew my day of adventure had taken a turn toward mortality. My ocean sojourn was being counted in singular gasps for air and life.

One solitary breath at a time...

I was completely permeated within the essence of the ocean.

The next set of waves, marching as rogue warriors, unleashed themselves as an approaching liquid storm. They were the *cleanup set* in surfer jargon. Substantially mightier, and exponentially more powerful, they longed for a shoreline to bite into. Focused and determined to chew off a portion of the confines they were captured within. Waves are never to be allowed to march infinitely forward, so they embrace their own destruction with a singular violent encounter against reef and rocks, cliff and beach. Unleashing their rage was their primary pursuit.

Today their violence had a small human impediment fighting for life along the way. As the gremmy, I had not a clue of what awaited me. I only knew one breath of life at a time.

As sand tumbles downwards, my allotted energies wound down as well.

My feet bled profusely. My lungs were on fire. My arms tormented me with anger for being forced to perform time after time after time. My options gone, I had nowhere to go. Only one more bite of air, one more flailing touch of life above the surface.

I managed to live to see the waves approach, stealthily, at a pace too slow to ignore, yet far too quick to escape.

With a newfound perspective on the danger I was encapsulated within. I fought for position.

I fought for my very life.

The first wave broke just behind me, falling as a liquid avalanche. It exploded with a cannon shot's fury, and I could feel it grasp its liquid tentacles around me. I forced myself to claw through it and over it. Now that I knew the super accentuated hydraulics each wave possessed, I desperately wished not to allow myself to be destroyed. Another wave past -- too many more to endure cascaded through my thoughts with overtones of impending doom.

The next wave arrived without mercy, found me in my distress, and lifted me upwards. Three concussions tore through my spirit. I felt my own mortality almost escape from my nearly shattered earthen vessel!

My entire world exploded as I felt that I had been thrust into the very hands of the Living God Almighty!

That is how I found myself quivering standing on a ledge of lava, a tiny leaf of safety with tumultuous waters on every side. I had been wickedly trounced, swept far away, and mercifully deposited on a tiny sliver of exposed reef at the entrance to the adjoining surf break known as Tombstones.

It was appropriately named.

* * * * * * *

This story is my best attempt at transcribing my very first encounter with real waves. For me, it will forever be impossible to do justice to the unleashing of the tremendous forces at work when Pacific Ocean waves - that have marched forever far - encounter a shoreline that refuses to yield.

I, a foolish gremmy, had simply gotten in the way of a raging and eternal war, an endless struggle as two violent foes clashed. Primordial forces, in mortal combat, as the vast ocean seas raged against one of the earth's immovable fortresses.

So foolish was I! I had attempted to learn the Sport of Kings without the sword of wisdom or the shield of knowledge. To this very day I feel divinely blessed to have survived such a deadly encounter.

7

Changes

"Change is the only thing that is constant."

AJG / 1976

* * * * * * *

I woke up in the *penthouse* of 1956 Kilauea -- after adjusting my monthly rate from $60 per month to $80 per month, paid in advance, as always. Everything seemed off-kilter and slightly wicked. While the exact cause couldn't be placed, my deep desire to effectuate some much-needed changes was starting to take hold in my thought patterns.

There was the constant pounding of noise permeating every inch of the Animal House. Then, there was the monster of a cane spider was just two inches from my bug-eyed expression when I screamed so loud that the Beach Boys renting surf boards probably heard on Oahu - 208 miles to the west. The encounter happened after rinsing the soap from my eyes in the fungi-shower. The Beach Boys were probably having a good laugh at my predicament and taunting, *"There's that stupid haole again.*

OK, that might be a bit of exaggeration, but I'm sure that I killed the next spawn of fungi with my death scream, setting it back a few weeks in its scummy spread of taking over the entire underneath of what was supposedly deemed livable.

I needed to change quickly.

One profoundly good change, which appeared unexpectedly, found me with two new souls, fellow residents of the Animal House, whom I could actually call friends.

Kenzo hailed from Kaneohe, Oahu. From the windward side of what we started calling 'The City Island'. Kenzo was a natural born people's person. Everybody loved Kenzo. He had an electric smile that easily drew souls into his orbit of unbounded joy looking for adventure! Thin and athletic he would often find himself in over his head since Hawaii's surf could pound anyone into submission, even Kenzo on his best day in the water. What I found astounding was he could get completely trashed in the surf and still come up wild eyed and laughing, just happy to have survived the ordeal. Chics love him. But, it appeared he could care less and continually looked past the one on his arm for the next best thing to appear over some mystical horizon.

My other newfound friend was from Surfer's Paradise, Australia. He was full-blooded Ozzie through-and-through! He'd tell us, "... it's Aussie! Not Ozzie, you stupid under educated Yanks!" But we didn't care. To us he had to be from the *Land of Oz*, since both it and Australia were mythological places never to be found on any map. Every morning he'd slog up to Kai Store (half a block away) and fetch himself a 16-ounce can of ice-cold Folger Beer to have with his Cheerios prior to classes. His bizarre non-stop beer drinking kinda' freaked me out, but he was a wonderful bit of fun and darned entertaining. Brian came with a pedigree of having been on the National Championship Rugby Team his senior year of high school and was an avid surf enthusiast. Brian preferred knee boarding, a type of surfing that you wore bodysurfing fins and knelt on a shortened surfboard instead of standing. His take was, "Allows me to get into smaller tubes, mate."

Kenzo was of the same mindset, although his was a uniquely local boy perspective. "When I lose my board, I want to have fins on in case I need to make it back to shore...alive!" The two of them enlisted me into their club of knee boarders. Having fins on, should I lose my board, would save me from having another *Hanoli'i death experience*. An event I never wished to replicate under any circumstances. I truly had become very sober when it came to Hawaiian liquid thunder.

"Allen, we've got to blow this place," Kenzo deadpanned on a melancholy morning. "We've got to get out of here. This house reeks of filth and I can feel its stench seeping into my soul."

He had a point. Even though the fungi may have been screamed into submission momentarily, it was relentless in its resolve. The break in the perfect weather wasn't helping.

Unbeknownst to me, we had been in a rather rare drought cycle with every day sporting puffy white clouds against a sapphire sky. The weather had taken a turn for the worse, and it started raining endlessly, day after day after day. By mid-October, Hilo had fully reverted to its true nature of being a saturated rainforest and it was apparent that GOD had turned on HIS overflowing heavenly spigot. During the drought it would downpour between midnight and two in the morning, then give way to glorious weather all day long that we all got to enjoy.

"I keep coming up short. Somebody's stealing everything not nailed down: food, change, and a pair of board shorts. 'Think I'm missing some checks, not to mention some of my mind. They stole my favorite Quicksilver board shorts! Punk bastards!" Kenzo went on with his list of misgivings concerning our decrepit living conditions and the Silva boys' propensity to take anything they could get away with.

"Me too. Quick and his cohorts?"

"Probably, but there's so many people stomping through here, we may never know. Hard to keep track of how many thieves there are amongst us. I'm done with this crappy, dirty, filthy, slime and mold infested situation." Kenzo finished his declaration why he would be fleeing to a better rental. He was going to move far from the Animal House of the Pacific with or without me.

Just about then, Quick walked into the house and plopped a six-foot tall *agricultural product* - planted in a black plastic container - on the indoor picnic table for everyone's viewing pleasure and admiration.

"Is that what I think it is?" I asked Kenzo while staring at the magnificent botanical specimen in total awe.

"I'll give you two hundred for it." Little Pat offered to Quick as he came out of his lair. Little Pat had no discernable means of income. Now we all had a much better inclination of why he always had extra cash and lots of time on his hands.

"Four hundred," countered Quick, while not missing a beat.

"Two fifty. Quick, you low life scum, we all know you stole it anyways!" Little Pat dropped the money on the table and proceeded to take the towering plant into the depths of his corner of the house where none dared venture.

Quick smiled with an *asphalt-eating-grin-of-a-road-splattered-mongoose*, as he exited our lives with his newfound bounty. To this day, I don't think I've ever caught a single glimpse of him again. Someone said he moved to Oahu and got into a world of trouble with some rough locals who didn't like him very much, subsequently beating the snot out of him and leaving him for dead.

Suddenly tires were squealing outside as Brian appeared doing a wild batch of three-sixties in the broken driveway. All the while he screamed out of his hammered VW Bug's open windows, "South shore's breaking! Let's go mates! Grab your boards you *American Wussies!* Waves-are-a-wasting!"

After piling into the car, we ended up at a place called Pohoiki just south of the eastern most point of the island. The waves were perfect, and the weather was considerably better than the torrential rains Hilo was unleashing in waves of endless downbursts of despair. It was all we needed to calm our souls after escaping both the Silvas and was turned out to be the scariest drive I've ever experienced. The Aussie panicked at every possible critical juncture on American roads.

I'd rather bleed to death than allow someone take the wheel who - when they got to every knoll or blind turn – would get seriously confused on which side of the road they should be on.

"Why on earth did you *Down Under Yoo-Hoos* decide to drive on the wrong side of the highway?" I asked.

"Maybe it's you *Damn Yanks* that picked the wrong side of the road!" He answered in his usual snarky Australian style.

Not wishing to be anything but factual, I gave him my "Damn Yankee' response.

"We invented the car and the modern highway system - and we chose to drive on the right side of the road, the correct side, to be precise. It's you *Kangaroo Morons* that decided to be stupid about it and put the steering wheel where it doesn't belong."

Brian deadpanned, "We blame it on the British and using us as their dumping ground penal colony. We can't help it if we're all a bit in-bred, every single one of us is obviously descended from a bloodline of renegades!"

That was the very last time I'd ever allow an Australian drive me anywhere.

* * * * * * *

"I think I just saw Noah's Ark float by..."

My comment hung vapid in the damp air.

I declared my sojourn into biblical analogy to whoever cared as the fortieth day of endless rains saturated our world. I got a melancholy response of grunts wrapped in angst. Brian cracked open a Folger to go with his stale *Cheerios* then let out a sordid bit of gas, a real one-cheeker. Kenzo just shook his head, rolled his eyes, and drove off in his trusty Dodge Valiant to start his day of absorbing the lessons of Communications & Public Relations, his chosen field of studies.

Getting prepared for another blast through the puddles and grinding rains, I donned my poncho and mounted my remarkably tough Sears bicycle. Right out of the driveway, next right at Kai Store, then right onto the main stretch to UHH, I peddled furiously while wearing my cutoff bibs and my

Dudley Do-Right t-shirt (my other prized article of clothing that I'd gotten with the cereal box-top-special). Having my distinctly unique fashion sense protected by a fifty-cent thin slip of plastic, I braved the elements, zipping along as fast as possible while captured below the biblical downbursts drenching my world.

"HEY! HAOLE! PEDDLE THIS!" I heard screamed directly at me from behind. Glancing over my shoulders, I saw a door-less Jeep with four of my classmates coming up fast. Its gnarly off-road tires swerved uncomfortably close as it hit a huge, deep, hundred-yard-long puddle that I was about halfway across. The wheels created a massive standing wave of hydraulics unleashed.

I braced for immediate impact, doing my very best to remain upright while expecting a drenching of epic proportions. That massive puddle wave threw me directly into the awaiting arms of a mammoth hedge, staunch and trimmed perfectly alongside the road. The impact was instantaneous. I found myself entangled and deeply impaled within a ten-foot tall hedge. Amazingly I was embraced within the matrix while still frozen on my bicycle in an upright position! But, from my knees to my ankles, I burned raw with emotions and from myriad scrapes and tiny punctures caused by the broken branches all around me. My cheap poncho was shredded to smithereens just like my newly vanquished self-esteem.

All I heard was my local-boy-antagonizers laughing hilariously. They continued to hoot and holler as they blew past me. An easy target so flagrantly abused, I felt like I'd just been jammed into a locker on my first day of school, a lowly seventh grader getting the backside of a senior's outstretched hand.

From this unfortunate episode, this blatantly unacceptable event, I came to a heartfelt realization. An epiphany of sorts, that forced me to acknowledge how so many aspects of my current circumstances totally sucked. How in the world had I allowed this turn of events to become my new reality?

Burning deep within me was a newfound deep-seated desire to change everything.

I knew exactly what that very first change was going to be.

My epiphany made me smile.

* * * * * * *

My mighty thoroughbred Forest Green VW Rabbit, ready for conquest, fortune and fame, awaited its new owner. It sat sitting silent, glistening, and perfectly drenched by the relentless Hilo rains. After my embarrassing crash into the *Towering-Hedge-of-Infamy*, I'd taken my bicycle down to Hilo's industrial section and found the VW dealer.

I had biked straight to the VW dealership and spotted my ticket to freedom.

"Sir, how will you be financing this?" The salesman asked rather bluntly.

"Do you take local checks? Please total it, I only wish to write one for the entire amount." I responded, annoyed with his lack of faith. "How long will it take you to prep it for me?"

"Here's the total," the salesman said pointing at the bottom line. I looked to see the line items, as he continued, "Tax, registration, floor mats, dealer prep and shipping were extra."

"OK." I summarily cut the check and handed it to him.

Immediately, he disappeared around the corner and called First Hawaiian Bank.

All trepidation gone upon his return with a skip in his step and a joyful bounce in his voice, he said, "It will be ready in about 45 minutes. Can I get you something to drink, Mr. Gourley?"

It appeared I'd garnered a new friend. Dad always said that paying in full could do that for a fellow.

"Can I help load your bicycle into the back? We can lay the seats down and double the storage?" My new best friend offered with a newfound enthusiasm and respect.

"Keep it." I tossed the comment over my shoulder as I blasted out of the lot, leaving my old decrepit ways behind me.

Arriving back to Kilauea Avenue, Brian wasted no time in taking a jab at the new wheels of which I was so proud. "Nice! Didn't know VWs came in vomit-green mate!"

"I prefer 'forest green', as it so clearly stated on the window sticker." I answered without waver or giving an inch.

"Maybe pea-soup-puke-green would be more accurate." Using a host of descriptive adjectives like his professors taught him, Kenzo got his quick hit in as well.

"Pohoiki?" I threw at them. "Let's see if three boards fit inside! Hop in -- I'm driving!" And off we went on our very first adventure with me as the pilot.

Finally, I had my own set of wheels. I'd been forced into other's schedules for anything that involved being more than ten blocks from home. My big purchase changed all of that. Now I was their equal and could take my rightful turn at the wheel for surf safaris and other needed shenanigans. My trusty four-speed-wonder-weapon-on-wheels sported the standard stick shift and optional racing-style steering wheel. It had four-wheel independent suspension - just like a Corvette!

Brand new. 71 horsepower. Untamed joy.

I left my broken and shattered self-esteem leaning against that VW dealership's wall. For all of my inadequacies were scorched onto that Sears bicycle and the limited lifestyle it had had me captured within. I yearned to be fully independent and unhindered by its profoundly slow motion lifestyle.

Now I had freedom!

I never once looked back.

Finally, I was back in control of my future.

And, just like getting rid of the tepid bicycle and finding a new set of wheels, it was time to find better - and less putrid - accommodations. My newfound best friend Kenzo was working on that very item. Along with Big Pat, who was another roommate and fellow wannabe refugee, who couldn't wait to make a dynamic change to a place far beyond the raging madness known as 1956 Kilauea Avenue...

* * * * * * *

Since that epiphany, so long ago, that I had concerning my deepest desire to own only hydrocarbon burning pieces of equipment as my main means of transportation and having nothing to do with a peddle driven slow-ride-to-nowhere, it has become abundantly reinforced daily that I was born for speed.

My quest for speed became apparent the day my Dad got me that go-kart. It helped me unleash my innate ability to not just control equipment but to make them scream. The list grew as the decades flew by. My first car was a deep blue Camaro Z28. I bought a Kawasaki PE400 dirt bike that could climb just about anything. I used it to blast around the sugar cane fields high above Hilo. A classic 240Z - done in ivory white with black accents - was one of my all time favorites. But it was the Honda Interceptor 500 motorcycle - that could delaminate the asphalt from the roadbed with speeds approaching supersonic - that gave me the quivers every time I got on it.

Eventually terrestrial speed limits became too confining and leaving the limitations of the earthbound highway system entered my world. When I was merely 15, my oldest brother Larry taught me entry-level aerobatics with his 150 Cessna at the local airport. There I learned wingovers, stalls, and recoveries, and with those introductory flights, I discovered that I loved the freedom flying allotted me.

Later in life I got my helicopter license, which, for me, was a type of right-of-passage. I yearned for a pilot's license to assuage my personal need to see if I could actually do it because it required all three disciplines: applied physics, very specific technical skills, and an advanced situational awareness in a three-dimensional space that few ever discovered.

My brother Keith summed it up best after a particularly wild flight-of-fancy dancing along the hardwood forest fringes overlooking the Allegheny River. After achieving staying alive for hundreds of hours as the pilot in command while flying with my skids in the trees and my heart in the clouds, he leapt out of the bird as the rotors wound down, looked at me, and stunned-to-the-bone declared, "You've got to quit flying like that or you're going to kill somebody!"

I presume he was actually worried about me...and not just himself.

Yet, I am still here. It appears that the "ancient adage"- that GOD will allow you to thrive until the very day HE decides to call you home - is absolutely true. It's a divine edict, for even people such as myself, who decided long ago that speed limit signs were for the least capable amongst us. And, that gravity is best overcome with pure power, applied skills, and, upon occasion, raw foolish courage.

8

What Happened to Fifi?

"Best not rush to judgment, since everything may actually be your fault!"

AJG / 1976-77

* * * * * * *

"We need food." Kenzo announced into the atmosphere with the refrigerator door hanging open and his need for caloric intake on high. Big Pat, another escapee from 1956 Kilauea, and I were sitting in the living room of our new digs we'd gotten to escape from the ongoing human destruction still taking place at 1956 Kilauea Avenue. We'd moved about a month prior to a new house Big Pat had been offered by a developer. Big Pat -- not to be confused with Little Pat -- actually had a discernable means of income. He drove bus for the County and fancied himself some type of chef. Kenzo and I were good with that since we were hungry all of the time and his cooking skills were considerably better than either of ours.

Life had thrown me an excellent person to call my best friend. Kenzo and I started hanging out more and more, surfing, snorkeling, and a bit of spear fishing. We were always doing something in between classes. Plus, his local boy knowledge and my propensity of being perpetually ready for adventure gave us a lot in common.

Big Pat gave Kenzo his list of needs, and I added Heinz Ketchup (the large 32 oz glass bottle) to the extensive list. We both tossed him $100 on his way out in his decrepit Dodge Valiant. Unlike my awesome VW Rabbit, the Valiant was kept in dirt-poor repair and in perpetual need of tires, wipers, oil, and gas. But, what was even more important to me was the fact that I could actually drive and Kenzo, at best, didn't possess a *feel for the road.*

Kenzo got a job stocking shelves during the four to ten o'clock shift at Hilo's Safeway Supermarket. As the produce clerk, he was rapidly becoming an expert in all things fruit and vegetable. Earning a living and getting the employee discount on foods purchased was both a win for him and a win for his roommates!

Back in the mid-70's $300 worth of groceries was at least two overflowing cartloads. It would last the three of us a few weeks of rotating between grazing and bountiful dinners. So, when Kenzo got his Safeway employee discount coupled with our monies, a few hundred bucks would stuff his Valiant to the brim with everything from toilet paper to T-bone steaks.

And, so long as he didn't forget to grab my jumbo Heinz ketchup bottle, we'd all get along splendidly. In fact, I went through so much ketchup that Kenzo and Big Pat started calling it "Gourley Sauce," which they leveled at me with friendly abuse and more than a touch of annoyance. They thought it was disgusting, improper, and just plain wrong to put ketchup on steak. I, on the other hand, grew up eating steaks cut straight from the cow, and knew true delicacy of said ketchup on steak.

The next morning Big Pat questioned me with a rather strange look in his eyes and a touch of mischievous knowledge. "Did you take a look at Kenzo's car?"

Checking the carport I asked, "Hey Kenzo! Where's your Valiant?" It failed to appear anywhere on the premises and certainly not where he always parked it.

Kenzo limped outside and stood beside me under a perfectly blue-sky morning. Birds were singing and flowers blooming. Hawaiian white ginger permeated the air. It was odd to see how he was more than a bit flabbergasted by the events of the previous night. He started telling me, in a very animated voice, with his arms waving wildly for emphasis, about his trusty Valiant's untimely demise and his accompanying tale of woes-gone-crazy.

"It was raining hard last night. Almost home, coming down Kahakai Boulevard - as usual - when I had to swerve to miss a dog." Kenzo became even more pumped up by his brazen wreck and loss of wheels. "Lost control, hit that little two-foot high lava wall just this side of the store. Next thing I knew -- I was upside down grinding the roof flush with the dashboard, diving under the dash to save my life!"

"So you're telling me you lost it on a straightaway?! I know your driving sucks, but don't you think that's a bit much?" Kenzo was not at all happy with my critique of his lack of driving abilities. Ignoring me, he went on with his story.

"Got seriously airborne prior to landing dead center in the middle of Kahakai. Then, after what seemed like years, I ground to a perfect stop pointing exactly where I wanted to be going in the first place -- just upside down!"

"You finished wheels up in the middle of the road in heavy rains? Wow! Are you OK?"

"Kinda' stiff and sore, but nothing broken. Except for totaling the Valiant, all is good. But, that's not the wildest part!"

"How can it get better than that? I mean, really Kenzo? You flipped the car, screeched to a grinding halt and lived to talk about it? Really dramatic, even for you." Giving it a second's pause, I asked, "So what else happened?"

"When I realized I wasn't dead, I dug my way through the huge batch of groceries, kicked out what remained of the back window, and crawled out onto the highway. Man, was I in some state of shock, standing there quivering in the downpour -- trying to figure out what to do -- must have been around 11:30 or midnight? My boss had me stay a little later for inventory, so I got out late and I had to buy all that stuff after my shift was over."

"Where's our food?!" It finally dawned on me that breakfast might not be in the cabinets.

"Screw our food -- I'm telling a story here. The food was torn to shreds in the crash. Man, you're going to have to deal with it! Anyways, I saw a light in the distance, a porch light on the nearest house a few hundred yards away. So, I trudged in the middle of the road to get there and ask for help. It was the only thing I could see, black as midnight with the light reflecting on the rain and puddles. So, there I was, walking along, and then I tripped over something lying in the middle of the road. It was that damn dog! I fell over it, tore my pants and scuffed my knees. And they still hurt…Man, I don't have any Neosporin!" It was on the list. One more thing…" Kenzo sighed with the realization of one more item lost to the night's confusion and sorrows.

"OK. So not only did you lose it on a straightaway, but you still killed the dog in the process? We've got deer in Pennsylvania, dude... You Never! Ever! Ever! EVER! Swerve!"

"Too late. Found that out way too late. Anyways, I killed the dog, fell over it, hurt my knees, and then got back up and walked to the light for help." Kenzo leaned against the post of the carport and proceeded to describe his next phase of the previous evening's list of woes. "Knocked on the door and this real local babe - think she was pure Polynesian - answered. She took one good look at me, screamed bloody murder, her eyes got real big, and then she passed right out! Fell over backwards on her living room carpet and didn't move! So, I bent down to check on her and that's when her husband, a huge moke, came around the corner to see what the heck was going on with this stranger being in his house. He was looking at me like some crazy freak out to get his wife in the midnight hour. He leapt across the room, grabbed me by my shirt, picked me straight up, and screamed 'what'd you do to my wife?!' In my defense I told him, while inches from his foul breath and directly into his face, that'd I'd been in an accident just down the road. And I wasn't sure at all what happened to his wife. She was starting to come around after feinting and appeared to be getting rapidly better while he cradled her in his arms after throwing me into the Lazy Boy while telling me, 'Sit still! You're dying, Man.'"

I gave Kenzo a look of pure confusion on his last comment since he looked plenty OK to me. Not dying at all...

"I know. I felt rather good at the time, in spite of my run in with the dog and my knees getting trashed." Kenzo had gotten my look and knew what I was thinking. "So, I took stock and looked down at myself now that I had some light to work with. I had blood from my face to my toes! Glass stuck all through my hair. Man, I must have looked like a victim of some lunatic ax murderer, right out of *Texas Chainsaw Massacre*! I looked like I didn't have a drop of blood left in me, all the way down to being stuck between my toes. It glued me to my slippers! So, by impulse, I touched the blood, which had been melted by the rain and was smeared all over my white t-shirt, and licked my finger. Turns out, your massive Heinz ketchup bottle flew up during the crash, took out my rearview mirror, and completely exploded all over me! Put shards of glass all through my hair, painted me in globs of thick blood red goo and made me look like I was gutted and left on death's doorstep. Although, I was on their doorstep and feeling rather fine." Kenzo smiled when he delivered that tidbit of factual information for me to digest and enjoy.

"Does your insurance cover my ketchup?"

"Get over yourself, I'm trying to tell you a story here!" Kenzo took back control of the narrative. "So, foolish me, I told the moke, who I found out was a Sergeant in the Hawaii Police Department – the guy musts been 6'4" - that not to worry, it's only ketchup! I was so relieved by finding out that I wasn't really dying after all.

"Well he certainly wasn't. He leapt across the room like a nuclear-crazed Godzilla getting ready to stomp Tokyo into oblivion! And, for the second time, he had me by the throat with my feet dangling, foaming at the mouth while screaming directly into my face, 'WHAT KIND OF SICK JOKE IS THIS?!' All I could get out between gasps was '...*car wreck...my car...middle of the road...upside down...sir.*' He proceeded to carry me over to the door, with me still kicking and gagging. I couldn't breathe. My feet didn't touch the ground as he looked outside and down the road where I was pointing. Neither of us could see my newly destroyed Valiant. It was completely out of sight, so far down the road that it was hidden in the pounding rains."

"Wow! So, what happened then?"

"He proceeded to frog-march me down Kahakai, his gorilla fist still latched hold of me by the back of my neck. Since, after all, I had the audacity to demand that the wreck had actually happened. At least his wife was now back in the land of the living and getting a grip on their couch. Then, as we left their porch light behind us, we both tripped over that same dead dog!" Kenzo was truly exasperated with the telling of this secondary event, "Stupid mutt got me twice!" Kenzo had a deep thought, "I guess three times if you count that it was the actual cause of the accident to begin with."

"At least now he knew you weren't lying." I offered.

"It was his dog! That monster huge, ticked-off-angry Police Sergeant - *that crazy moke brudda'* - knelt down, cradled the dog in his arms, and started sobbing uncontrollably. He completely turned to mush with tears and all! Turns out that German Shepherd was his baby. He'd raised him from a pup. And now, with this turn of events, the shoe was finally on the proper foot. All of a sudden, he became my newest best friend. Man was I pissed, he'd screamed at me, frog-marched me all over the place, only to find out that it was his stupid mutt that almost got me killed! After the 'it's his dog' bombshell revelation, immediately we all got along much better. He called his buddies from the Pahoa Police Station, and they swept everything under the rug quickly and quietly. Zero anything. Like it never even happened. Immediately, got me a wrecker and carted my destroyed car off to who-knows-where, and I might add, at no expense. Seems like those Pahoa Cops had a lot of practice making their mistakes disappear, if you know what I mean. Squeaky clean. They even used brooms to get every little piece of glass and reflectors."

"Did you have insurance?" Big Pat asked off to the side, really enjoying the re-telling of the story, chuckling all the way through it, much to Kenzo's chagrin.

"Why bother? It's useless to insure a ten-year old Valiant. My car's gone. With no insurance money coming my way, I'm screwed 'til I find something else to drive."

I nodded. "Don't worry, I'll get you to and from classes and work. Want to go get some groceries?" I smirked. "Do you think that the bald tires had something to do with it?"

Finally, Kenzo admitted the Valiant was junk; I'd been telling him that since my first ride in it.

"Sure, but I think the wipers were even worse. Never saw that dog until it was way too late!" Kenzo confided in his analysis of the previous evening's events-gone-bad. "Big Pat, you want to ride along?"

"No. I don't trust either of you driving me anywhere. I'll stick to my bus. But, I'll get you a new list so you can remember what we need." He laughed without remorse as he added, "And, please, don't forget a jumbo bottle of Heinz!"

* * * * * * *

"Wow! Nice ride, Kenzo." I was inspecting his brand-new Toyota Land Cruiser painted in some weird taupe color, sort of military like. "Maybe I should give you lessons on how not to lose it on a straightaway."

"Just get in, redneck! Let's see if Kalapana's Left Point is breaking. I already put our boards on the rack. Nice not to have to put them inside, isn't it?" Kenzo was so happy with his purchase, seems being gainfully employed had its benefits when it came to financing a vehicle.

Kenzo promptly dumped the clutch in reverse, blasted out of the low-hanging carport and summarily peeled our boards off the roof racks in the process! They landed with a thump right in front of our faces on the hard cement.

I laughed so hard I thought I'd lose my cookies!

Kenzo was aghast.

We got out to inspect the damage; Kenzo didn't want to look. He hadn't even thought of glancing upwards to see if clearance was an issue. I, on the other thought, was thinking how it would be hard to blame this one on me, especially for being on the fringe financially day-by-day. Both of our boards were custom creations and not cheap.

"Look at that! Zero damage! Not a mark on them." It seems as though Kenzo had tied them together, and they came off as one single unit.

After a sigh of relief (mostly from Kenzo) and readjusting to being outside of the height limits of the carport, we ratcheted them back down. We quickly found ourselves blasting up Kahakai Boulevard as Kenzo got Land Cruiser to speed. He looked over at me while declaring, rather profoundly, "I'm never swerving for another dog again IN MY LIFE!"

Just as those words escaped Kenzo's lips, a house on the right, with some little old lady dressed in a housecoat and full frump, threw open her door.

Out jumped Fifi.

Fifi, being a tiny fur ball with ribbons in its hair, was one angry Pomeranian. She immediately decided to take her hostilities out on Kenzo's Land Cruiser. Running full bore, past the grasp of her frumpy owner's outreached arms, Fifi leaped to bite into Kenzo's front right tire, and promptly got sucked over the falls. The next thing we felt was her getting mangled by the back tire, where she did a double loop through the wheel well assembly!

When I looked in my rearview mirror, I saw Fifi exit the back getting twenty feet of air and landing dead as a doornail. Fur flying everywhere, the Pomeranian skidded on its back down the baking hot blacktop of the infamous canine-killing Kahakai Boulevard on a crispy-clear Hawaiian morning! Basic physics claims that it is impossible for a Pomeranian to stop a Toyota Land Cruiser going 60+ miles per hour by biting into its front tire. Now, it was proven fact.

I looked over at Kenzo and gave him the look that said: *I can't believe you didn't move over half a lane to give Fifi a fighting chance!*

Kenzo shrugged his shoulders, put his foot on the gas, and stated without an ounce of remorse, "Told you I wasn't going to budge."

And that is what happened to Fifi.

* * * * * * *

Often, when I've found a lull in a party or get-together, I'd tell Kenzo's story "What Happened to Fifi?" as a means to keep everyone engaged and laughing. Usually I'd enlist a bit of help from one of the guests by asking, "So, what happened to Fifi?"

As decades have passed, I've used this long rambling story as a means to an end. I've used it to teach many of life's lessons as well as a few Biblical truths that are easily garnered from the events captured within this absurd tale of Valiant woe.

1. *Being ill prepared (bald tires, funky windshield wipers, etc.) can cause a lot of grief.*
2. *Going too fast for conditions can get you killed, especially when using bad equipment.*
3. *Never – ever -- swerve for a critter on the road; it is always better to hit the deer than the tree.*
4. *Go to the light for it will save you, especially the Light of the World -- Christ.*
5. *Misinterpreting events and anger falsely unleashed can lead to bearing false witness. Kenzo's being "greeted" at the front door. The whole exploding ketchup saga. The husband's leap to judgment and getting fired up multiple times while assuming that Kenzo was lying and playing some type of sick joke. And, of all things, the husband's assumption that everything was Kenzo's fault when it was his dog that actually caused the entire series of tragic events to unfold.*
6. *Unwarranted rage kills. Fifi's suicidal death-leap at a moving vehicle speeding down the highway that was at least one thousand times her size.*

And, my final bit of wisdom, one that needs to be clearly front-and-center in all of our lives: it is vitally important to show mercy when and if possible. Kenzo should have, and easily could have, moved over and given Fifi the slightest of chances to survive.

9

Brothers And Sister

"Not all brothers are related, but all brothers are blood."

AJG / 1979

* * * * * * *

Yes! It is true that I have a sister. I have a wonderful sister. She is both awesome and discreet. But, maybe even more importantly, she could be mischievously helpful when called upon. With four brothers it was important for her to be a touch mischievous on a daily basis. She used to turn off the lights, flush the toilet and slam her bedroom door exactly at midnight so Mum and Dad believed our oldest brother had managed to get home on time. Now that's a good sister!

One day, when I was merely ten years old and she was just hopping into a car with some young man fortunate enough to take her out for the evening, my older brothers handed me something and told me, "Quick run out to there and give these to her before she leaves!" Just before she pulled out to go on her date. All flush from the sprint to catch her, I shoved what my brother's gave me in her open window and very excitedly declared, "Here, Shirley, you forgot these!" I didn't even know it was funny, but my brothers howled with wild abandon as I sheepishly returned with Dad's false teeth still in hand. Shirley glared at me for the better part of a month.

With all of the crazy things all of us boys got involved in, fast cars and flying machines, she often gets overlooked in all of the hubbub and wildness. Yet, she was right in the middle of the fray.

Sister Shirley is a wonderful soul. She has patched us up with Band Aids and Steri-Strips, then dusted us off and sent us right back into the action of whatever craziness we'd discovered that day to entertain us.

Although she is ahead of me in years, I often refer to her as "My Little Sister".

We all claim to have taught her how to drive. But, to quote Dad, "It appears that she found the gas pedal all by herself."

Shirley routinely drove through weather unfit to be out in, often to get to work. She's been a nurse forever: ER, Telemetry, Floor Rounds. No matter the affliction, she was there to help whomever needed to be brought back from the brink and then get them discharged as soon as possible.

Eventually she ended up as the school nurse at our high school alma mater. We couldn't have been more fortunate since it was often our kids that needed fixin'! Our children had Shirley to protect, look after, and help them with a bit of extra subterfuge (if and when needed) as they all worked their way through high school's long and perilous, strange, and winding "teenage wonderland" of pathways to choose.

Her stories are legend, but I am sworn to secrecy and shall never divulge them to anyone without her permission. I've often teased that my next book is going to be called *Confessions of a School Nurse*. She typically becomes indignant when picked on, and occasionally threatens to get physical! I'd rather have her hit me than give me 'the look' that only an older sister can give to a little brother.

My sister is awesome! After all, she was a cheerleader who blended right in with the hot chicks of her era. When she was tasked to make something for the varsity cheerleading squad, one of her favorite quick items to fulfill her assignment was chocolate fudge. Unfortunate for her, us boys loved chocolate fudge. We'd first nibble at the corners – because, of course, who'd miss the corners? But corners turned into edges and then into sections, and then into...

Well, in her ability to adapt to having brothers that knew no boundaries, she would make a double batch and hide one away using one tray full as bait. We caught on to her malfeasance and would tear the place apart until we could have a double portion. Only thing better than one batch is two.

She'd scream and tell on us to Mum, who would chastise us and inform us not to ever do it that again.

We didn't, until the very next time. The only thing better than tearing down the highway at speeds beyond compare is a fresh batch of chocolate fudge while you're heading out the door to escape prior to being blamed for her lack of being able to fulfill her cheerleading obligations. We were the best - and the worst - batch of brothers that homemade fudge could buy!

One day she came home with her report card, as we all did. Unlike us, she was excited to share her grades with our parents. Keith summed it up best when he sadly lamented, "That stupid Shirley got straight A's! Now she's making us all look bad."

Shirley was always ready to enjoin the ongoing shenanigans: muscle cars, planes, hot air balloons, Harley Davidson bikes, sandrails and side-by-sides. No matter the Toy of the Day, she hopped aboard and screamed the entire time!

We've done our best to protect her, while shielding her from the criticisms we more than likely deserved. So, when people comment that they didn't even know we had a sister, all of us brothers simply laugh. We change the subject as a means to protect her from a world that needs more-than-a-few secrets kept. So many tales, events and shenanigans that are best to forever remain hidden.

We'd like to keep her safe to write her own tales of what it was like having so many crazy brothers while surviving the same. She would know as best as anyone what we were really like. Now that would be quite the adventure taking a walk in her shoes! Maybe she shouldn't say too much, keep her deep-seated knowledge confidentiality intact. Besides, not everything we did was kosher; anytime you woke up in the ER from being knocked unconscious it was nice to see Sister Shirley hovering over you along with her caring smile of assurance that you weren't dead yet.

Sister Shirley has been sainted, after all.

Love you, Sis. You're the best!

And, always remember... I am your favorite.

* * * * * * *

I have many different sets of brothers -- some, -- who have been thrust upon me by time, events, and circumstances often out of my control. I have been fortunate to be so blessed. All of my brothers are so profoundly different. There are the three who have Gourley as their last name.

Then there are the chosen brothers like Kenzo. Along with another sojourner named Frank Lee, who somehow found us and became one of our regular surf-mates, we too were a team of amigos with a wild side and a propensity to immediately enjoin the fray: surf, scuba, skiing or cliff jumping. No matter the locale or terror, we were pushing each towards more and more radical elements of behavior and outcomes.

Kenzo found his limit for surfing on a small minus tide day at Pohoiki. Tiny crystalline tubes broke in shallow water perfectly, as the waves peeled over razor-sharp reef in water merely inches deep with pockets loaded with Hawaii's formidable needle-sharp vana spines. Kenzo decided to take off and show me how to do quick snaps off the top lip of the liquid rolling thunder. His skills were on rampant display.

Then he lost it, got sucked over the falls, and disappeared from sight.

There was nothing unusual until I caught a glimpse of him belly crawling across the inner boulders to safety from the foaming mass of the inner bay. When I got to him, after flipping my board and riding it upside down so the skegs didn't snag, I found him whimpering and looking forlornly at the bodysurfing fins on his feet. Blood seeped out from all the punctures where the long-barbed-brittle-nasty purple-black organic vana spikes protruded out the tops and bottoms of both of his feet!

He looked at his fins, knowing they had to go, and proceeded to rip both of his fins off simultaneously. I could hear the vana needles snap loudly in the process; it was wicked to see and gruesome to know how much that must have hurt.

Kenzo lay back on the hot lava boulders, closed his eyes, and took a series of deep breaths trying to gather his strength.

What a gorgeous day!

Blue.

Blue.

Blue.

Pohoiki was alive. Endless blue skies with tiny sets of translucent turquoise waves, all dazzling in the sunlight, danced in synchronized perfection. A pod of spinner dolphins lazily played just outside of the breakers. Yet, with his poor launch and rather unfortunate landing, Kenzo had managed to transform everything into a sea of pain.

I put him on my back and carried him to the hot springs. It was his desire to be in warm waters, under the shade of eighty-foot palms lightly swaying and wrapped in elephant ear philodendron vines. It was the perfect place for Kenzo to get a grip on his current condition. With a shrug and a toss into the pool, I helped him achieve that simple goal, and then went to retrieve our boards.

It was so small that Frank refused to even bother, strapped on scuba gear, and went blue water hunting while Kenzo and I surfed Second Bay. When I got back, Frank had appeared with his bountiful harvest of a few lobsters. He too was floating, catching up with Kenzo and his newly pierced feet and accompanying tale of woe.

Between their discussion of all known methods of how to remove vana spines and survive the process, I broke in, "What's it like scuba diving?"

Frank pointed nonchalantly, "Try the gear on." I looked at him intrigued.

"There's a few hundred pounds of air left, at this depth should last twenty minutes or so. Easy. Just never ever – ever -- go up fast or you'll explode. Even in here, in four feet of water, you can still form an embolism or worse, like rupturing a lung. So always breathe out as you ascend." Frank got real intense and looked me in the eye, "Never forget that most important rule." Then smiling and lightening up a bit, he finished, "Go for it. Think you'll love it."

With my newfound underwater freedom, I lingered on the bottom and discovered that I loved scuba gear and the underwater freedom it so easily allowed! It would become the basis for how we'd end up spending so much of our energies over the course of the next years.

Plus, while I was down there, I got to inspect Kenzo's perforated feet.

Upon surfacing (slowly, as Frank had so pointedly advised), and with more humor than Kenzo desired, I shared my sound medical advice. "Looks bad, brah! Might need to amputate...".

"Dibs on the Land Cruiser!" Frank offered as a means of condolence.

There was no humor in Kenzo's world as he chose to ignore us. And continue his downward spiral into a world of hurt...

But, after a few days of soaking his feet in vinegar, Kenzo healed enough to return to a life of extreme sports and wayward friends. The black barbs of vana - being some form of invertebrate chalky substance - had finally dissolved from the acidic properties via a multitude of vinegar soakings. Although, Kenzo still sported black dots on the tops and bottoms of his feet, reminders that would last a lifetime.

* * * * * * *

Amongst us closest of friends, we rarely ever said hello or goodbye. To us it seemed that "hello" invoked the feeling that you'd been somehow separated. And, by declaring a "goodbye" to a dear friend, you may never see them again, at least not on this side of the veil. So we started our conversations with personalized catch phrases, which often appeared absurd to those adventurous souls who happened to be within earshot. They had zero prior knowledge of our past conquests and exploits, losses and triumphs, and certainly not about our current arena of dangerous pursuits.

"Bamboo." I deadpanned as I answered the phone on a melancholy morning.

"Luau!" Kenzo answered brightly. His joy annoyed me greatly.

"What are you thinking?" I asked.

"*Trifecta*! Tomorrow at sunrise. See you at 6 am. Be prepared for a Hawaiian winter -- going to be awesome! I'll call Frank."

"He's here. I'll bring him with me. See you before sunrise."

Our *Trifecta of Adventure* was a day of adventure virtually impossible anywhere else on the planet. It was to be only found on the Island of Hawaii - our Big Island - and only during the winter months. It appeared we were all suffering under the ancient Hawaiian curse: "May you suffer through many a Hawaiian winter." When it is 85 degrees Fahrenheit in the water in the middle of winter, it is most difficult to think of it being any type of curse or bad omen of things to come. Yet, as in all ancient sayings passed through the epochs of time, there is always a grain of truth wrapped into a warning of how even the most benign things can go astray.

For us, we knew not the seasons of life and were trapped into a perpetual version of *Endless Summer*, just like the movie we'd grown to love.

First, we'd go surfing just as the sun evaporated the dawn. We chose Honoli'i, with its massive and heavy north shore point break. Somehow, I'd managed to get past my first experience there with Quick Silva and my near-death experience while being dragged towards the entrance to Tombstones. I always remembered that sordid event, and how close I'd come to drowning. I kept that valuable lesson learned firmly at the forefront of my mind when anywhere near those treacherous waters.

After dawn patrol, we'd get *loco mocos* and the 10,000+ calories they provided at Cafe 100 to prep for what was to come. Frank would get a double; his insatiable appetite allowed him to consume massive quantities while never slowing down.

The next activity was skiing Mauna Kea, above the cloud layers. The time was best as close to noon as possible, to give the sun the opportunity to break apart the ice pack into some semblance of snow. It rarely happened, mostly just pellet snow and ice patches, but it provided us with a single line through the slush. Mauna Kea's summit was at 13,803 feet above sea level, sitting alone in the vast Pacific, and created its own dynamic wonder of amazing presence and unique challenge with a couple thousand feet of vertical drop.

Sometimes, when the air was crystal clear, you could see most of the main islands of the Hawaiian Archipelago laid out like a relief map stretching far to the western horizon. Only Kauai and beyond would remain out of sight. Today was one of those obscenely clear days.

"Dude! How on earth did you ever work up here?" I gasped between breaths while trying to buy a moment of time.

"Wasn't that fun! We used to bring wine and beer and use UH's telescope to play *Pong* - just like our personal gigantic video arcade to the cosmos." Frank answered with casual indifference.

Frank wasn't flushed at all, and earned his moniker, Neanderthal, daily. He seemingly was impervious to injury, fatigue, or failure. I'd seen him get completely crushed by waves, come up laughing, and reel in his board. Then he'd go right back into the lineup. Meanwhile, Kenzo and I gasped for every breath of the rarified high-altitude air.

Reminiscent and not nearly as indifferent, I challenged, "That telescope was awesome!"

Frank just grinned.

I continued, "I couldn't believe there was anything on the planet that powerful. I mean, we had to put it on auto-track just to stay on the crater; otherwise those craters would just fly past in the eyepiece."

It was true – we needed technological assistance to stay focused on the chosen moon crater as we could never keep up. Now that was power.

"Hey! How'd I miss all of that?" Kenzo jumped in, completely forgetting about his lungs being on fire or his feet that still stung from our last surfing adventure.

We both looked at him and simultaneously explained the obvious with a singular word: "Chicks."

Immediately, Kenzo knew exactly why he'd never gotten to enjoy the stars like we had. And, we understood exactly why he really didn't care.

We'd alternate turns since there were no ski lifts and we had to pick each other up after each run. Launch was between all of the scientific community's telescopes gracing the summit. Manmade structures of stark white spheres silhouetted by the glacier-blue sky overhead dotted the run. The skiers would slide over to the access road at the bottom, and we'd all drive back to the top together.

"Go ahead. I'm done." Kenzo motioned for us to get out of his Land Cruiser.

"Kenzo! What! Still nursing your vana wounds?" I laughed as we got out.

Frank just grinned, snapped into his skis and barreled full-bore down the frozen tropical slopes without even once considering looking back.

Finally, we found ourselves down at the broken boat ramp - shattered by a seismic event -- just north of South Point. Far from everything civilized and doing a wall dive were the Big Island met the Hawaiian Deep. The wall along this section of coastline fell abruptly into the awaiting arms of the abyss, which was over 17,000 feet below us.

Sitting on a bench of black lava shelf, in the wash zone of the surge of the ocean, I adjusted my Mares mask, soft as could be, to a perfect fit. To add to my ensemble, I pulled out my brand-new spear gun, a Mares snub nose with the super-sharp trident tip. It was a pneumatic and had the stopping power of a real beast.

I felt invincible and ready to fetch dinner.

Tanks good. Gear set. Spear in hand. It was my turn to leap into the water. Following the vertical streams of bubbles, I chased Kenzo and Frank into the bottomless deep prior to becoming even more separated.

The ocean was exceptionally clear - like liquid air. Passing 60 feet, I got approached by a pelagic fish, a kahala. From a distance, it looked small. But then its curiosity got the best of it, must have been all of the bubbles trailing from my descent into the deep blue, and came over to check me out.

Perfect shot -- right in the gills! The kahala hung limp on the end of my retrieval cord. As I wound him in, it became readily apparent he was at least 25 pounds of fine dining. Man was I excited as I pulled him closer...

All of a sudden, I could feel a wild type of anxiety rush through me - *Obi Wan* would say, "a disturbance in The Force."

Out of the corner of my eye a shadow approached fast. And, to make the situation fully dynamic, the kahala reanimated, snapped back to life and ripped my gun right out of my hands!

Forgetting everything else, I swam after my prized possession, which was now spiraling down into the deep blue, trailing a brilliantly lit stream of green blood. The green blood trail – caused by a lack of spectrum at depth – added a surrealism as I kicked wildly. The fish and my gun remained just beyond my grasp, past my yearning fingertips and just out of reach…

Somewhere around 140 feet, give or take, with everything cast in various shades of the deepest blues, that huge shadow blew by me. It was at that precise moment that I decided that my fish and the attached gun were both gone, never to be mine again. For that disturbance in The Force was – in fact -- a monstrous hammerhead shark hell-bent on eating my dinner with or without my permission.

I said a silent goodbye to my beloved speargun and the kahala in its final death spiral, plummeting into the dark blue of the Hawaiian Deep, with one very focused and hungry thousand-pound shark, giving chase, jaws wide open, getting ready to chomp it into oblivion.

Upon finding Kenzo and Frank, I did the massive double-handed shark jaws underwater signal and waited for them to follow me back to the surface. They looked at me, took a moment to gaze around, saw nothing, and went right back to searching for dinner, spears firmly in their hands. They could care less about my tales of the hungry Kraken and monsters of the vast abyss.

No longer having a spear gun to defend myself, I felt very naked and totally exposed. Surveying my surroundings, I swam back to the shelf and climbed out. Still quaking in my fins from my wild encounter, dry land provided me the safety I yearned while I waited for my brothers to join me.

All to live another day, *Trifecta of Adventure* firmly behind me and hoping my intrepid brothers would provide a nice touch of seafood to go with our dinner plans of having garden salads and two scoops of sticky white rice prior to all of us collapsing from that day's journey of survival above and below the clouds and the waves.

* * * * * * *

It took a rare convergence of weather, waves, and seasons to be able to pull off a true Trifecta of Adventure. Everything had to align and then you needed capable friends who could endure the stamina and required physical capabilities, as well as the technical skills to thrive during every phase of the journey.

I've been fortunate enough to know more than a few souls – many of my brothers included -- that fit the desired characteristics and wouldn't end up as road kill along the way.

* * * * * * *

Loco Moco = one scoop rice, one hamburger patty, one over-easy egg, all smothered in brown gravy. Best found at Cafe 100 in Hilo on Kilauea Avenue.

10

My Sansei Princess

"She almost smiled at me. That alone made all of the difference!"

AJG / 1977 and Forever

* * * * * * *

"She almost smiled at me!" I nearly screamed at Kenzo as we skateboarded down a freshly paved subdivision in Upper Hilo.

"...And?"

"And what? It was awesome! She totally reminds me of your mother!" I grinned ear-to-ear with my latest revelation and carved a long arc across the asphalt.

Kenzo nodded. Everyone who had ever met his mother knew she was not just a little bit pretty; she was downright stunning.

"So where did you meet this stunning babe?" Kenzo moved on. Then added, almost as an afterthought, "Must be pure Japanese -- sounds like a *Sansei Princess*. Man, you are digging deep into a world of trouble!"

"It was so weird. She was trying to hide behind her sketchbook. We were doing this really weird assignment: *Charcoal on Paper of the Human Form.*" I smiled as I continued to walk back up the hill, skateboard swinging under my arm, large smile beaming in the evening's cool air.

"That's the class that they cover the windows with newspapers and won't let anybody near, isn't it?" Kenzo stopped and asked pointedly.

"Yeah. As usual, I showed up late -- just as this dude steps onto a pedestal in the middle of the room and promptly proceeds to drop his bathrobe! Perfectly posed buck naked so we can draw him in all of his heroin-addicted-naked-butt-glory."

I shook my head as I recounted the morning's events that were so far from my farm-raised childhood upbringing.

"Looked like the guy had been using hard drugs forever. He probably gave up years of daily acid abuse and eventually settled on heroin as his newest and best friend..."

Kenzo cut me off, "Back to this local babe..." He dropped his board and tore down the street hooting and hollering to the world at large as he sweepingly embraced the moment.

Barely keeping up, I breathed, "Really cute. That is… while blushing to the max and hiding behind her charcoal drawing as best as she could. Think that naked haole guy totally freaked her out. After all, she was on the full frontal side." Then I added as an afterthought, "So weird..."

I drew some smooth lines right behind Kenzo, lost within my deepest desire to find my unidentified *Sansei Princess* once again. There was something strangely familiar about her; something I couldn't quite identify.

It was almost like a dream wrapped within a primordial vision.

Or, perhaps it was simply a profoundly deep yearning of the heart.

* * * * * * *

Somehow, I'd misread my summer's class schedule and showed up 20 minutes early for Oceanography 101. It was the beginning of my sophomore year and I had formulated a plan spawning from a very deep thought: watch for the cutest girl in the class, follow her into the classroom, and sit down beside her. Having learned one of the strangest phenomena of the known universe, it appeared that wherever everyone sat on the very first day - everyone would forever gravitate to that exact same seat throughout the entire semester. This time I would employ that *Cosmic Law of the Same Seat* and have an entire semester to get to know at least one of the fabulous babes on campus. Besides, I never showed up with either a pencil or piece of paper, so hopefully a smile and my lack of preparedness could work as a means to an end.

Such a simple, yet elegant, plan.

And then, there she was! The predicted cute girl was walking towards me in the morning's joy, wearing a sundress while sporting an electric smile. Better yet, she danced up the steps and went into Oceanography 101! I leaped up, followed her in, and proceeded to declare the desk on her left as my own feudal territory for the entire upcoming semester.

She looked longingly familiar, effervescent golden-brown eyes that sang a tune of mystery wrapped in radical kindness. I was immediately smitten to the point of having a difficult time asking her for the requisite pencil and paper. Trying my best to formulate entire sentences, but having a ridiculously difficult time doing so. Then I realized it was the exact same babe I'd seen blushing and hiding in the naked heroin dude art class the previous semester.

She was the very same girl who had almost smiled at me!

One item I didn't know, however, was that our Oceanography class would only ever meet in the room three times throughout the semester: today and then to take the midterm and final exams. All other classes would be field trips for the simple fact that this was Hawaii. What better possible place to learn than down at the ocean discovering ocean stuff?

Upon the proclamation, I leaned over and asked my Art Class Blushing Angel if she would be kind enough to go with me on the first field trip. Acting like I didn't know how to find the great Pacific Ocean and praying that she'd consider me a mission of mercy, I gave her the most hopeful look I could muster.

She gave me a piercing that resembled an x-ray scan from top-to-bottom, smiled, and softly answered, "OK." That near whisper held a hint of going completely beyond her upbringing's pronounced warnings (from her parents, friends, family, cousins, priests -- virtually every single person she'd ever known) about haoles like me. Her eyes danced to a tune of somehow having gone completely rogue and venturing far afield from her sheltered existence about everything she'd ever been taught about boys like me.

As for me...

It was the very best class I'd ever had IN MY LIFE!

* * * * * * *

Kenzo and I We were busy prepping for the evening's surf session, waxing our boards and getting ready to battle our way through the inner shore pound at this really exotic place we'd discovered called Hakalau Nui. Being a hidden bay with towering cliffs on both sides. Completely covered in lush jungle, which dripped in strange ways off of every conceivable angle and possible place to cling to, the break was just off a tiny beach of tiny black sand black as midnight beach. With a vibrant stream cutting a channel to the ocean thundering right before us. Soft sand black as midnight; smooth lava pebbles along the rims of the beach. If you picked but the smooth lava pebbles it up in your hands, you could see a myriad of olivine crystals -- red, green, brown and gold -- along with the vibrant stream cutting a channel to the ocean thundering right before us; all there and creating a dazzling display enthralled us of why the Big Island's continued to enthrall us with its mesmerizing beauty.

"You do know that you have a real battle ahead of you? She must have a boyfriend, and her girlfriends will dissect you into a million pieces. I'm telling you -- our local *Sansei Princesses* are in a class of their very own. They all pack together and nothing and nobody breaks into their world without the entire pack's permission.

Especially some hillbilly white boy from Outer Mongolia!" Kenzo filled me in on the challenges I unknowingly faced.

"What the heck is this whole *Sansei Princess* designation? And, I am from *Pennsyltuckey*, thank you very much! You misguided, annoying, uninformed, local boy punk."

"*Sansei* - third generation Japanese. They're fully Americanized and fully weaponized. I'm telling you, be careful you foolish naive farmer! She is soooo above your pay grade." Kenzo laughed out loud as he sprinted down the beach to embrace the pounding waves going off like canon volleys. Sitting outside of the shore pound, waiting for one of the real sets of waves to arrive, he continued on with his dissertation of all things *local*, "Believe me, she is a true princess in all that matters. Boys have been trying to marry her since grade school. Probably the most sought after, and impossible to obtain. They're Hawaii's finest natural resource known to all of mankind. Men travel far to find a girl like her."

"I'm from Far. Heck you yoo-hoos don't even know where Pennsylvania is on a map." I jostled for position while carrying on the conversation.

"The reason I don't know is… because…who cares! Nobody says, 'Hey, let's go to Pennsylvania. I hear it's awesome'. That is exactly why nobody can find it, and why nobody ever will." Kenzo turned and proceeded to disappear down one of the giant liquid tornadoes barreling through. We had the place to ourselves. After all, who would be crazy enough to paddle out here? With massive northeastern swells exploding onto a lost-in-time black sand beach, we were all alone in the middle of the vast Pacific Ocean's endless domain.

"It's so strange. Every time I ask her to go on one of our field trips, she brings a friend along. Don't get me wrong, her friends are really pretty too, but we're never alone, like ever. What's with that?" My question hung in the air as we both caught our breath from each catching a ride and scratching our way back into the safety of the channel.

"*Sansei Princesses* always bring a friend. It's their own version of protection, a form of armor from unwarranted advances and smiling haoles who have the obvious intention of stealing their virtue! You really don't get it. I'm telling you -- they always travel in packs. You're lucky she only brings one friend with her." Kenzo went on, "She already has a boyfriend; I guarantee it. And, he will be very disappointed when he finds out that his girl is being pursued by somebody that is over here to plunder our natural resources and steal our most valuable assets."

Ignoring the second part of his comments, "Well, sometimes she brings two. You'd like Karen, she's smoking hot," I offered.

Kenzo smiled as he piled on to his version of my ongoing stupidity, "Let me guess, Karen's third generation Japanese too?"

"Of course." I nodded yes, while keeping my eyes focused towards the entrance to the bay for the next set of waves to cover the horizon.

"Why aren't you dating blonde girls? After all, there are plenty of Southern Californian beach babes all around. They're everywhere. Sometimes I think we're being invaded by them..."

Kenzo shook his head, and immediately proceeded to answer his own question. "I'm not going out with Japanese girls for the exact same reason you aren't chasing blondes. I grew up with them. Just like you grew up with mainland farm, raised, lily-white, Girls Next Door, I grew up with *Sansei Princesses* all around me." Kenzo knowingly smiled and concluded, "All they want is to get married and raise your kids while taking your paychecks, like, forever. Every single one of them reminds me of my mother, just two generations deeper into being full-blooded American. Princesses all."

"Your mother is so hot." I smiled.

Kenzo just shook his head. He'd heard that exact comment from all of his friends his entire life.

Contemplating all things female, which completely confused us, we both turned to embrace the next set of waves. They lifted high -- magnificent before us -- feathering translucent blue in the evening's twilight. They softly called our names to participate in a ride of a lifetime.

We understood waves very well -- unlike the young ladies around us, who totally freaked us out.

* * * * * * *

"This entire time -- I thought we were dating!" I was so exasperated from my discovery that Faith, my *Sansei Princess,* was under the impression we were just hanging out. "I took her to Liliuokalani Gardens and everything." I looked at Kenzo and Frank while telling my sob story over a beer at The Poly Room, the local disco.

"Who cares? Hot babes are a dime-a-dozen! Take a look around. They're everywhere." Frank could care less. His lack of empathy was being honed to a rather sharp edge. He guzzled his beer and ordered another round.

"That's not dating. You told me earlier it was for a class assignment... Something about Suisan Fish Market? And the auction price for that day's catch?" Kenzo admonished me with facts.

"Oceanography 101. Observe the day's catch and do a spreadsheet. Kind of fascinating, really."

"So, you took her to see a bunch of dead fish. Blood, guts, and gore all laid out in a row. Other than that wonderful event, did you provide lunch or some other type of activity?" Kenzo probed my technique, thinking maybe I was flamingly obtuse in all things dating.

Suddenly I felt a little bit stupid. "She brought a picnic lunch, we ate it buried deep in the Japanese Gardens by the stand of towering bamboo -- near that ornate bridge overlooking the tidal pools." I tried to defend my position. "Surely that's a date? Me, her, food, exotic location - Asian to the max - Hilo style."

"Not a date." Kenzo sipped at his beer, not a big drinker Kenzo. Me either. Frank made up for us with his proven ability to consume all things in mass quantities that were put before him.

"What on earth do you see in this girl, Allen? Simple local girl without a brain, devoid of logic, and caught up into her tiny-local-world." Frank was brazen in his attack.

"Besides the obvious? Like she's actually everything you're not. Clean, kind, refined, sweet, nuanced to detail... I mean, the list is endless when you put her credentials beside yours. Even her sneezes are cute." I, once again, defended both her and my interest in everything about her.

"She is hot...super cute...kind of like a Japanese version of Valerie Bertinelli," Kenzo chimed in.

"History major. Excellent grades. Can paint, draw, sew, cook. She's polite to a fault -- unlike you bozos and your Neanderthal tendencies." I went on with my nearly infinite list of attributes that she had and they didn't.

"You're in love -- admit it!" Kenzo blurted out blowing beer out his nose and making a bit of a mess that nobody cared about. The Poly Room was used to messes - usually much larger ones, and Kenzo's foaming nose barely qualified.

Frank just belched out a full-bore monster and ordered another round. Everybody glared at him. He glared right back.

I declined the beer, wondering how to get my point across to these numbskulls. Then I captured a bit of brilliance and added, "She looks like Kenzo's mom, but thirty years younger." I allowed the comment to hang in the air.

Frank's head snapped my direction. He had a strange moment of being flabbergasted, like an electric blast of a deep-seated epiphany ripped him a new pathway of brain connections. Finally, he really started to understand the implications of it all.

I was, too. It stunned me to my very core.

* * * * * * *

The term "Sansei Princess" refers to the gorgeously cute third generation Japanese girls who were fully acclimated to living in Hawaii. They often spoke little, if any, Japanese due to their parents' desire for them to completely immerse themselves into being all things American. They were all that and so much more, for they loved to have a foothold in three different worlds. In some ways they were all things Hawaiian -- knowing how to blend easily between the various factions of Japanese, Filipinos, Chinese, Portuguese, and all of the other ethnicities of the local population, including (fortunately for me) mainland haoles. They easily flowed between the Pidgin English of the local dialect while being able to abruptly switch to Standard English mid-sentence. Also, they were all things Japanese when it came to being perfectly polite, soft spoken, and delicate in all things Asian regarding art, food, and elegant service. But then, they had a third world they easily inhabited: their wild side for they loved the joy of partying under the starry skies like a Southern Californian beach bash gone fully native.

And, their stunning beauty and island girl mystique was legendary. Sansei Princesses *will always be sought after by men searching for the finest wives from the furthest ends of the earth.*

As for me, I am so fortunate to have found my very own Sansei Princess, my wonderful wife, Faith. She exemplifies the very essence of aloha daily. She sings the morning alive. She embraces adventure and is a joy to behold. My greatest gift from heaven is having found a loving wife who makes an entire room light up with her presence.

And, amazingly, she simply loves me for who I am. That alone is the miracle. I have married the sweetheart of my quest to make my childhood vision a reality from a time long before I even knew that such a place as the Big Island of Hawaii existed.

To this very day, seeing black sand on my hands causes me to drift back to days gone by, far ago longings when I had the dreams of my youth and the simple joy of living in a singular moment of time.

11

The Incredible Quest for Surf

"Some journeys last a lifetime, even long after the waves have gone astray."

AJG / 1979ish

* * * * * * *

"Bamboo." I answered forlornly.

"Luau!" Kenzo once again declared brightly.

"Please bail me out of this place." I asked with hope in my voice.

"That's my job. Two o'clock here?" Kenzo made my day.

"Perfect. I'll bring my board and fins."

And so it began...

Or, to be more accurate, our quest continued unabated.

Kenzo and I used our cryptic (and yet obvious to those in-the-know) phone greeting to set a time to meet. When? Where? Both needed clarification, but why was never the question -- it always involved the ocean's welcoming embrace. We were living in two worlds on one island. He was still in Hilo staying in a bungalow deep in the rainforest. I was babysitting a spec home my brothers and I bought hoping the market would continue to climb. The resultant outcome would be the next step to move forward with our plan for world domination.

Bamboo & Luau was the actual address of a two-bedroom two and one half-bath Lindal Cedar Home that two interior architects out of Beverly Hills had built on the slopes of Mauna Loa. Then they split up. Then they died. It was such a typical Hollywood ending, replete with cheating and scandalous facts wrecking any semblance of love that they might once enjoyed. Their children sold it to us, allowing their parent's sordid tale-of-woe to evaporate from their lives.

The house was located dead center in the middle of nowhere and sat on the longest running ridgeline in the state, Mauna Loa's southern flank. The location provided an uninterrupted stunning view of the southernmost point of the Big Island, which happened to be the most southern point in all of the United States of America.

In our world, it was simply known as South Point.

It was spectacularly, magnificently awesome! And, it was profoundly lost in every other possible way. It was near nothing and far from everything that mattered in the real world. Newspapers came in odd batches every one to two days. It was exactly two and a half hours from Hilo - no matter how many speed limits you destroyed along the way. Or, going clockwise around the island, two hours of torturous twisting roads would get you to Kona and its one blinker light. The entire coastline of overgrown coffee fields was sparse to say the least and led to little else but a few restaurants and one good body surfing beach appropriately named Magic Sands. When it was big, the sand would completely disappear and you'd end up surfing on exposed lava rocks, leaving you feeling like it was a magical experience if you came out of the water alive. And, even more importantly not crippled for life from the neck down.

From the lanai, you could see forever. When the weather was typical, you could see the sunrise bursting forth right out of the ocean. Then, as the day waxed fallow, the sunset would fall into the easy presence of the ocean once more, releasing a myriad of stars under perfectly clear skies, unparalleled for clarity. Stars, dripping with divine purity, fell far to the very edge of the most distant horizon. In the winter months, the Southern Cross made its grand appearance, allowing you to realize how far you'd traveled both in time and space.

It was such a strange location, Bamboo & Luau. I was captured in a home that most anywhere else in Hawaii would be worth a true fortune. But, out here, in Hawaiian Ocean View Estates (HOVE), it was simply a very nice home intertwined in a far-flung community built by psychedelic dreams of second-generation hippies and purposely lost souls. People who either did not wish to be found, ever, or those who hoped the Statute of Limitations would run its course before they were discovered to still be above ground.

Civilization was both undesired and unwelcome.

Two bedrooms with glass everywhere allowing the views to permeate everything. Decadent decking completed the designer accommodations. It was completely off-grid before anyone even knew what that meant. Equipped with propane fridges and stove, as well as a having an Onan diesel generator for electric when needed.

Bamboo & Luau was a sojourner's dream. That is, if there was someone to share it with. And that is exactly when our fellow sojourner, Frank Lee, filled the breach with his presence and witty observational skills. Frank had become a friend when we kept bumping into each other at some co-ed student housing. He was chasing the blonde from Alaska. Me, well I was much more interested in the *Sansei Princess* with the golden-brown eyes.

We'll come back to that later...

"Frankly my dear, I don't give a damn." Frank had a habit of quoting *Gone with the Wind* whenever he felt like it, even when it made zero sense (which it hardly ever did). Like now after I'd asked him if he wished to ride into Hilo, meet up with Kenzo, and find some waves.

Time did not flow along a linear pathway in HOVE, being so far removed from reality. It mattered not the day. They all blended, and rarely did we know what day of the week it was, let alone the date. We usually had the month right, but not always.

"Leaving in ten minutes. Up to you. Looks like an eastern swell with a southern component bouncing off of South Point. Pohoiki and Kalapana should be breaking. Gonna' coast in Hot Springs after. Who knows? Maybe not? Don't care. Find Kenzo and decide best way to put our fins in the water."

Melancholy deeply infected our conversations. Rarely did they involve full sentences. Mostly they were punctuated with grunts and words that were only capable of being deciphered by some weirdly adapted type of Bamboo & Luau guttural code known only to us. We thought we were cool; looking back I simply acknowledge that we were stubborn to a fault. Somehow we'd become locked on a course not of our own making.

"Think I'll sit stalwart, ponder the intricacies of life, hang with the dogs and play my guitar. I could use a little alone time." Frank decided his fate, as he took a good look around and embraced his inner Zen. Frank was trying to be cute with his answer; Frank and cute never really matched in any venue. Sometimes a loner needs his seclusion delivered in an obviously raw format.

"Well then, bye. Frank Lee, I don't give a damn either, Scarlett." I smiled, fluffed the dog's ears, and flogged it down off the mountain in the trusty Rabbit. I would not be missing much; Frank's guitar playing sucked. I never heard him string enough strums together to remotely call it music. Besides, tracking down Kenzo on our perpetual quest to find the perfect batch of waves was all on that was on my mind.

The three of us had even given our ongoing journey, our self-imposed exile from all things civilized, a title: ***The Incredible Quest for Surf.***

We'd been at it for the better part of three years.

Yet, somehow, it already felt like a lifetime.

* * * * * * *

"Off to Maui. I am out of here. I need human contact with people who know what planet they're from." Frank explained why he was packing and fleeing the premises for a better gig, far from the hippies and hermits crowd.

"I'll miss your guitar skills." He knew I was lying.

"Give me a couple weeks, then come on over. Should have wheels and a place by then." Frank grabbed his duffle bags and his guitar case, a man of few possessions. His nickname was Neanderthal. It was appropriate in every possible dimension.

"Got some type of plan? Other than flight from this place of solitude and contemplation?"

"Science City on Haleakala is hiring, might get back into astronomy. Put my astrophysics degree back into motion. Got to do something with my brain before it atrophies and turns to dust." Frank took another good look around and shook his head.

"I've only got three more weeks of this self-imposed exile from the human race. New owners are chomping at the bit to move in. You'd like them. The husband is old but cool. The wife is completely baffled by his desire to live this far removed from the world at large. OK with me; it's now theirs. I no longer have to feed the dog, find Gertrude's eggs or pluck the weeds out of the rock formations."

"What are you going to do with the dog? I love Sheri. She's the best dog ever!"

"My only caveat to their offer was they had to keep and take care of her. She has freedom here and is safe. I mean, where else in the entire state can you own a German Shepherd and never have to put it on a leash? Call Kenzo and give him your number as soon as you're not homeless."

"Frankly it's time to go." He chuckled to himself, as always.

"Don't forget the guitar, or I'll launch it off the pali down at South Point and make it the southern-most *Les Paul* in America."

Frank Lee the Astrophysicist knew I meant it.

* * * * * * *

After a few false starts with weird housing and strange friends, Frank found his footing amidst a touch of serendipity. Somehow, he got a place in Kapalua and an obnoxiously fun roommate that worked the bar at The Blue Max.

Kapalua, snuggled perfectly into the base of the West Maui Mountains. What a glorious upgrade! Million-dollar condos with billion-dollar views. Three beaches, a multitude of surf breaks, and nobody actually lived there. For almost all of the owners, the condos were speculation and a place to park some of their winnings from whatever their day jobs were. They came and went like the wind and the rain - some for days or weeks. Most were escaping from everything that haunted them. Celebrities were a dime-a-dozen.

"Hi, Stevie," Frank threw out to the nice lady going into the adjoining doorway.

"Hi. Having a good day?" Stevie Nicks replied with a well-worn smile.

"Always," I replied. We could care less. She was in her thirties and we weren't.

Later, we'd go to The Blue Max open mic nights and listen to this odd trio play blues and jazz. The very ad hoc, and yet, strangely wonderful, tune with complex melodies wrapped within an inherent nuance of perfection always entertained. The trio had really long shaggy unkempt beards and spoke in grunts and nods - much like our days in HOVE and the stunted conversations that we produced there. After long exposures of time with the very same people, such communication styles appeared, a natural development amongst the male sector of the human race.

Week after week, George Benson, George Harrison, and one of their unknown buddies played for the nearly empty bar save for Frank, a few wayward souls and me. They played away on a sax, guitar, and minimalist drum set.

* * * * * * *

It was really strange to sit and chat with the most famous sax player on the planet and have a former Beatle chime in with his own version of Maui humor. George Harrison's British accent lingered from days gone by.

Only on Maui in the late seventies would that even be possible. The best part was, that even if people knew, they simply chose not to care.

And, yes, our neighbor really was Stevie Nicks of Fleetwood Mac fame...

12

Umi-Gumi-Ungawa

We'd all gone adrenaline junky rogue.

Each and every one of us had acquired some very risky proclivities...

AJG / 1980s

* * * * * * *

"Umi..." I left the announcement of my presence linger after giving Kenzo a call at his new digs on Maui. He, too, couldn't handle the relentless rains of Hilo one single cloudburst longer.

"Gumi..." Kenzo laughed as he answered. "When are you coming over?" Kenzo knew my imminent arrival to Maui would be forthcoming.

"Two hours. Pick me up?" I asked.

"Not a chance. Got a photo shoot. Get here yourself." Kenzo had a job doing underwater filming for Atlantis Submarine, and he was having way too much fun getting paid to scuba dive in Maui's pristine waters. He showed no remorse in stranding me at Kahalui Airport to fend for myself.

I was jealous, although I'd never admit to being any such thing.

"Ungawa!" I hung up with blunt finality.

The phrase had come about on one of our quests for the perfect set of waves in Puna, on the Big Island, we happened to be entertaining my brother, Bob. Stopping to fill up the trusty Rabbit with gas, I glanced over to see Bob in an animated conversation with the owner's adult son.

The son was autistic long before the term was ever coined, and greatly challenged in life. One of his biggest hindrances was his inability to formulate words into any language known to man. But having a difficult conversation was not that far out of the norm since Puna's strange mixed-breed of soul created such a bizarre reality of many languages and dialects intersecting within an awkward clash of cultures gone astray. So Bob's conversation eventually became extreme with his arms flailing and questions flying in rapid succession.

"What on earth did you do to my brother, Kenzo?" I asked completely dumbfounded from watching my Appalachian brother interact with the man we knew hadn't formulated a coherent word - much less a sentence - in his lifetime.

"Sent him over to get directions to Hot Springs!" Kenzo lost it laughing as we both observed in awe as the Rabbit's tank filled and our humor meter burst at the seams. We both knew not only how to get to Hot Springs, but that Bob had his linguistic skills twisted beyond anything he'd ever encountered, on or off the farm.

"Hey, time to go." I shouted over to Bob while waving for him to come join us on our Incredible Quest for Surf.

To his credit, Bob thanked the young man, shook his hand very properly and trotted our direction.

"What on earth where you two talking about?" Kenzo asked with a wry smile, trying real hard not to lose it laughing.

"Did you get the directions? I mean, how are we ever going to find Hot Springs? Might get lost - Puna has so much jungle. It's easy to drive right past the place." I piled on.

Bob wasn't just a little perplexed; he was completely befuddled and in his own world of deep thought from his strange encounter. Eventually Bob blurted out, "Honestly I couldn't understand a single word that guy said...it honestly sounded like...*Umi-Gumi-Ungawa*...to me!"

It appeared that Bob needed to invent a new language to describe his encounter with the confused soul Kenzo had thrust upon him.

And thus, the *Legend of Umi-Gumi-Ungawa* was born.

* * * * * * *

"I'd rather be the guy they make the movies about than the guy making the movies." Frank stated as fact to Kenzo and I as we prepared for that evening's risky behavior. We were sitting on the wall down at Front Street in Lahaina. Doing not-much-of-nothing while watching the entire world's tourist population cruise past in one rented Mustang convertible at a time.

"The Man!" I declared.

"The Myth!" Kenzo added.

"The Legend!" I finalized the newest string of pronouncements that summed up Frank's current state of mind, and his latest moniker. His antics had generated somewhat of a mythical personification about him that we poked fun at every possible chance, but in reality, Frank Lee had truly become his latest moniker. Frank just looked at us, smiled, and continued with his rant, "I mean it. Been around way too many *movie stars* to ever desire to be part of their spoiled-brat-wimpy-ways. All they actually are is a privileged pack of deadbeats that can't surf. What a bunch of incompetent losers. All wimps. All soooo over rated." Frank shared his unvarnished opinion, which he gave with or without asking.

"I mean it. They ought to do a movie about me! I'm awesome, and they aren't." Frank stood up, did a chest thumping *George of the Jungle* roar, and declared himself awesome to the entire Central Pacific. "Look at me: surfing huge waves, scuba diving wild spots with heart-pounding surf going off overhead while dating hot babes those losers wish that I'd introduce them to." He flexed his muscles and strutted his stuff against the backdrop of Molokai and Lanai silhouetted on the horizon.

"Are you actually trying to call that dating?" Kenzo blurted out. We both burst into spontaneous laughter as he threw him a verbal bomb. "I mean, has a girl ever allowed you to take them out a second time? Or, do they immediately discover your cave bear tendencies while they beg for mercy -- hoping that you would move to some far removed and distant abyss? Somewhere like the deepest point in the Marianas Trench?"

Frank brushed off Kenzo's verbal barb and continued, "Found a nice girl. Smart girl. She's working on her Masters. Might even go on to get a Doctorate."

Being an Astrophysicist, Frank thought that all girls were devoid of grey matter. That is - it appeared - until this one. He Frank defended his lack of true love, while never acknowledging his Neolithic ways.

"This super-smart-whiz-babe got a name?" I asked, not really caring but trying to buy some time while I pondered where best to go night diving for lobster.

"Wendy. She's that crazy-good surfer's older cousin. You know the surfer I'm talking about, Mikey? Out at Caves?" Frank half questioned, half answered all the while still pondering the possibilities with said smart girl.

"Mikey, that scrawny kid that surfs dawn patrol with us? Man is he ever good! I've seen him almost totally inverted in the tube. He's got a whole new way of shredding a wave into submission." I answered, knowing exactly whom he meant. "Seems like a good kid. Isn't he still in high school? I've seen him out in some pretty heavy stuff." I shook my head in disbelief at how comfortable Mikey was riding monstrous surf exploding along the cliffs of Honolua Bay. And he did it with a big smile on his face while never saying anything. "OK then, we'll meet at Fleming Beach. Dive its outer reef section. Me, and the guys I've been working with, have started calling that chunk of reef, Honeycombs. See you there just after dark," Kenzo stated, leaving Frank and I no room for barter. Obviously, Kenzo was clearly focused, unlike us. He got up and left without saying goodbye, knowing we'd all meet as scheduled to acquire lots and lots of lobsters for both food and barter.

* * * * * * *

Honeycombs was like a multi-layered cake of Swiss cheese. Everything was interlocking holes in layers of reef, an underwater grotto wonderland. In the daytime, the holes created skylights of brilliance into the depths of the reef's rampant critter population. At night - it created a myriad of strange groupings of reef dwellers, some cowering in fear of the night terrors shredding their brethren into tiny little pieces. Bits and chunks that fell to the bottom and littering its floor.

It was those tiny little scraps that fed the lobsters. They loved to march out on the darkest nights and feed boldly along the ocean bottom. Predators ate the fish, lobsters ate the remnants, and we ate them both. It seemed that every creature in the ocean had at least one thing in common: we were all looking for dinner.

About three layers down, 100,000 candle power light creating its own brilliance of reality within that portion of hidden reef, I bumped into a tiny cavern full of crustaceans. Lobsters on lobsters upon lobsters. They were all frozen stiff by my light exploding into their pitch-dark world.

I did exactly what I'd been taught to do: I grabbed the biggest one first. I latched on to him with two hands, not realizing that he was a monster and did not wish to enjoy my embrace or be my dinner. That huge hard-shelled monster took me on a wild ride, galloping around his subsurface kingdom by running inverted laps with me firmly attached! I was not going to let go, being the "dominant" species and all.

Finally, after having a few of his legs and one antenna torn off in the rampage, I got him wrestled into my dive bag. I felt victorious and proceeded to rediscover where all of my gear had flown during my encounter with the largest lobster I'd ever seen, much less caught.

I was so proud of myself.

Twenty minutes later, tanks empty, and sitting huffing and puffing on the beach with Kenzo and Frank, I pulled out my massive catch by his one remaining antenna to proudly display it for all to admire.

"That's rather nice. Do you want to see what a real lobster looks like?" Frank offered as he pulled out a lobster at least a few pounds heavier.

"Me too." Kenzo had one nearly as large as Frank's. Neither had appendages torn off and remained fully intact.

"So, I get a five plus pounder and you both beat me?" I was exacerbated. "Looks like I'm buying dinner. Kobe's?"

We all trudged over to get some sushi. After all, we were way too tired to cook for ourselves and sushi with ice cold Asahi Super Dry beers was properly in order to polish off the perfect Maui day. Plus, we bartered out back with the chef for some of our "bugs" that we'd caught, which made it much more affordable.

Our Incredible Quest for Surf had evolved into long days and longer nights. Our daily surfing adventures were slowly morphing into scuba diving adventures. Unless, of course, the waves were absolutely perfect...and huge.

* * * * * * *

I am still somewhat miffed about getting the largest lobster I had ever caught and coming in third in our ongoing contest: smallest catch buys dinner.

Frank got his job with the Department of Defense (DoD) up on Haleakala, a group of observatories known as Science City. He shot laser beams at satellites, redirecting their orbits for war games and such. By this stage of his life he was toughened to the point of being obnoxiously callous in most everything human. Living in an oceanfront million-dollar condo with stunning views, rubbing elbows with the rich and famous wannabes, whom he could care less about, Frank declared his original deep held belief that Hollywood should make a movie about him, and begrudgingly, about us.

Although, with tenacity and persistence, he eventually got to take out his Wendy more than once, to the point of becoming somewhat of an item. I only met her one time, years later when they were building a spec house together along the Kona Coast. They never got married; she always kept him a bit on ice and somewhat at arm's length. To me she was brilliant but cold, distant and un-engagingly aloof.

Yet, what is too often true: as humans we are clueless to what is really going on in another person's personal life. In essence, we assume poorly. What I did not know was that she was battling a brutal form of aggressive cancer. And, sadly, she passed away not too long after I met her.

Frank didn't know either. Her pushing him further and further away, coupled with her untimely death, broke his jaded heart. Along that particular journey of his life, Frank Lee actually did give a damn...

It seems as though that Wendy was the Scarlett in his personal saga of Gone with the Wind.

* * * * * * *

As for that scrawny kid, who we all called Mikey... well he had a real name after all. He was (and is) the legendary Michael Ho. He went on to win about every possible surfing contest and title a professional surfer could ever acquire, including the ultra prestigious Pipe Masters. Mikey was actually our age, but because of his boyish good looks, small frame and charming smile, Frank and I improperly assumed he was much younger than us.

Michael Ho righteously became known as a world-class surfer. Something that we knew long before the world piled fame upon him, claiming him as one of their very own.

* * * * * * *

Michael Ho has an effervescent daughter named Coco. She too professionally surfs with outrageous passion and style. And, like her father, has won many contests and well-deserved accolades all across the globe. She, just like her father, exemplifies the very essence of being Hawaiian. She freely casts out her aloha for the entire world to embrace the joy known as Hawaii Nei.

Our brilliant daughter Tiffany, also effervescent, loving and kind, our surfing lawyer -- two-time winner of the Land Shark surf contest -- would upon occasion bump into Coco Ho while out in the line-up. Together they'd surf the liquid thunder crashing all along Oahu's pounding shorelines. Rarely speaking, just smiling and reveling in the moment as the setting sun caressed the passing ocean swells the two would simply allow the waves to be the conversation while carrying away the cares of the world.

Fortunately for us humans, interlocking patterns emerge, creating generations of overlapping contact points in the most marvelous of ways.

We all inhabit such a tiny planet that transcends time.

13

Santa Has A Balloon

"I can't remember exactly if it was the family's first or second hot air balloon, but I am sure it was a blustery biting cold winter's morning. It wasn't just any day, but Christmas morn with nary a whisper of wind. There was the tiniest touch of light appearing over the eastern horizon - our intended direction of drift - if everything worked as planned. My brother Keith laughed under his breath 'this is a good time not to screw up!' He kept laughing as he hit the thunderously loud burners and de-weighted the balloon for a rapid ascent into the approaching dawn..."

AJG / 1982ish

* * * * * * *

Anytime you're launching a craft that flies, it's always good form not to 'screw up'. We settled in for a soft drift towards the sunrise. We searched the ice crystal blue skies with the wind at our backs. In a balloon you only ever have one direction to proceed, and that was wherever the wind should take you.

Today, on this lovely Christmas morning, the wind was taking us towards a wee bit of Pennsylvania known as Frogtown. The tiny smattering of homes was difficult to find on a map. Yet it was a most excellent choice to shop if you needed penny candy and something to work a field, mow a yard or play an extra-short round of golf on the Frogtown Five. The micro-short golf course was kept in excellent condition in order adjust the mowers from the regional John Deere dealership that needed to be kept to spec prior to handing back to the local customers, who had a penchant for exacting standards when it came to yard, field, and farm appearances. Seems it was cheapest golf course on the planet. No charge was ever made to any patron. A simple smile and appreciative wave would do if the owner's wife saw you hacking your way by!

But, in late December, the course was frozen silent. The store was closed. The John Deere dealership was appropriately void of activity, and this sliver of the world was perfectly at peace.

Keith looked at my lovely sweetheart, Faith, and deadpanned while pointing at the critical connector points holding us all in the air, "Did you check those cables?"

Faith, wise to his off-the-wall one-liners of snark wrapped within implied doom, answered, "No. Was I supposed to? Oh my! This one looks a bit undone..." A hint of a twinkle shown in her eye and my *Sansei Princess* smiled as she shook one of the four major cables.

Undoubtedly boys had been trying such shenanigans all of her life, which she took with a grain of Hawaiian salt, all as she attempted to adjust to the polar vortex that pressed icy hard against her tropical comfort zone.

Typically, our flights in the balloon were at way greater altitudes, seems that one to two miles was the norm. Yet, this day, for no apparent reason, we skimmed the surface from a relative height of a few dozen feet, dancing along the tips of the barren oaks and maples. We might as well of been plowing the snow compared to how we usually went straight to being a speck of color in the vast blue skies.

So, there we were, floating along. Keith had his favorite toy within its flight parameters. I had my favorite girl intoxicatingly wrapped around me, and then something magical happened!

When the air is stark quiet and the snow freshly dusts the ground, the burners scream with volumes of blue flame keeping us aloft, "HERE WE ARE!" A bit of intrepid sojourn meets divine plan. We drifted past a rather large dairy farm, then over a random house...

And, between a thunderous burst of flames, things went perfectly serenely silent. Keith, Faith and I looked down to see a very young child in his Holstein cow onesie pajamas gazing in awe. His soft tracks trailed behind him in the pure white snow with the door hanging wide open behind him. Then, with perfect childish joy, he pointed with profound delight skywards, and squealed, "LOOK MOMMY! SANTA HAS A BALLOON!"

So, what are intrepid-wandering-balloon-warriors to do? Well, of course there was but one thing we could do. We all hunkered down inside the wicker basket, and while the balloon drifted dead silent - we all shouted in unison, "HO! HO! HO! MERRY CHRISTMAS!"

Last we saw, peeking over the edge as we climbed for higher altitudes, was a young boy wrapped in his mother's arms while our small world embraced this magical moment in time.

* * * * * * *

When reindeer are preoccupied, Santa has a balloon.

14

First Time Dead

The first time I died I didn't know I was dead. It appears that it is such a shock to one's system that being dead doesn't really sink in for a while...

1983

* * * * * * *

We were just having a bit of fun for the day, my buddy Greg and I, out for an adventure. We were going diving to look around underwater, see the sights and find something new. It was a simple plan, at best, but then the simplest plans are the easiest to adhere to. We tended to be strict when it came to scuba diving: stay in the profile, watch your gauges, keep an eye on each other, don't get lost, and most importantly, don't die.

We found a dive operator sitting on the fringe of Lingayen Gulf, a huge bay in the northern part of the Philippines. Hundred Islands National Park sounds majestic, but being on holiday from Hawaii, we were far from impressed. What I do remember, prior to death, was that the atmosphere was heavy. It had a tinge of dense silver cast in metallic blue. It smelled off. Not polluted exactly, but somehow corrupted. The ocean was slowly evaporating under the equatorial sun that heated the water into the high 90s. As I look back, it wasn't so much a stench, but a foreboding of tranquil opaqueness disguising hidden dangers.

A lone NAUI flag hung limp from the entrance to the brand-new dive center owned by an expat, who looked very happy to see us. Maybe we were his first English-speaking customers, wayward compatriots at this far-flung outpost that few sojourners found and in which fewer stopped. Everything was absolutely pristine. We could still smell the paint drying as we sized some gear and bartered for two tanks, a boat with guide, and a half-day excursion. Part of the deal was the sun-baked Filipino gentleman had to speak at least passable English, possess *local boy* knowledge of where to go, and of far more importance, how to get back.

At this stage of our lives we had spent a lot of time both on and under the waves. It was an extreme relief to see that the shop was brand new with clean gear. After seeing the profound squalor of Metro-Manila, decrepit survival on a scale I had not imagined, it was as if we'd found a touch of home wrapped in a fresh breath of safety in this American-owned dive center.

Just as we departed the dock, the gas engine for the air compressor on the upwind side of the building kicked on. Its primary use was to fill the tanks with 3,150 PSI of compressed air, universally known as Aluminum Eighties for the next souls seeking adventure, exactly like the ones we were about to strap on our backs.

There we were, skipping across the placid waters to anchor for our first dive not too far, a mile or so from the dock. Somehow, I expected to go farther out. Maybe, somehow, we expected too much. This minor disappointment would prove to be profoundly important. Not for us, but all of those who would dare to come after. We unceremoniously set anchor on some underwater barren flats near a rather stark island with a half-moon beach glaring in the noonday sun. We were diving an inner bay filled with small islets and hosts of bizarre, odd- shaped rocks, all with tufts of lime green, stunted vegetation on them.

Greg looked at me and without saying a word, transmitted everything that needed to be said: *better check all of the gear at least twice; we've got strange waters all around.*

Dead canaries save human lives. Greg and I simply did not know that we'd been designated as that day's version of disposable avian (it would became readily apparent that the dive shop owner didn't know either). Later we found out that the tiny island we dropped anchor beside was of all things, called Devil's Island. And, by its ancient character, it sat in wait to kill, steal, and destroy.

*　*　*　*　*　*　*

Immersion into the inland sea felt like bath water! It felt so inappropriate that the usual rush of hitting the water was not refreshing in the least. Immediately, I unzipped my wet suit and tried to adjust to being too warm in the ocean. A very unsettling feeling came over me. At least I had my brand-new Mares mask, I thought. Masks are very personal; it is difficult at best to find one that fits, let alone one you can wear for extended periods of time. I loved my Mares mask. It never got tight or rubbed me raw, one thing going for me, or so I thought.

I dropped to the bottom and started a slow, lazy pattern to find something, anything, of note. All I saw was hard-packed sand, off-color and pale, some rock outcroppings with hodgepodge stone white coral heads littered along the barren flats. A tiny number of small colorless fish, all loners, passed by. It was stark. Void. Barren. Everything was bland-on-bland. The water itself was of limited visibility, - maybe 25 yards or so. We could barely make out the boat gently wafting above us on the placid waves.

I looked over at Greg, gave him the two-outstretched-hands-palms-up signal with a questioning look of *why are we even here? This dive site sucks*!

Greg returned my look of annoyance. We had both hoped for much more. He turned and started working the various outcroppings in hope of some kind of entertainment. I was a bit less inquisitive with my approach. I simply allowed myself to sink and stand on the bottom while taking a long look around. Where was a good ol' black tip shark when you needed one?

Time crept past, and I kept an eye on my gauge array while Greg squirmed deeper into the sub-structure of a reef outcropping. He was coming up completely empty as well. We were twenty minutes into the dive, down a 1,000 pounds on the tank and hovering along the bottom at 65 feet deep. There wasn't a cloud in the sky, and I was well past comfortable wearing the unnecessary wetsuit in what I was internalizing as the Tepid Sea of Barrenness.

At least the wetsuit was keeping the tank straps from digging into my shoulders. So far the equipment appeared to be working flawlessly. The regulator and gauges were fine. As far as the technical aspects of the dive, we were good to go.

The first major hint of malfunction entered my murky world unawares, my new Mares mask, my baby, slowly allowed water to infiltrate and annoy me as it sloshed into my nostrils. I cleared it with very little notice. At this stage I'd been on hundreds of dives with most of them being two-tankers -- maybe approaching a thousand hours total underwater. We'd done a lot of diving along the eastern and southern coasts of the Big Island. Places from tame to extremely wild, most of the dives were becoming night dives for lobster, menpachi and kumu. Even if we were perpetually tight on funds, we were spoiled rotten food wise, as were all of those around us. Anytime you're complaining about having lobster "again", life is good. We'd even dive off the backside of Lanai, after a 4-hour boat trip across Au'au Channel from West Maui's Lahaina Harbor. Once there, we strapped on our dive gear and dove one of the most exotic unknown dive sites on the planet, a place we nicknamed *Lobsterminiums*. Located at the base of massive sea cliffs towering high above with gargantuan broken rock formations stepping down into the deep blue abyss, many of them honeycombed with intertwined caves spilling over with myriads of lobsters clambering over each other.

We'd immediately grab the biggest ones first.

The second time my mask filled up it gave me a chance to take stock. I did my best to ignore this boring Filipino dive we were on, and, with real purpose, I leaned way back to clear it. What was rolling around in my brain was that my very favorite piece of gear must have cracked a seal while in my luggage. I'd just have to deal with it, like so many bits-n-pieces of marginal dive gear that had become obsolete by usage, or, flat out abuse.

When I arched backwards, with the noonday sun directly overhead, I cleared the mask and watched the liquid world above me turn blood red! I was bleeding from my nose profusely! Shocked to the core, I was stunned by the sight and even more by the dreaded reality confronting me. Immediately I swam to Greg, pulled him out of a mini-cavern by his fins and did the universal signal of - I AM OUT OF HERE!

He shrugged and went back into the cavern, for what I will never know.

So I yanked him out again, this time without room for barter. I hit my chest with my fist and pointed up. Then, without delay, I started going there. Surface was only 65 feet away. I did it slowly so as not to explode, but I did it as fast as possible because I instinctively knew that my time was running short in every possible dimension.

All I remember was that once I got to the surface, the boat seemed impossibly far away. That small skiff came in and out of focus. Troubling elusive. Just like quicksilver. Forever unobtainable. Never did it get any closer, no matter how much I struggled to get home to its perceived safety...

No matter how hard I tried to remain in the land of the living, I was gone.

* * * * * * *

I found myself being transported at an immense speed and at a stratospheric altitude towards home. My soul was completely untethered from any type of reality. Going to Pennsylvania; going to say a last goodbye to my parents. I had no hint of concern or pain, just on a very simple mission to say goodbye. I had done it once before when I left for college. This time was of no difference.

I was actually looking forward to seeing them again. I loved my parents, and anytime I got a chance to be around them was counted as a good day.

I'd been out of the house for nearly a decade, and I wasn't going to see Mum and Dad until the wedding coming up in few months' time to marry my sweetheart. The tiny wedding followed by a big blowout of a reception was going to be epic!

As I accelerated towards home, I was encased in a dense whiteness all around. Miraculously free of all concerns or cares, I had a very deep thought and decided I had better swing by Hawaii to say goodbye to my wife and daughter, for I knew that it would be a long time until I saw them again.

Then it dawned on me; I didn't want to say goodbye to them at all. My life with them was yet to begin, and I desired that reality more than anything else on either side of the veil...

And that is exactly when I heard a thundering pronouncement reverberating through my entire being: **"YOU DON'T HAVE TO!"**

* * * * * * *

"DON'T DIE ON ME NOW, GOURLEY! WHAT AM I GOING TO TELL YOUR PARENTS?!" Greg screamed directly into my face at the confounding circumstances thrust upon him, and to the entire world at large.

I found myself back in my body with my best friend sitting on my chest, pounding my whole body on the deck of the boat. Greg was employing a type of highly modified Neanderthal CPR, but it apparently worked.

It will forever go down as the single most bizarre way I've ever been woken up. I shrugged him off of me, and made my weak -- but very honest -- thirst-driven request. While not profound in the least, it has gone down in our personal historical records as an all-time great quote to be used only in the direst of circumstances.

"I think I need a beer."

The current state of affairs were alarming: I was bleeding out of my nose, ears, and eyes, but the flow rates were quickly winding down to a trickle. Then I discovered a subcutaneous emphysema bubble, air trapped under the outer layers of my skin, the size of my hand on the back of my neck. I immediately became outright queasy.

To add to my dire circumstances, I felt like the ocean had picked me up by my ankles and pounded railroad spikes into my forehead. Ensconced in a type of whole-body trauma, I sat there squinting, trying to shield my eyes from the pain of the equatorial sunlight.

We were done diving for the day.

One good look and the local guide needed zero encouragement to hightail it back to the dock, where the owner was more than concerned by our rapid abandonment of the day's activities. Greg, being slightly heavier than I was, hadn't fully developed the symptoms that I had so fully embraced and was downright livid. At some point amidst a very animated, arm-waving conversation Greg yelled, "What the hell is wrong with your dive gear?!"

Once Greg got past his high decibel phase of the one-sided conversation, he and the stunned dive shop owner, a long-time avid diver with military experience and training, settled into a bit of forensic analysis. Once he was apprised of all of my symptoms, the answer was readily apparent to him. He hung his head in shame as he announced, "Your friend got a poison bottle. He's fortunate to be alive."

Greg looked around the shop as the owner continued, "My intake for the compressor is too close to the exhaust of the engine. He got a full dosage of carbon monoxide! He was delivered carbon monoxide under pressure while at depth. Lucky to be alive..." He was so contrite when he added, shaking his head in despair, "I am so sorry. I had no idea." He took another look at me in my pale weakness, "Should I call an ambulance?"

It was beyond obvious that my body had absorbed the full effects of one of the poison bottles given to us. Being lighter, I'd succumbed at a far faster pace than Greg. He too had been poisoned, but his was only a taste with minor consequences that were quickly dissipating.

I shook my head, "No, I just want an ice-cold beer and a cool place to lie down out of this sun." My lips and throat tasted of blood, and I felt an internal fatigue that wouldn't allow me the pleasure to deny my immediate need to get horizontal.

* * * * * * *

The next few days were a complete blur. I drank one ice-cold San Miguel beer, as per request, and stayed in the dark drinking tons of water until I finally bled off all of the effects and could emerge, anew, into the light. I slept almost continuously.

Finally, I asked Greg what had happened. I only remembered *my heavenly flight homeward bound.* That reality was so strange that I didn't share it with him, or anyone, for years to come.

"First of all, I couldn't believe you were done. I mean, we had just started our first dive, maybe 15 or 20 minutes into it. I know the dive sucked, but we'd come all that way..."

Greg started with his recall of events. Greg was always a very straight shooter when it came to describing something that had occurred, since most of our adventures rarely needed any type of embellishments.

"I followed you up cause you looked really strange to me -- something in your eyes that second time you pulled me out of the rocks and signaled to go up. When I got to the surface you were already at the boat. You gave the guy your fins, your tanks and BC. Then you climbed onto the bow with his help. At that stage I was probably less than a minute behind you. And I have to admit; I was more than a little ticked off. So I gave the guy my weight belt, my tank, and climbed on board. Still had my mask and fins on -- lucky for you I might add. That's what saved your life!"

Greg got real serious with his next bit of information and hesitated to even discuss it. "You know, I think I saw you die. Your eyes rolled back, you went ghost white and fell backwards off of the bow of the boat, with your weight belt still on, and plummeted lifeless into 65 feet of water trailing a stream of bubbles."

By this time in the story I knew I didn't remember a thing he was describing. I was on my own journey to place that doesn't exist in this time or realm.

Greg quietly continued on his own path downwards along his tale of terror, "I dove off the boat and chased you down into that cursed water, caught you by an ankle at somewhere between 30 to 40 feet and dragged your butt back to the surface." By this stage of the story Greg was truly spooked as he recounted what happened next. "You were dead near as I could tell. Not breathing, pulse gone, stark white, eyes rolled back, and I didn't know what else to do other than to start beating you off the deck and screaming at you! I was so mad at you for dying on me! I mean, what the heck was I going to do with you? And then what, call your parents from half-a-world-away and explain to them how you decided to die on a perfectly clear sky day on calm waters! How unacceptable is that? What the heck was I going to chisel onto your tombstone?"

+++ DIED FOR NO APPARENT REASON +++

Forever after that trip into the death-waters off Devil's Island, both Greg and I never took off our fins and masks until everyone else was either onboard or onshore and safely tucked away. Our Devil's Island dive burned into our souls a learning experience, to be used as a form of safety net for those around us. To this day, my *first-time dead* experience at Hundred Islands National Park remains a subject we only discuss upon rare occasion and with limited detail. Mostly Greg and I simply drink an ice-cold beer and communicate via grunts and shrugs when the events of that day attempt to raise their ugly memories.

* * * * * * *

I owe Greg, the best man in our wedding, an eternal 'thank you' that can never be repaid. For Greg saved my life that day. He allowed me to go on and get married to the love of my life, have three gloriously wonderful children and embrace a future that otherwise would have never been possible without his instantaneous response and heroic efforts. Also, as the designated "canaries" in this nearly terminal story, who knows how many others we saved by finding out the flaw in the design for the dive shop operator. Maybe the next intrepid souls wouldn't have fared nearly as well. He had rows upon rows of poison bottles all lined up, lurking in wait for whomever may have appeared at his door. It could have been a bus full of innocent tourists...

As for my "flight towards home," God calls each of us personally home to Heaven. Fortunately, He abounds in both mercy and grace! And, He is willing to overlook a multitude of foolish endeavors to allow a future to unfold for His children.

No matter how far astray they have roamed.

As for choosing not to say goodbye to my wife and daughter, this is where it gets purely Biblical...

You see, I wasn't married yet! And, our first child, our oldest daughter, turned out to be awesome!

15

Jan Ken Po

Patience is a virtue. Virtue is a sign of a good moral being. Good moral beings make wise decisions... Or so the ancient proverb goes...

We probably wouldn't have been even remotely confused with being wise.

But sometimes patience will save your butt from being eaten.

AJG & FKG / 1983ish

* * * * * * *

"I still can't believe she married you. You stormed the fortress and captured a real-life *Sansei Princess* after all. Bravo!" Kenzo patted me on the back.

"I prefer liberated!" I offered. Kenzo ignored me and continued on.

"See your kingdom's going to expand due to natural causes," as he nodded towards her *delicate condition*. We both smiled while we donned our scuba gear to take a quick look underwater during Faith's lunch break. Adjusting his mask after dipping it in the tidal pool, he asked, "Where'd you pop the question, somewhere exotic? Oh, that's right, you were in Backwoods, PA."

"Becky's bedroom! I just got back from checking on a gas well I'd invested in, trudged right in, found her there and asked the big question."

"Becky the flower girl?"

"Yea. Do you remember the ring bearer's reaction when he took one look at little Becky - so cute - as he 'bravely' walked down the aisle?" I chuckled and continued checking gear.

"That was unreal, he took one look at her, saw she was blonde with blue eyes, immediately whooped the pillow-ring-combo over his shoulder, dove under the pews and latched hold of his mother's ankles in sheer terror! Screaming MOMMY SAVE ME! Never saw anything like it...Had to peel him off to continue with the ceremony," Kenzo laughed as he put on his fins.

"That wasn't the funniest part..." I left the comment linger. I too was nearly complete in our process to get underwater. Taking a good look around, I smiled over at Faith as she basked on the shore, six months pregnant and looking like a wonderfully cute, super tan, beached-mini-whale. She was trying to figure out how best to get comfortable in the noonday sun. The palms were too far away for any type of shade, but the electric green grass on the fringes of the interlocking tidal pools provided a touch of soft for her to lounge upon.

We both smiled and continued with our analysis of how our wedding had a life of its own.

"What on earth did I miss? I was there for the entire event. After all I was your emcee." Kenzo was a little confused on how he could have missed anything." He glanced over at Faith, who smiled and struggled, trying her best to adjust to grass on lava, "She's still awesome even pregnant; most ladies are just plain fat," Kenzo bluntly declared as he started to crank his air valve to the on position while doing a final equipment check.

I shook my head and refused to engage in his generalizations of pregnant women...having learned many valuable lessons about acceptable adjectives when it came to describing *being with child*. "During the ceremony Karen and Faith completely lost it giggling, it was borderline obnoxious. I gave them stink eye, trying to remind them that this was supposed to be a solemn ceremony and all. After the dust settled, as we braved the rice and got into the rental Continental, I found out what set them off." I looked right at Kenzo, who was very curious by this stage, and continued on with the tale, "I guess I was too preoccupied gazing at my gorgeous bride to notice the honking big fly that landed on the priest's nose, then leisurely did a few laps right in the middle of it all!"

"Really! You didn't even see that? Wow! That priest never missed a beat, the rest of us didn't notice a thing."

"So, there's more to the story..."

"And..." Kenzo was very engaged by this point in the dissertation of all-things-wedding.

"You do know that Greg was driving after the ceremony? Coming into town we all decided it was vitally important to toast the blessed occasion with some champagne. So, to celebrate, we stopped in Papaikou to get a bottle at that little Mom & Pop store on the corner. Found out we had zero cash with us, so after a deep thought, Faith remembered she had a twenty tucked into her garter for the Lucky Bachelor Toss later in the evening. Should have seen that mamma boy's bug-eyed look when she lifted her leg onto his counter right in front of him, slid her dress to the side and pulled that twenty out of her garter belt! He completely lost it and turned 18 shades-of-confused!" I smiled and stretched as I started struggling into my wetsuit. "Then, to top everything off - you know how we all drive - Greg blasted into the hotel's roundabout from the wrong end, smiled over at Karen, punched the parking break and did a sweeping 180 to park the Lincoln Continental two inches from the curb directly in front of the manager's desk! Karen screamed, leaped out of the car, and immediately went into a tirade on how she never - in her life - was ever going to ride with some crazy lunatic driver from Pennsylvania again!" I looked at Kenzo and we both completely lost it in the moment laughing so hard Faith took notice and tapped her watch to remind us she was on a clock and we needed to stay focused so she could make it back to work on time.

"Can you blame Karen? She's ridden with you, and your brother Bob and now with Greg. You are all nuts -- only guys I know that can four-wheel drift at will, do bat turns and sweeping 360s. Never met a Pennsylvanian that didn't drive like they were being chased by the creature from *Alien*."

"That's because you city kids can't drive - or dive - worth squat!" Then I threw him into the water and dove in after him.

"Did you know we even had tourists at our wedding?" I laughed while delivering one more morsel of info. Leisurely kicking on our backs towards our goal to get past the inner tidal pools.

"Really? They are everywhere..." Kenzo shook his head. To him, his island homeland was being totally consumed by one group of really stupid tourists at a time, asking really stupid questions while taking pictures.

"Yea. Two full tables in the back; two whole families. We found them while making our rounds after dinner. I thought they were from Faith's side and she thought they were with my family - but they thought it was part of their tour package and were greatly enjoying the food and the show. They mentioned that it wasn't until midway through your rousing speech that they figured it out. Even then, they were having such a wonderful time that they decided to stay. And, of course, there was the free bar." We both laughed at the reality of all things tourists that saturated our world. After all, Hawaii was where the entire planet came to play. "By the way, thanks once again for being our emcee, you were magnificent. We really appreciated your help. Although, some of the comments you made, although very true, my loving parents are probably still trying to process it all. Maybe a bit too much information for Presbyterians!"

"Music was great. Food was better. My honor to help, thanks for including me in your reindeer games." Kenzo loved making my parents nervous.

We were at Keaukaha at high noon with blue skies, prepping for a rather nice, easy wall dive just 30 yards off shore. Faith was reading while we took our very best attempt at obtaining dinner. Pushing past the interconnected sheltered tidal pools, we easily got out into deeper waters.

Kenzo and I proceeded to work the steep underwater wall, separated by nothing but crystal-clear water and little else.

Not long into the dive, I glanced over to scan for Kenzo. I'd caught a brief glimpse of motion off to my side and thought it was him. As I turned to get a better look, a little confused why he was right beside me, I saw that it was anything but him.

A mako shark stared right at me with his head hanging down, full vertical and his back arched in a kill-strike position! Teeth dripped from his gaping open mouth, suspended in time and space with the vast Hawaiian blue framing his primordial body. Where he came from didn't matter, nor how he got there.

My very first reaction was to drop my jaw, allowing my regulator to fall from my mouth! An instantaneous cloud of bubbles free-flowed from it creating a mass of rising gases all around me. Then I swung around and pointed my new Mares Snub Nose at him, while slowly swimming backwards away from the hungry beast, which was now a bit put off by his lunch's ability to create a cloud of confusion.

I saw Kenzo about 50 feet away and swam at breakneck speed his direction. When I looked back for the shark -- the huge monster of the deep -- it was gone. Somehow it had completely disappeared in unlimited visibility waters...

What his intentions were eluded me not at all.

I firmly grabbed hold of Kenzo's fins, popped him out of a tiny indention in the wall, did the universal massive shark double jaws sign with both arms fully clamping together with my fingers as shark teeth, snatched him by the elbow, and headed straight up to the surface. When we climbed out, we found ourselves sitting on a tiny islet, a barren chunk of jagged lava rock with minimal protection from the wild beast I'd just seen 40 feet from shore.

But we weren't getting eaten by a shark and successfully were out of the water, which was a really good start as far as I was concerned.

"What the heck! I just found some menpachi -- Faith loves those things. They make the best soup. I can't understand why some tiny, little shark freaks you white boys out so much," Kenzo spat out at me once we climbed ashore. "You Pennsylvanians might be able to drive like *Smokey and the Bandit*, but you are all wimps when it comes to our native sea life."

"Thing was huge... mako... with teeth dripping everywhere... suspended head down... eyeing me up like feedstock for a piranha," I could barely get out as I unzipped my wetsuit and adjusted to baking under the noonday sun.

We both waved nonchalantly at Faith who gave us the look that said: *what the heck are you stupid boys doing sitting on that rock? Get some fish or let's go.*

We smiled, turned, and ignored her -- never a good thing to do with a pregnant girl under any circumstances, but we still had a lot to learn.

After about ten minutes of minimal discussion -- me still freaking, and Kenzo getting very impatient -- Kenzo decided, "It couldn't have been that big. You do know everything looks 40% larger underwater. It's called optics."

"Monster... Big..." I wouldn't budge in my opinion of size and danger while being completely unable to make full sentences.

After another few minutes passed, Kenzo offered, "Let's call it. We'll just swim over to Faith, not tell her why - hate to get her so excited that she goes into labor - and declare victory."

"It's still deep between us and her - what if it's still hungry and it doesn't eat you instead of me?" I countered.

"Jun Ken Po to take a look and see if your *supposed monster* is still here?" Kenzo extended as a means to appease me by using the localized Japanese name for Rock Paper Scissors.

"Sure." I answered, knowing what the stakes were way more deadly than he did.

So we hit our fists into our palms while Faith pondered why we were being such stupid boys and unwilling to cede to her demands of getting back to work on time.

"I win!" I declared, feeling triumphant.

Kenzo donned his mask, begrudgingly proceeded to take a gander from the safety of kneeling on our mini-rock islet, and stuck his head in the water to see if my 'monster' had gone to more productive hunting grounds.

He leaped up, eyes on fire, and screamed, "IT'S RIGHT THERE!" Pointing straight down two feet away. Kenzo was quivering like a leaf and standing dead center in the middle of our miniature rock sanctuary.

"Told you he was big." I looked at him and scooted over to join him in the center of our tiny bit of shelter, as far as possible from the edge and the jaws-of-terror that continued to circle us in the noonday sun.

Faith was starting to guess that all wasn't right, but then shrugged it off. She figured we were nuts as usual and went right back to reading.

After another undetermined period of time, we decided to play Jun Ken Po once again, to take another look and rescue ourselves from baking to death in the sweltering heat. This time we both knew that fun-n-games were not the reality, but life and death were. I won and felt really good about it. Being chomped into pieces had zero appeal to me, probably my least favorite way to die.

Kenzo, not so much...

"Remember, deal is you have to check in all four directions. Nice knowing you..." I sort of laughed, as I demanded he adhere to the parameters of our bet, serious as it was.

Kenzo stuck his head in the water, looked one way, then another, then a third - then he immediately leaped straight into the water and swam towards shore as fast as possible - leaving me unprepared. I guess I had just become the 'slow swimmer' (literal shark bait) while he escaped and evaded.

Wise fellow that Kenzo -- using me as a white-boy-decoy!

I suppose he could console Faith and raise our child if I ended up getting shredded and eaten on the perfect Hawaiian day.

A potential outcome that did not console me at all.

We both made it to shore - a miraculous feat - but not without aging a few decades in the process. I think that's when I got my very first white hair.

"What happened? Why on earth were you both acting so weird sitting out there on that stupid rock?" Faith wanted to know.

We told her after childbirth.

* * * * * * *

Our ring bearer, who is now six foot two and looks like a chiseled version of Hawaiian Superman, is still totally freaked out by blue-eyed blondes!

He's Hawaiian, Chinese, Filipino, Norwegian and host of other ethnicities, a living example of the United Nations. Yet, for some crazy deep-seated reason, blondes turn him into a quivering mess.

Faith and I really have a great time with him, often teasing him about his fear factor concerning all things Scandinavian. It's amazingly fun to see him squirm.

We love him dearly.

* * * * * * *

Faith still believes that Kenzo and I were overreacting to the whole mako shark encounter thingy and were just playing some type of foolish game, as we often did.

Kenzo and I know better.

I've never played a game of Jan Ken Po since that had so much riding on the outcome.

And, Kenzo still can't believe he lost, not once, but twice!

16

Two Worlds

It is such a simple choice to make:

We can either curse GOD and die or we can praise GOD and live.

As for Faith and I, we choose to praise GOD.

AJG & FKG / 1984++

* * * * * * *

"We can afford this lifestyle for about six more weeks." I softly announced to Faith as she rocked our daughter to sleep. "Japanese have pulled out of Hawaii. Market's flat-dead...Kenzo's somewhere on Maui, found a girl and is so far gone...His little brother, Kanzi, is opening a business, selling water, never has any time to surf, or dive or do anything but work. No fun going to Oahu any more. I tried three interventions! I mean, who on earth is going to buy *water* of all things? Hope he doesn't lose everything...Wade and his family are somewhere in Colorado. Why? Don't know... Jeff found some Latina babe, moved to Kona, and is like... busy… for like... forever. Eddy's been gone a long time, heard he's in Nashville doing radio. Brian the Ozzie is somewhere unknown, not sure even how to find him. I'd probably have to go to Surfer's Paradise and ask around. After he went to Chicago to finish college, we completely lost touch... Chucky ran off with identical twin Filipino bombshells. He's on Oahu and not coming back anytime soon. Found a job at the docks, union wages…"

"I like Mai. She's really nice, Faith chimed in.

"I think he *likes* them both," I sighed. *(Chucky was every guy's hero, but we weren't allowed to mention that to any of our wives or girlfriends).*

"Willy got married... probably not for long..."

Faith simply nodded. It was so sad. We all liked his wife, but when you put the two of them together you got a human form of napalm. If a marriage is flamingly explosive, its life expectancy is greatly diminished...

"Clarence finally got a good job paying really well. He's about the only one left on the island that's sane."

"You call that sane?" Faith almost choked offering her response. Everybody liked Clarence, but his habit of swimming in alcohol was becoming a real factor in his day-to-day world.

"Greg's got a good gig being a concierge on Maui - working with American Express. Never comes over to visit anymore since he's *important and all*. Plus, his future wife is there now, and better yet, he doesn't even know he's getting married sooner than later!"

Faith and I both could see the *writing on the wall* with his pending nuptials since his Pennsylvanian girlfriend had joined him on Maui permanently. We really liked her and thought that with her concentrated efforts, she could help him move past some of his caveman tendencies.

"Frank somehow wrangled a fishing concession for halibut and king crab up in 'Polar Bear, Alaska.' He's in reality *gone fishing* forever. I know you really don't care even in the slightest..." I looked over to my bride.

Faith simply smiled and nodded; she never cared for Frank much as she thought of him as crude, rude and lewd - basically obnoxious. Him going to Alaska was plenty OK with her. Her *Sansei Princess* upbringing had a total disdain for those particular attributes in men. Yet to me, he was one of the original crew. I'd miss his blunt oratory rants and witty observations on all things human. Although, I wouldn't miss his wailing on his electric Les Paul guitar. How could anyone play that often and still be that far out of tune?

Putting our daughter into the crib and coming over to comfort me in my borderline depressed state of mind, Faith wrapped her loving arms around me and asked, "So what exactly are you saying? Are you just whining or do you have something more important you wish to discuss?"

"We can afford this lifestyle for about six more weeks..." I mumbled as the sun set over Mauna Kea and the sky lit up huge. We had a rather Spartan condo with a gazillion dollar view. The volcano had decided to erupt spectacularly; both mountains, Kilauea and Mauna Loa, were putting on outrageous displays of spewing lava. With the sun down, we could see both volcanic events simultaneously from our lanai. Kilauea had a needle fountain roaring like a primordial jet shooting over 1,000 feet high on the ridgeline to the southwest. Mauna Loa had a huge flow coming from its 13,678-foot summit that towered above us. That monster flow was progressing slowly. But, it was aimed directly at the heart of Hilo and had the entire town's population on a knife's edge. The Civil Authorities kept issuing warning after warning. But what are you to do if a flaming wall of lava enters your world at the speed of a tortoise strolling downhill? You get out of the way and watch it destroy everything it touches.

So, just like me in my melancholy mood, the entire east side of the Big Island pondered what the future would behold.

As for me, and my small family, I knew I needed to get a grip, grow up, and discover a future that I had never met.

It was 1984. Our entire world was exploding, just like the mountains on fire before our very eyes. We were all running from our past lives while trying to find a pathway forward. All of our friends were searching for an escape from our youthful decadence of partying and chasing risky exploits while dodging reality. Each and every single one of us needed to make our best faith efforts of becoming productive members of society.

Take our best shot. Move rapidly and boldly into the future.

It had become flagrantly apparent that everybody's next series of choices needed to include the adventure of growing up. It was time to quit being the people our parents warned us about.

I hugged Faith as the stars came out one by one, and the lava roared softly from a distance, consuming everything it touched. Our entire world was on fire from events cast down upon us like flaming showers of volcanic embers igniting everything they touched.

Change was on violent display as I softly whispered; "We can afford this lifestyle for about six more weeks..."

* * * * * * *

A two-story brick house, refurbished, small but rather comfortable, sat nestled in Western Pennsylvania, USA, aka, the Heart of the Known Universe. Or, at least, that's what Faith and I tried to convince ourselves was our new reality. We often suffered in silence.

I missed the ocean. She missed the food. Well, OK, we both missed the food and the ocean and the waves and the weather and our friends and… and… and...

In reality, the new adventure of growing up was brutal hard work amidst really long days: delivery boy, gas well tender, gofer, paint, fix, plumb, mow in the summer and plow in the winter. Make hay, shovel everything from manure to grain - the work was never ending and relentlessly repetitive. Truck driver, salesman, packing and shipping - any and all assigned jobs started at 6:00 am and ended when the sun went down.

Buying production and pipeline systems on the side, fixing leaks and moving natural gas to market while staying inches in front of the bills that were every bit as relentless as the work.

Day in, day out, all roads led to trying to force enough business risks that were being taken towards a reality that would afford a lifestyle worthy of betting everything we had towards that goal. Everything we owned was constantly on the line. With each deal we were perpetually all in. Hopefully with each risk we'd be closer to independence from the treadmill known as the rat race.

Many days we lost ground. But then - while replacing an ancient gas meter along a new stretch of pipeline we'd replaced - serendipity happened and a whole new world of possibilities was miraculously thrust into my world.

Two monster red oak trees hung over the meter site. They had been stripped by the ongoing gypsy moth invasion and were standing stark dead. An extreme hazard, they needed to be removed so as not to eventually fall onto our new live high-pressure gas meter and cause a catastrophe. So I trudged up and knocked on the landowner's door, hoping to pay, not much, to her for them. But they obviously had to go; it was the right thing to do.

"You one of those gas boys working behind the house?" It was more of an announcement than a question. The elderly woman at the door was all of 5-foot- tall and had the presence of a saint that tolerated no fools.

"Yes, ma'am. I am." I smiled. "Ma'am, you have a few trees overhanging our meter site. We're changing everything out and will need to remove them. I was hoping to give you a check for them. We'd like to get started immediately. We'd be very appreciative if you would be so kind. They are dead as can be; it appears to us that the moth ate their foliage. They are standing stark in a place that when they fall, they'll crush our new gas meter or even worse. When they fall, they are threatening to cause a catastrophe, ma'am."

And, just like the retired school teacher she was, she took it all in, had a deep thought, looked me square in the eye, poked two of her fingers directly into my chest, and pronounced her judgment on both my request and my immediate future, "Sonny. You just buy them all."

Then she firmly closed her door in a total show of who was boss.

Having dealt with many of Pennsylvania's finest souls, even a few exactly like her, I did not need to ponder the fact that either I complied with her demand or I would be picking those trees off of the meter at some point in time in the not-so-distant future. And she did not care how that fact affected my current need or my future reality. She simply did not care; she had a need and I had better comply. I think she expected me to see her as my elder, and she darned well better be respected by some upstart young gas man like myself.

So, I did. Got the plat map out, found out the rough boundaries of her property, got my oldest brother Larry involved, and proceeded to make an offer on her 10 acres of hardwoods that included the two danger-zone red oaks. Almost every tree was dead or dying; the gypsy moths had wrecked havoc on her tightly packed stand of timber. If there was ever a time to harvest her -- what I learned to be -- red, white, black, and scarlet oak, it was now before the bugs turned them into Swiss cheese and their combined value equaled that of a huge pile of firewood.

So, I found a guy from a local sawmill that wanted to take a look. I paid a fair price in American dollars and took a massive chance, hoping that Larry's numbers were accurate and the desire from the local sawmill was real.

Turns out, I sold it for fairly nice profit 48 hours later. A new reality burst into my world. I had just made a month's wages in two days! That was my first real taste of being directly involved in an enterprise that had actual potential to set Faith and I free from the endless grind of brutal hard labor with a slow-motion return on effort.

Hallelujah!

We were free at last!

I started buying timber for the local export market, which was a huge supplier to the world. What I had never known was that Pennsylvania's hardwoods were considered the finest wood products for high end furniture, veneers, cabinetry, paneling, interior finishes and were even used for trim in Learjets, Bentleys and Rolls Royces. The world shopped in Pennsylvania for its finest wood products. From Japan to Italy, and all points in between, we provided the globe with the finest oak, cherry, maple, walnut, ash, poplar, and sassafras as well as many other hardwood species. Massive quantities of logs and lumber were shipped daily, which made the industry's demand for standing timber virtually insatiable.

And, even though timber was the second oldest industry in the world -- *it appears that the oldest industry in the world needed a bed* -- I had just now discovered that simple fact.

Of all things, my new business enterprise had been firmly beaten into me by a retired schoolmarm.

In some ways she saved my life...

God bless retired schoolteachers!

* * * * * * *

"Dad, thank you for providing a place - a home really - and work for me to do and actually get paid. You've provided me with a future and allowed me to be part of building the gas company on the side. Both you and Mum have been a godsend for us. I don't think I'll ever be able to thank you enough."

I was sitting at my parent's dinner table on a Saturday morning with two of my brothers trying to figure out how to fix the meat packing company's lackluster performance. It obviously wasn't happening, we'd been hemmed in by larger entities and their ability to undercut us on every front. We had a better product, but our customers enjoyed the reduced prices the larger companies could provide. As for me, I could see the end coming.

My analysis was that the actual light at the end of the tunnel was an oncoming train and our pathway was cascading towards some type of annihilation.

Fortunately, Dad was a true visionary; he knew it long before we'd identified the need to change. He had coaxed us into the natural gas industry, college housing, real estate, and now timber, one tiny step at a time.

"I officially quit. I'm going to start buying timber full time. Once again, Dad, I can't possibly thank you and Mum enough for everything you've done. It has been a real learning experience... I think we'd have starved without all of your help."

Dad smiled with a type of deep-seated pride. While he knew it was coming, my brothers probably didn't. I got up and shook their hands. I had work to do and looking for timber could be done as long as the sun was shining, especially on Saturday mornings.

* * * * * * *

"Will you look at that!"... Frank, Kenzo and I stood in complete awe at the spectacle unfolding before us. Kilauea's east rift zone was exploding in liquid fire, with lava flowing down the pali (cliff) in at least six major lines, all headed to the sea. A couple had already made it to the base of the steep grade, rejoined, and slinked along the road we were standing on.

My family and I were on vacation, and Frank was temporarily back on the Big Island from Alaska. Turns out, it's hard to fish in the dead of winter when the sun never shines and the storms across the Bering Sea are horrendous. Kenzo was living in Kona. He'd become the head of the second largest Century 21 office on the planet and enjoyed having more than 400 licensed realtors working under him. He also babysat a mansion for a client and got a small percentage of whatever the crew sold. Everyone loved him. As for them, he wished they were better at their jobs, and way less demanding.

Eventually he figured out how to avoid them all on a regular basis. He'd simply explain to them, "Sorry, I have a court appearance later today. I won't be able to make it." What none of them knew was that his "court appearances" were actually at a tennis court tucked away on the backside of one of the Five Star resorts along Kona's Gold Coast. Kenzo played so much tennis that he eventually got astoundingly good at it. Maybe even won himself some accolades and a few trophies!

Frank and I were so proud of him.

"Hey! What on earth are you doing?" I yelled at Kenzo. He had his back turned to us and was half-a-step from the edge of the glowing flames-from-hell lava flow.

"I've always wanted to do this…," he trailed off as he relieved himself and watched it explode into a vaporous cloud off the glowing rocks.

We gave him space when he was like that.

On down the road, just past Sea Arches, we bumped into a park ranger. He had the hat and all, looking very official. "Gentlemen, if you are going any further, please be aware that the lava is now entering the ocean and causing huge billows of poisonous gases. We are currently upwind, so we are safe for now. If for any reason you feel the wind shift, or your eyes get irritated, you must rapidly go back the way you came and seek safe shelter by driving back up Chain of Craters Road. Go all the way back to the park. Don't stop for anything."

We all smiled and nodded, then sauntered down to see raw live 2,000-degree Fahrenheit lava attack the great Pacific Ocean. There were a multitude of stars out and horrendous noises piercing the air. Huge concussions overlapped creating an atmosphere gone insane with volcanic rage.

Sitting on a high promontory overlooking the onslaught - the ongoing epic battle - we sat quiet and took it all in. No matter how hard the lava tried to gain a foothold, the ocean held its superior position by casting wave after wave upon it. Explosion after explosion ensued and the age-old war continued, a war that had formed the entire archipelago throughout the ages.

Then, as if things couldn't get any more awesome, a full moon peeked over the eastern horizon, backlighting the entire primordial event!

"Are we going to see pterodactyls…" Kenzo whispered at the full moon rising. Frank and I sat silent, taking in the spectacle, completely lost in our own separate worlds.

It was flat out amazing. And the three of us got to enjoy it together, just like old times; something we hadn't done for years.

* * * * * * *

Decades later we took a Bell 407 helicopter to the summit of Mauna Loa to check on Halemaumau, the stunning caldera of the very active volcano. We were absolutely at the edge of the craft's acceptable envelope. Helicopters don't like altitude and 13,678 feet above sea level was keeping us all very focused in every possible way.

Far above the clouds, the sun illuminated everything. Layers upon layers of a multitude of volcanic eruptions created a stark reality of how eruption after eruption shaped the largest mountain on the planet when measured by volume, from the base of the Hawaiian Deep on which it rested.

We gazed in awe at the blowout on the eastern edge of the caldera. The exact same eruption and flow that had almost consumed Historic Hilo Town back in 1984 had completely crushed its way through a two hundred foot portion of the caldera's sidewall. It performed that task and made its run towards the sea. With such immense forces on display, Hilo was simply in the way and most likely would have been completely destroyed from the onslaught of lava cascading down through the mountain's lush rainforest slopes. However, legend claims that the only reason it stopped was because some righteous souls gathered and prayed, invoking the name of JESUS CHRIST to GOD ALMIGHTY, in a heartfelt plea to halt the wall of lava headed directly at Hilo Town. It was obvious it was about to destroy many people's lives, their businesses, and everything they had ever known, including the beautiful place they called home.

Hearing their prayers, the eruption and lava flow immediately halted.

* * * * * * *

Kenzo housesat a doctor's mansion, built on the slope of Hualalai Mountain, located just above Kailua-Kona. It was huge, and the room they gave him was on the side of the house where the neighbor's equally pretentious estate had their TV located. Every evening they'd blast the TV 'til the wee hours; they appeared to either be very hard of hearing, or they blared it while they moved about from room-to-room as a means to keep themselves company.

Kenzo eventually couldn't take it anymore, so he formulated a deep thought and instigated a two-step plan. First, he made cookies and took them over to his neighbors. As a realtor, he asked if he could be shown their fabulous home. They were more than happy to oblige, and showed him all about their architectural masterpiece, which, of course, included their TV room.

Kenzo noted the make and model of the set, went to the local electronics store, and bought the appropriate remote. That night, and every night thereafter, he'd hear the neighbor's TV blaring, and proceed to aim his newly purchased remote out the window. Click, click, click, the volume magically dissipated to an acceptable level.

Now and again he'd simply hit the mute button.

Kenzo started to sleep a whole lot better.

One day a moving truck showed up, dropped the tailgate and started unloading a brand-new TV at the neighbor's house.

Kenzo rushed over, caught the owner's attention, and asked what they were doing. The lady answered, "Every night we're watching our favorite show and suddenly the volume falls all by itself. We put it up, and it goes right back down. WE THINK OUR TV IS POSSESSED!" She was visibly shaken. "So, we're getting a new one to replace it."

Kenzo noted the make and model and drove straight to the electronics store...

* * * * * * *

Sometimes Faith and I think the only things that Hawaii and Pennsylvania have in common are that both inhabit the same planet, circle the same sun, and enjoy the ambiance of the same welcoming moon.

When we speak of Hawaii to our friends from Pennsylvania, they think we're bragging, lying or obviously confused in our descriptions. To them, Hawaii is a mythological creature, like a unicorn, never to be found.

An exotic land determined as too impossible to imagine.

To our Hawaiian friends, they think that Pennsylvania is unworthy of comment or consideration. It's an East Coast location on the outskirts of New York where Amish plow the fields and knowledgeable people avoid for every reason known to man.

To Faith and I, as those who easily flow between these two separate worlds, we know for a fact that both can be awesome, fearsome, beautiful, and cruel. Both worlds have astounding features and touches of GOD's divine nature woven deeply into their souls.

Faith and I live in two worlds.

Two separate worlds, which have nothing in common. Yet, they have everything in common.

Now when people on the Big Island ask us, "What is it like in Pennsylvania?"

We answer, "It's like one huge honking Waimea." They easily understand the correlation since Waimea is the home of lush rolling green hills filled with happy cows roaming amongst stands of huge timber.

When our Pennsylvania friends ask us, "Is Hawaii really like they say it is?" We tell them, "It's 86 degrees... in the water!" which is usually enough information to assuage their curiosity. If not, we politely offer, "There's a flight every morning at sunrise."

And, if they appear indignant, I tell them, "Be careful, the turtles have fangs!"

17

Trillion Little Things

Parenthood is a subject of countless movies, stories, books and tales told since the dawn of time...Such a joy, so many 'wow' moments, and so many extended periods of exhaustion occur at the same time. Nothing new, just this time it happened to be us.

Our oldest, Domino, has raised us as best that she can. No parent - us included - actually raises their oldest child; the oldest child raises their parents.

For it's the wild embrace of becoming everything that our children need that allows us the wholehearted joy of chasing a far greater destiny.

AJG & FKG / 1984 - ongoing

* * * * * * *

"Throw that to Daddy..." I smiled, held out my arms and hands, and waited for her to gently toss me the toy she held in her tiny paws. With a full overhand windup and massive release, she drilled me right between the eyes with the hardwood block. It dropped me like a fly.

I don't think I underestimated our oldest daughter ever again.

Trying to be the good parents, doing our best to obtain a small slice of culture for our children, whom we were attempting to raise as best as possible, we took the kids to the Carnegie Museum in Pittsburgh. After the joy of unloading them with all of their gear: strollers, bottles, diaper bag, clothes, stuffed animals and other essentials we finally made it to the coat room where we could unpack the non-essentials and proceed to the heart of the day's enterprise. Rocks and fluorescent minerals seemed to be a bit of a hit, but when we got to the Hall of Dinosaurs, the kids got really animated and loved the displays. That is, maybe too much, as security had to chase both Domino and Tiffany away from petting the petrified bones of the frozen-in-time beasts. Appears that having a five and three year old pawing at the toes of monsters cast in stone was inappropriate behavior.

Oh the damage they could have done!

As our young family continued exploring the various rooms with the master's paintings and works of art collected back in Carnegie's acquisition phase, we discovered the finest specimens of oil on canvas. He purchased as he pleased and stocked his namesake museum with priceless relics.

Tiffany played and romped and Talon rode in the stroller with a firm grasp of the nipple on his bottle, which stretched to the max as he giggled and swung it with wild abandon over his head. Poor Faith, the frazzled Mommy, tried her best to keep them from causing a catastrophe. And from petting anything else that looked expensive, old or fragile - which was literally everything in every room. She had her hands full while silently scheming how best to vacate the premises and find a local McDonalds, preferably with a playground.

But as for me, I was with Domino. She was enthralled by everything hanging on the walls. Even at age five she absorbed every little facet of the master's works. Asking zero questions, she was absolutely mesmerized by the perfectly displayed paintings and sculptures all around. I allowed her to take her time, and simply followed her lead as she brazenly went from artwork to artwork.

Then, finally, Domino stopped dead still in a hallway between galleries where a Russian traveling exhibit was temporarily on display. She froze and stared at an obscure Russian artist's painting hanging alone. A single spot illuminated the rather small painting as Domino gazed intently. So I asked her, as a good father would, "Honey, what do you see?"

After having a very deep thought, with pure heartfelt emotion she answered ever so softly, with a quivering voice, "Daddy, the artist is so lonely..."

And, once again, she left me speechless.

Years have gone by, she's grown through childhood and become the woman we've always hoped and prayed she'd become. To this day her eye for detail is extraordinary. She sees far beyond what most perceive as reality, and can often, with little effort, pinpoint exactly what lay upon the canvas of life.

Domino paints, and sculpts and works magic with materials to create works of art that many who know her consider of master's quality.

Faith and I couldn't be prouder. Sometimes parenthood has benefits far beyond anything imagined or dreamed.

* * * * * * *

Our second daughter, Tiffany, was absurdly light on her feet. And, always had a plan with very specific goals.

She still does.

One night, at bedtime, I was sitting on the edge of her bed getting ready to tell her a story and tuck her in, when she got this extremely focused look in her brilliant greenish-brown eyes. You could see that she was formulating a very deep question. I smiled, got her to relax a bit, and asked, "Tiffany, what is it, darling? It seems you have something on your mind."

"I want to be a cheerleader." She declared in her trembling voice. She always had her own language, we called it *Tiffanese,* but this articulate request was wrapped inside of a very specific goal and was impossible to miss. Every word came out perfect.

After revealing her deepest dream to me, I took the prerequisite amount of time to keep the moment reverent, then responded, "My dearest Tiffany, YES! You can be a cheerleader! I know you can! We'll get you signed up for next season." She smiled, rolled over and went soundly to sleep, clutching her blanket - which she called *Yynee* (we think that meant 'mine'). Her prized possession's name had been adapted to her uniquely personalized language.

She loves that blanket. It has been around the world with her.

* * * * * * *

The third time Faith told me, "Allen, can you please sit down, I have something to tell you..." By then I had noticed a trend. This time, unlike the previous two times, I knew what it meant; she was pregnant, and we'd have one more bundle of joy to help raise us into the future.

We were young parents and still learning. Why learn from just two children? When three would exponentially increase our joy of being parents! Just for the record, raising two children is not easy. But at least there were two of us and we could each claim one apiece if things went bonkers. With three, all bets are off. 'Bonkers' became the new normal, and chaos reigned supreme.

Talon arrived screaming, happy, brilliant and healthy.

Yet, that is what we assumed, until the doctor walked into the room ashen faced, very serious with Talon's chart in hand. Bracing himself against the wall, he said, "Mr. Gourley, can you please sit down, I have something to tell you..."

Usually a trillion little things are cascading through a parent's mind when they have two toddlers and one newborn baby. Logistics, timing, requests, and demands all run rampant competing for brain capacity to deal with so many moving parts. And, to add to the list of emotions gone wild, a newborn son fulfills the dream of having our dreams within our grasp; what a wonderful set of turmoil and joys abounding!

Every single one of them evaporated from my reality, as I processed the horrid news that the doctor, using his best bedside manner, thrust into my world with his unvarnished opinion of his medical analysis. He held it tightly against his chest as an ice-cold chart of information, none of it good. When he said, "...your son has between eight and nine hours to live...," everything else was of no matter.

Our beautiful baby boy, our newborn son, was being consumed from a blood incompatibility - his billirubin count, a form of neonatal jaundice, was skyrocketing. He had mere hours to live. Every minute counted. Every hour critical and flowing towards a terminal ending. Decisions needed to be made, and the doctor, looking spooky serious, wasn't going to leave the room without those decisions firmly in hand.

"What are we to do...?" It wasn't so much a question as a desperate plea for guidance. I felt so mortal. A stabbing hurt tore into my soul.

"We need to get your son to a Neonatal Intensive Care Unit (NICU) -- and we need to do it immediately." The doctor gave Faith and I his instantaneous response.

"I presume that involves helicopter transport." I answered for both of us.

"Not today. All flights are grounded in the tri-state area. We've got Level 4 and Level 5 thunderstorms all around us. Nothing is flying, certainly not within the timeframe that your son needs them to."

I simply lost it and put my head into my hands. Then slowly lifting my eyes, I saw Faith crying. I got up and walked over to be with her. She was exhausted, and now destroyed from the ordeals of the day.

"Where is available? What are our options?" I pressed Faith's hand.

"Erie, Pittsburgh, DuBois... All have world-class NICU teams. All are available for your son's arrival." Once again, the doctor answered with zero hesitation. His immediate response was a bit of a balm to our wounded hearts. Obviously, he'd been in this position before.

"Which one do you recommend?" I asked, fatigue starting to creep into my mind; suddenly I was becoming exhausted from the reality of the moment.

"I can't prescribe one over the other. It is, and has to be, your decision alone." He looked directly at me, then down. He wisely refused to allow me to pass such a momentous decision back to him.

I sat down, once again put my forehead into my hands, and allowed the information to become all things. Somewhere I must have gotten a prayer cast towards heaven because I had a very deep thought form within me.

I softly asked the doctor, who was showing extreme bravery and standing stalwart in the corner awaiting my decision, "If this were your son, which team would you choose? I assume they all have the same equipment and facilities to work with." I took my very best shot, not for me, but for our son and my loving wife who was in a flagrant display of stunned anguish.

The doctor actually cracked a smile. It appeared I had asked exactly the right question, for his answer was instantaneous. "DuBois is where I would send my son if he were in this situation and needed immediate attention. Their head doctor is awesome as well as the team that he has surrounded himself with. They are all hand-picked by him and they have a proven track record with wonderful results." His countenance lifted, and he asked the question he'd been waiting for, "Should I arrange immediate transport to DuBois?"

"Can his mother go with him, please? I would hate to have them separated for any reason. Especially now...only hours old..." I very quietly requested. My internal ability to process everything was fully compromised.

"Maybe the only good thing about the weather is that I can make that happen for you. I agree -- best if we can keep them together. It would have been impossible by helicopter."

No smile. No nod. He just turned and went to work.

Time was of the essence. All the cares of our world - all trillion little things - had fallen far behind us, for the urgency of the moment had us firmly in its grasp.

Getting Talon to the NICU was all that mattered. Getting him there as fast as humanly possible was our singular goal. The nurses, the staff, the doctor (GOD bless his soul), Faith, me -- we all had the exact same objective. As did the ambulance transport team, which was in route. This is what they did - and they hopefully did it very well. We presumed that their link in the chain to get Talon to the NICU was strong, just as all of us were being.

But then, now and again, the twisted reality of humans being incompetent buffoons bursts in to destroy the finest plans put into action by incredible humans.

Weak links always appear at the worst possible time.

* * * * * * *

My first inkling that all was not right with the ambulance crew was virtually immediate. Having brought the trusty Ford Taurus around to follow them to DuBois we left the ER loading area and proceeded straightaway down the highway into Franklin proper. In the pounding rains, the driver drifted right, tight against the curb, with no traffic in sight on a four-lane stretch of wide-open highway, and hit the deep divot of a water runoff drainage opening. For no apparent reason! He hit it so hard that the entire ambulance bounced two feet in the air. Pulling over, with me utterly confused, the driver got out, got soaked by the downpour, and opened the back doors to climb in.

Faith was fully incapacitated by the painkillers and was mumbling some type of questions concerning, "....are we there already..." Talon was snuggled into a portable incubator and I was out of the Taurus gazing into the mess the impact had caused: stuff flown about, the nurse confused, and the plug in auxiliary power feed ripped out of the socket.

Alarm sounding and the driver fumbling to get the incubator plugged back in, it was self-inflicted mayhem with lightning dropping and thunder roaring. Surreal stupidity was on rampant display.

We hadn't even gone one mile!

Faith laid her head back down and softly faded into the Never-Never-Land of drug-induced oblivion. I stood in the downbursts and made eye contact with the driver as he closed the doors tight. He put his head down and returned to his assignment of driving his precious cargo to the destination.

I was too much in shock to say a word. Seemed we were "pre-disastered" - as they would say in Hawaii. Meaning that whatever could go wrong had just done so and therefore all would be well with the rest of the journey.

I couldn't have been any more wrong in my assessment.

Taking the extended longest possible way to get to I-80, the driver decided that going 45 MPH in the left lane on the Interstate, with all of his lights on, while being the slow guy in the fast lane, was his very best option. Spray, rain, and road mist enveloped everything. My wipers on max and my temperature rising, I kept the Taurus directly behind my wife and son, who were in the process of being transported by slow motion idiots. I was fuming.

"Why is he in the fast lane going 20 MPH under the speed limit!" I screamed out loud to myself -- just me and my boiling blood -- as everything dear to me rode at wrap factor zero, in and out of raging thunderstorms. My confusion had given way to a perfected awareness that the person driving the ambulance and his helper were sent to destroy every hope that the doctor and his valiant team had put into motion.

As my temper flared, I saw a tractor-trailer, an 80,000-pound behemoth, flying up fast behind us! He did not care if the ambulance had on its lights -- it was going slow and he wasn't. So, he swerved to pass on the inside, just as the driver decided to commit suicide and take everyone with him! He switched lanes - finally after all of this time - directly into the path of the massive truck barreling through. I dove behind the ambulance, figuring that I could lessen the impending impact, at least a little bit. Maybe give Faith and Talon a fighting chance in the crash...

Fortunately, the truck missed my back bumper by the thickness of a sheet of paper. He blew by us with all 18 wheels locked up and horn-a-blazing. I'm sure he had the exact same opinion I did of the driver of the ambulance.

At this stage I didn't think that the driver was simply incompetent; I knew he was downright dangerous and couldn't be trusted for anything.

What should have been a straightforward easy transport was now turning into a deadly situation with a touch of diabolical carelessness. We proceeded along the path to DuBois, shaken but at least going east on I-80 to the hospital about one more hour away. It appeared that hope, albeit slow, was still within relatively easy reach.

Then, after what felt like decades of tepid progress, he drove right past the exit! Not knowing exactly where the hospital was - DuBois was unknown to me - I (once again) assumed he knew what he was doing and that the hospital must be located at the far end of town. But after taking the far exit, he proceeded to drive the entire length of town back towards the original exit's entrance, all the while slowing, then stopping, for every possible light along the way. This was profoundly ignorant driving! My anger was giving way to rage as this all played out. By myself, with zero outlets for my frustrations, I pounded the steering wheel and screamed at the fool, "HURRY YOU INCOMPETENT MORON!"

Turning left, he found the railroad crossing that had just started to blink. With no train in sight, he decided it was best to wait for one. If you wait long enough, eventually a train will arrive, and of course, one did. A 100-plus-car coal train came sauntering towards us at less than 5 MPH. Since it was over a mile in length, it rolled past like a glacier on holiday.

So, we sat. And sat. And sat some more. By this time I felt like we'd been on a journey to the ends of the earth while riding on the back of a yak with a flaming batch of hemorrhoids.

Things had deteriorated from the surreal to the absurd.

When we got to the hospital - thank GOD, finally - I watched as the ambulance found the ER loading dock entrance. Knowing that we'd arrived, I rushed myself to the front entrance, went to the desk to get directions, and found out the worst possible news: somehow -- in the driver's infinite wisdom -- he had brought my wife and my newborn son to the wrong hospital!

By the time I got to the ER, they were gone. Having been summarily shooed away and sent to the proper hospital that actually had an NICU, which was all the way on the other side of town.

Back where we'd been before the wrong exit...

And the train...

All as the clock continued to tick.

* * * * * * *

112

Making my way across town, having lost my *precious cargo* to forces unknown, I finally discovered the real hospital we'd been dispatched to. It sat stark in the rain. I circled it looking for the ER entrance. The most likely place for my loved ones to be, but, alas, even after two circuits no entrance was to be found! Eventually, in my pure frustration, I took a chance that the loading-dock, under a full rehab demolition/construction. Unmarked with an ambulance tucked in beside it - no lights, no markers, no nothing - there was a door. Nothing else. Just rain and a non-descript side door half-opened. Must be it!

When I got there, I saw a tightly packed group of professionals whisking Talon away in the incubator. The entire team of NICU nurses and doctors focused on the tiny newborn that was supposed to have arrived hours earlier.

And, to my horror, they left my lovely bride, mother of my children, in the hands of the driver and his assistant. Forlornly, the two incompetents were assessing the latest dilemma facing them. They had to lift Faith up a flight of stairs to get her beyond the loading dock, into the hospital proper and down the hallway.

Seeing that she was about to be "lifted" by the driver and an EMS chic who was absolutely tiny. The driver was leaving the downside heavy end for the mini-EMS chic to handle! I proceeded to pick her up and summarily cast her aside. She was stunned by my brazen disregard for protocol. With one look of fire shooting from my eyes, she got over it.

Once I helped get Faith up and into the building, I happened to see whom my nemesis actually was up close and personal.

What bar they'd dragged him out of was unknown. But the fact that he'd been dragged out of one was not. I shook my head in disgust and glared at him until he grabbed his stunned assistant and went back the way they came, never to be seen by me again.

Once in a lifetime was plenty.

No wonder he was all over the road, couldn't drive and made horrendous judgment calls all along the way -- he was incoherent and lost. I wish I could say he was simply fatigued and in over his head, but I would be lying. He was a slow-motion disaster, which almost cost me everything that mattered. Being a *weak link* would be the kindest of descriptions. As for his sidekick, she couldn't help that she was born height challenged. But, just like the driver, she needed to seek more appropriate employment.

And they both needed to do it immediately as far as I was concerned.

* * * * * * *

"Hear your son is doing well..." the hospital Chief Administrator of trailed off as he tried to diffuse the situation with facts.

I sat there a while and let him squirm.

"Your nurses and doctors are world-class excellent. Everything is coming along just as hoped. I wish to thank them for everything they've done. Wish I could say the same about the ambulance transport here and your lack of having the ER properly marked." I just shook my head in disgust as I relived the longest day of my life, just a few days prior. I was still seething at the mere thought of it.

"Sorry about all of that. Some things are out of our control, Mr. Gourley."

"The ER markings aren't. I presume that those will be flagrantly well marked by the end of the day." I demanded, with a forced calm in my voice.

"Yes, already being taken care of. Might I offer you a coffee?" Once again, he deflected. Changing subjects appeared to be a regular portion of his job description, as well as risk assessment and risk management. Obviously, I was both types of threat to them. Any type of righteous pending litigation always caught the upper-echelons-of-power's attention. Hospitals were no exception and were acutely aware of that fact in the modern world.

"Don't worry. I'm not suing you or this hospital. Why on earth would I? You've saved my son's life, and you're doing it in style. It appears that *his future's so bright, that he's gotta wear shades.*" And with that, I broke the tension hanging in the air like a thunderstorm threatening annihilation, and we both had a belly laugh from the joke that was so specific to the reality of the moment.

Talon was in the NICU under lights with a mask to protect his eyes. The lights were slowly helping him rebuild his blood to the needed levels and helping to combat the neonatal jaundice, which had threatened to destroy him. After the full body transfusion, that had been performed the night of his birth by the best doctors and nurses on the planet, he was doing excellent and was scheduled for release in the next few days.

They were awesome to watch in action. Their attention to the minutest details was profound. We all prayed, then they performed their medical miracle a few CCs of blood at a time. A gift of life, found for his super-rare blood type, given by a retired military man who had been married for over thirty years to the same woman came just in time. That very same blood was transported across the length of Pennsylvania, by Pennsylvania's finest State Troopers, at extreme speeds to arrive in DuBois as quick as humanly possible. Pounding rains, thunder and lightning, they knew the sense of urgency and performed the task assigned at great risk to themselves in weather conditions that were violent and profoundly intense.

To this day I never say anything bad about our State Troopers. To me they are permanently exempt from verbal abuse and deserve the utmost in respect. They are often unsung heroes. And, most importantly, they were a very strong link in the chain of souls that helped in saving our son's life.

All is well that ends well. My anger at the drunken transport from Hades slowly evaporated with time. And the advent of bringing our son home from a journey that started the day he was born - while a trillion little things in world collapsed in upon itself - gave way to what truly mattered. Our son was safely at home with his family that loved him dearly.

Talon was, and is, healthy, happy, and full of life abounding!

* * * * * * *

Faith and I learned a profound reality upon the birth of our third child: always pray first then act, for it is the only way to connect to Heaven's wisdom while placing your fate into the CREATOR's hands.

* * * * * * *

It will forever be impossible to commend the DuBois NICU team enough. Their professionalism and delicate care were heaven sent. We shall forever be in their debt as long as time exists.

As for the doctor that delivered Talon in Franklin Hospital, his guidance in a tight situation was perfect in both method and technique. He quietly coached me to come to the best possible decision while allowing me to think it was mine. He also steered us an hour closer to where the donated blood came from. Which, in essence, bought us two hours of precious time -- time being the most important commodity known in the universe during that ongoing slow motion medical emergency.

As for the Chief Administrator of DuBois Hospital (the "correct" DuBois Hospital), well we ended up on a friendly basis. We enjoyed long discussions on a multitude of subjects, only one of which was the need for better signage.

As for "The Future's So Bright, I've Gotta Wear Shades" reference, that song was a major hit in America at the time and played endlessly on all channels of the radio. I think I heard it two to three thousand times on my many drives to and from DuBois Hospital. It was so supernaturally appropriate. To us it was obviously GOD having a bit of fun within the realm of our personalized universe.

And, vitally important in this saga of so many being there for us in our time of need -- the WW II Veteran who donated the blood on the far side of Pennsylvania. He did it without payment or recognition. Well sir, you are our unsung hero! You are a valiant warrior in the links of the chain known as humanity.

Which brings me to the Ambulance Service. We received a bill from them for "Transport Services Provided" a few weeks later. I flipped it over, gave a short account of all that had transpired during that fateful journey to DuBois, and mentioned that if they thought in any way that I had used overly descriptive adjectives or adverbs, they should check with their driver to confirm. And, that they could probably find him in the exact same bar they'd originally dispatched him from in the first place.

I never heard from them again.

* * * * * * *

Talon didn't turn out just OK.

He turned out absolutely wonderful!

Just like his two older sisters.

At the end of his senior year, doing his best to garner new heights in the pole vault for the varsity track team, he qualified for States.

So, just like his sister Tiffany, who had a few years earlier been on RVHS's record holding 4X100 relay team, Talon competed against Pennsylvania's finest athletes.

With every height that he cleared, he set a new personal best along with a new school record. Our family was out in force and chanted TALON! TALON! TALON! As his sisters waved signs saying "He's TALON-ted!" for everyone's enjoyment.

Talon flew through the air with poise and style, did most excellent and brought a medal home for his wall, having cleared 14 feet while winning eighth place (a height that had won States the year prior). In between jumps he sat there under the baking hot sun, wearing his trademark sunglasses because his future was truly so bright he absolutely had to wear shades

A few months later, with Tiffany home on break from CU Boulder, they were comparing notes during a family dinner. "Did you go to the All School Dance while you were out at States? It was the very best part!" Tiffany declared to her brother with a big smile. Tiffany, who held six school records simultaneously (which may have been a school record in and of itself) wanted to remind her brother who was the best athlete in the family after all.

He looked at her, laughed with a real hint of sibling rivalry, and replied, "I guess you weren't on the medal stand..."

Talon's record still stands...as do many of Tiffany's.

18

A Mean Squeegee

"Sometimes friendships are discovered during the weirdest of circumstances."

AJG & FKG / 1990ish - ongoing

* * * * * * *

"Can you take a look at my property?" I fielded a random call while in the office - just another day. Another block of timber offered to me by a random stranger for the insatiable global market forces wishing to acquire oak, black cherry, maple, and so much more from Pennsylvania's forest.

"Might I ask who's calling?" He gave me his name and title, which happened to be the CEO of a rather large heavy equipment company. Somehow, they'd obtained a property during the course of a court ordered settlement.

I asked only one question. The only one remaining of any substance: "Do you wish for me to buy the timber, or do you want to sell it land and all?"

"I would like to sell the land outright. We have no use for it."

When I met him there, about a month later, he arrived in a freshly polished Lincoln Continental. It was black, and he was annoyed that he had to take the time from his regular day's schedule to meet with me. "What do you need from me, young fellow?" He asked.

"Only a few things. I've pulled the maps -- plat, topographical and aerial -- so I'm good to go as far as that is concerned. Did you bring the deed, Sir? I'm curious to what it is that you actually own." I smiled. I'd just gotten back from Hawaii a day earlier and was in a rather good mood. It was perpetual summer there and it was summer in Pennsylvania, so I was in my element since my tan wouldn't immediately freeze dry off of me like it did in the other three seasons.

"Got it right here." He handed it over, and I glanced at the *Provisions: Exceptions & Reservations* portion.

"Only thing you own is the dirt and the trees, everything else has been carved out long ago. No gas. No oil. No coal. No minerals. It appears that any and all of your potential subsurface rights have been retained by others, is that the same conclusion you've come up with, Sir?"

He nodded. "How long should this take? I've been working long hours, and if you need a couple days, I'll be on my way." He answered, looking tattered in every possible dimension. *Maybe he shouldn't have worn a suit to a timber showing* I thought. But after seeing how uncomfortable he was, I decided not to mention the obvious.

"According to the maps, and if my experience tells me correctly, this should only take a short walk on my behalf. Everything appears to be somewhat homogenous in characteristics of stand and composition. Give me an hour, and I'll give you a price. Maybe we can finish this right now and not take up any more of one another's busy schedules." I offered as a means to an end. At this stage of my acquisition phase of buying natural resources, I had grown very observant of micro and macro expressions - and this gentleman was one of the easiest "reads" I'd ever encountered. He just wanted this task done. Price wasn't the point; completion of divesture and the permanent removal of this property from his books were.

Less than an hour later, I woke him up from his nap in his idling Lincoln by tapping on the window. He sat up, frumpy and startled, to find himself in the middle of Nowhere, Pennsylvania. I smiled. He did his best groggy representation of a smile and stepped out into the heat of the day.

"Will that work for you?" I smiled as I made the offer and put out my hand to on it.

He smiled with what looked like great relief and shook my hand with his first showing of real enthusiasm since we met.

"When can we expect payment?" He asked prior to leaving.

"Soon as you call and tell me the deed is ready for transfer." I answered, happy to be adding another tract to the list.

He blasted out of the dirt access road and headed south, back to his corporate world of heavy equipment and hundreds of employees with their insipid demands, needs that apparently weathered him raw like the dust hanging in the air from his rapid exit.

* * * * * * *

A few weeks later I got a call from Mr. Heavy Equipment CEO's secretary with instructions to meet at his lawyer's office in Downtown Pittsburgh. Not a problem I told her and made sure I had a sheet of company checks as I proceeded to adhere to their desires.

I parked and walked into a skyscraper known as the Oliver Building. I'd driven past it a thousand times, at least now I knew one of the tenants was a group of lawyers I'd never heard of. One item I noticed immediately was the tight security, and the strange looks they gave me when I asked to use the bathroom prior to going up to the floor I'd been given. The security man looked me up and down, and then begrudgingly pointed to the men's room. As I washed my hands it was impossible for me (as a good timber-man) not to notice the doors and trim were done in solid walnut. The floors and walls were all marble, brass and mirrors buffed to the highest polish. The fixtures were gold, not brass, and the towels were real. Nice. Maybe I'd bumped into a touch of class for a change. I had become so used to the rough-sawn world that being around loggers and sawmills provided me on a daily basis.

Off the elevator, through the cut glass double doors, I was immediately scrutinized by the coifed lady sitting at the oversized desk directly before me. "None Shall Pass" might as well have been tattooed on her *just right* indigo fingernails as she tapped them in synchronized fashion, for she was the type to only allow access into her domain at her personal prerogative. It was readily apparent she allowed access sparingly and at her soul discretion.

I sized her up: grey Chanel dress, 18 carat gold necklaces dripping with real diamonds, matching earrings dangling. Her hair was perfect, and her demeanor was crisp and staunch. 'Barter' was not in her vocabulary and lighthearted had never been used to describe her since her birth decades upon decade's prior.

She returned the favor, with even more intensity; seeing me in my exquisitely comfortable Quicksilver board shorts, my favorite sun-faded Pro Leisure Circuit t-shirt while sporting Reef slippers. Meanwhile I cast a touch of joy into her world with my trademark smile (which I'd obviously inherited from my father) all highlighted by my fresh Hawaiian tan.

I simply took a seat, smiled and said nothing, wishing to hear what she was going to come up with. It appeared I had disarmed her with my choice of summer wear. After all, it was the middle of August outside these hallowed walls, and somebody had to embrace the reality of that fact. As she inched her way to a question, I took a good look around. Huge windows allowed the natural light to fill the massive office space. A four-wide spiral staircase wound its way two floors up to a suspended glass room, which I found out later they referred to it as The Fishbowl. I assumed it was probably for important staff meetings and such. It was obviously vital, since it was impossible to miss.

This over-the-top office interior creation looked like it was straight out of Hollywood and the set of *L.A. Law*.

I continued to say nothing. I just sat and watched her fidget while she contemplated *why on earth has this individual been allowed to reach my desk?* She was far too important to deal with comfortably dressed commoners such as myself. Beyond that, how dare I be someone who had actually been outside while having the audacity to enjoy natural sunlight!

"I presume, young man, that you are here for the job interview." She stated as fact, blunt serious in her demeanor, finally having determined why I was in her space. "I will be happy to point you towards our Human Resources Department."

"Ma'am, what job might that be?" I asked sincerely intrigued. I kept smiling while I leaned in to give her the attention she so demanded.

"Well, we do have a janitorial position available." She continued with her offer by dangling the joys of obtaining a regular b-monthly corporate paycheck. But, with the piercing look she gave me, she thought I might just be a bit under qualified for even that mundane task. All the while she tapped her indigo fingernails to an annoyed staccato rhythm.

"That sounds wonderful! I do believe that I am highly qualified of performing that exact job, Ma'am. I have much experience in cleaning up other people's messes. And, now that you mention it, I think that maybe I actually miss mopping floors -- it can provide a person with a form of stress relief. Also, I might add, I've been known to run a mean squeegee." I honestly answered, thinking of how best to continue. "But, unfortunately that isn't why I'm here. I was contacted by one of your clients to be here at this appointed time. I'm to attend a real estate closing..." I let that tidbit of information hang in the air, then after the appropriate lingering pause, as she had a nice rosy flush starting to show, I finished my bombshell answer "...because I am the buyer."

It looked like she was hit by an electric cattle prod set on max and thrust directly into her spleen! She leaped up, turned a thousand shades of indigo to match her fingernails, instantly pirouetted in her Jimmy Choo high heels and disappeared to points unknown.

It immediately crushed her perception of me while casting her into a frenzy of confusion in a realm previously undiscovered.

So, I calmly sat in my Quicksilver boardshorts and tapped my Reef sandals to a lingering Jimmy Buffet tropical beat on the polished floor. All with my trademark smile beaming. I came from a place so far outside of her reality that she could not fathom it.

I may have been displaying just a touch of too much joy from our off-kilter encounter because when she got back, she refused to make eye contact and had one of her many legal assistants (vassal servants) take me past her desk for the real estate closing awaiting my arrival.

* * * * * * *

Mr. Heavy Equipment CEO exited the huge conference room, and I took another look around. I sat alone with his lawyer at the huge table that could seat over thirty. The conference room was massive, two sides floor-to-ceiling glass, looking directly into Pittsburgh's Financial District, which unfortunately, from our perspective, were competing skyscraper glass towers. Their walls obscured everything being directly across the narrow alleyway.

"Nice building. Thought we'd have a much better view, maybe over the Allegheny River or The Point or something other than those walls of mirrored glass." I broke the ice with minor conversation. "Although, I do have to admit, I think I could land a small fixed wing aircraft on this burled walnut table. Very impressive." I laughed as the ever-observant lawyer -- sitting at the table with the strangest look on his face -- sized me up. I could easily tell he wanted to comment on my choice of business wear. But, he'd been groomed since birth not to mention such strange anomalies. No matter how brazenly displayed and certainly no matter how they came barging into his professional world.

"So, Mr. Gourley, how well did you fare on this purchase? Good for your company? I do hope that our client didn't take too much advantage of your backwoods country graces." He smiled and helped to return the conversation to the topic at hand. Being an elite attorney and all, he knew how to stay on point.

I took a really good look at him. He was an obviously mischievous soul wearing a witty curiosity. So, as I often do, I made an instantaneous decision to like him. And, by doing so, to allow him into my world. After all, I'd completed the purchase and had the deed in hand. My work was officially completed after I handed payment in full over and got all of the relevant notarized documents safely into my possession.

"How much truth can you handle?" I laughed with my question.

He smiled, shrugged his shoulders, and answered, "Try me."

"Your client just paid me to take his property. I pre-sold the timber earlier today and got his land for free. In fact, he actually paid me to take it." His jaw fell and I continued with my analysis, "Got the real estate at zero cost, plus garnered a substantial amount of bonus money, all done pre-purchase. And, even better, we have yet to cut a tree or drop off a piece of equipment. You just witnessed a true *Class A+ Timberland Transaction* with zero expenses outlaid. My only costs were a bit of time and a brief encounter with your receptionist that will go down in history as one of my all-time favorite job interviews!"

"I take it you met Ms. McKrackhausen? She runs this place with an iron presence." He got a somewhat stunned look in his eyes, then continued, "What exactly happened with her?" He was a bit confounded with my news about their elegant receptionist who manned the helm of their very prestigious legal firm like an admiral of a battleship in a war zone.

"She offered me a job when I came in." I smiled, again, and started chuckling to myself. I couldn't help it.

"She offered you a job! What on earth was that all about?"

"Well, your perfectly groomed Ms. McKrackhausen - in Chanel, gold and diamonds, I do believe - was kind enough to offer me a janitorial position! It seems you have one available, and she obviously assumed that I fit the profile of having capabilities in that specific service industry. You know, she must be a good judge of character since I've been known to run a mean squeegee!"

We both lost it laughing so hard that we couldn't get a grip for quite some time. Then we got up, walked to the all glass corner to admire the "view" while trying to figure out how to top that bit of information.

"You really had my client pay you to take his land? And, on top of that, our firm offered you a job to mop our floors!" The lawyer finally was able to spit out his newest batch of revelations with an absolute flabbergasted look on his face. Stunned to his well-groomed core.

"You aren't going to tell him, are you? I am entrusting you with a bit of discretion here..." I said, after getting my composure back on line.

"Can't wait to tell him! He's a bit of a prick anyways, always so demanding in how he treats both me and the firm."

"Can you wait until the deed is recorded?" It came to my mind that I still had a small possibility of exposure if they all wanted to take things sideways.

"I sent the deed over for immediate recording as soon as we signed. My legal eagle assistant is probably already at the courthouse."

"What about Ms. McKrackhausen? Hate to get even deeper into her wrong side. Think it's already awkward enough." I thought I'd better make everything crystal clear since I had already created a vivid history of being misunderstood by his firm.

"Believe me, nobody - me included - ever wants to get on her bad side!" He answered while rubbing his hands through his curly locks and looking totally lost on multiple fronts, a place as foreign to him as my clothing choices were to his formidable gatekeeper.

Switching gears, "This building has so much character, but the views suck. What on earth were you boys thinking when you bought this monstrosity?" I asked since we were on the topic of all-things-real estate.

"I'm on the firm's board for real estate acquisitions and transfers..." He couldn't believe my audacity and how irreverent I was concerning his lack of attributes when it came to his specialty field of law. Yet, he knew I was right, and the view really did suck to the max.

We looked at each other, started laughing once again completely out of control. We took our time to exit the conference room, since we'd instantly become the best of friends...

* * * * * * *

I loved my unexpected "job interview". To this day I'm not sure if I'd ever been capable of meeting Ms. McKrackhausen's (not her real name) exacting standards should I have made the cut by the Human Resources Department to get the position. Although, I am sure she would have made me change my choice of work clothes if I was to ever be in her presence again as an employee of "her" firm.

My nephew often kids me to this very day that after I'm gone, he's going to have my tombstone replaced with one that will have the following epitaph chiseled boldly upon it:

++++ HE RAN A MEAN SQUEEGEE ++++

* * * * * * *

As for the lawyer, the jovial-happy-real-estate-specialist, he became one of our corporate attorneys and dearest friends. He will forever go down as the best thing that I gained from that particular A+ Timber & Land Acquisition. Once again enforcing the simple universal truth that close friends are always more precious than mere silver, gold, real estate, or hard commodities.

As our dear family friend, he eventually helped mentor our brilliant daughter, Tiffany, as she fulfilled her lifelong dream of becoming an attorney herself.

I even got to the point of never being billed for his counseling. I simply bought him lunch while enjoying witty conversation wrapped into friendly banter. He gave me world-class advice concerning techniques, methods and structure, while I provided him with some comic relief from his daily grind of buying viewless properties for his ice-cold humorless corporate clientele.

* * * * * * *

Years later, who'd have ever known that my corporate lawyer buddy and I would be sitting on a spacious lanai overlooking the vast Pacific Ocean while sipping homegrown Kona Coffee and eating the world's best homemade blueberry muffins? The owner provided the sustenance as we enjoyed the large family estate that -- just like back in what seemed like a previous lifetime, during our "Incredible Quest For Surf" days -- overlooked South Point laid out like a relief map far below.

My friendly lawyer, who had become both a dear friend and fellow sojourner, accompanied me to the Big Island to see about possible scenarios to expand our natural resource holdings while generating a bit of adventure along life's journey's way.

We sipped away all while doing my very best to figure out how to acquire this overwhelmingly massive property, being one of the largest privately held remaining intact ahuapua'a (from the mountain to the sea) land holdings in the Hawaiian Islands. Both the owner and I were listening intently and trying our best to decipher what exactly my friendly lawyer's dissertation meant, some type of the latest version of using international monies by employing a newfangled loan-to-value methodology called "Black Box Financing".

Our eyes were fully glazed over when he finished. He sipped his coffee while we pondered his oratory skills concerning the nuances of international financial instruments. None of it made any sense near as I could tell. When I looked across the koa table, I could see that it might as well have been a foreign language to the owner, who wished to sell the family's magnificent estate to me.

Muffins consumed and fresh coffees in hand, we were all lost in our own worlds. This particular epoch of my life, filled with vast open spaces above a sea of blue, was most difficult to grasp and impossible to determine where it was truly heading.

That particular transaction never got done. It had become too complex and way too expensive to ever find an ending that could work for all involved.

Seemed everything was nebulous, faintly reminding me of the feeling of having quicksilver flowing through outstretched hands...

19

Pathways in the Sky

"It is vitally important that you choose not to be risk adverse."

AJG & FKG / 1992ish - ongoing

* * * * * * *

Northwoods Helicopters would dispatch a Bell Jet Ranger from DuBois Airport to pick me up in my front yard. Goal: Elkins, West Virginia and the timberlands prevalent on every side. Huge forestlands encircled Elkins. It had become the heart of West Virginia's wood products industry.

Once landed, I strolled up to the rent-a-car counter's hole-in-the-wall window. "I'll be needing a rent-a-car for the day." I mentioned to the Avis rep. She was obviously annoyed with me being there but begrudgingly tore herself away from her dime store novel, which was as beaten-around-the-fringes as she looked, stuck her head out the window, gazed into the parking lot, and offered, "You can have the brown one or the red one." Then went back to reading. I looked where she was looking and had a difficult time discerning which was which, both were covered in mud complete with huge chunks of goobers on the roof!

"Do you need a Visa or something?" I asked, wanting to keep her engaged since she showed obvious signs of being anything but.

"Keys are in it. We'll take care of that when you get back." Never missing a beat from her engrossing cheap novel about a taboo vapid love triangle and someone's dog dying, I'm sure. She didn't look up or give a rip about protocol.

Things were absurdly different in West Virginia, so I learned to roll with the punches and continued on my quest of expanding our mini empire. I headed to meet up with a local acquisition forester for a huge global conglomerate in the wood products industry. We cut three different deals for a hand-full of timber tracts and got assurances on payment. Since noon had come and gone, he reverted to his hillbilly upbringing and offered me a *snort-of-shine* (moonshine) to cinch the deal, which I politely declined since I had a 'real journey ahead of me' to get back home before the sun went down. I did it in such a manner so as not to pollute our ongoing business relationship by being too snotty or appearing aloof.

We parted ways, and I hustled back to the airport - using my early childhood acquired skills for bad roads and treacherous terrain - to turn in the limpid lizard rent-a-car. Off I went to track down my pilot who'd probably be reading his own version of a dime store novel or sleeping under the shade of a tree on the fringe of the airfield.

"How'd you do today, dear?" Faith asked me after getting dropped off in the yard a few hours later.

"Like printing money. We did very well. Sold five tracts of timber, won three deeds for the asset list and made a bit of money in the process. How were the kids? Get them all off to school this morning? Anything planned for this evening?" I smiled, gave her a big hug, and headed to get cleaned up for whatever her schedule demanded.

"One more thing. You're going to love this one!" My *Sansei Princess* smiled as she waited for me to show a bit of enthusiasm for what was happening on the home front.

"Alright, what do you know that I don't?" I could tell she was just dying to tell me something she thought was either strange or profound, or both.

"After you left this morning, I got a call on the Leatherwood Church's Prayer Wheel. It appears that someone called in this morning's helicopter arrival as being an Air Ambulance Med Evac Flight for our neighbor, Merle. One of the ladies must have figured that he'd had a heart attack and needed immediate medical attention, and a flight to Pittsburgh's Trauma Center!" She smiled and started to laugh with me, both of us flabbergasted by the obvious lack of knowledge being displayed by our wonderfully naive neighbors and their assumptions gone completely astray.

"They are getting up there in years. You know, it could have been Pearl instead of Merle. Why do they always assume it's us husbands that have the proverbial heart attack first?"

"Maybe it's because girls are smarter than boys..." Faith smiled and started getting the kids rounded up for an early dinner and some type of sporting event in the world of elementary school athletics.

* * * * * * *

"Dad, we've got to talk." Talon obviously had something he needed to get it off of his chest before anything else could interfere with it.

"What's that? How may I be of service? Did I do something wrong?"

"Not really, but could you please not drop me off at soccer practice in the helicopter anymore? Sometimes, Dad... it is too much..." I could tell he was being most serious by the tone of his voice.

"Why? Sometimes it's the most convenient way of getting you there for me, when it is on the way to whatever the task-of-the-day is." I had gotten my pilot license and bought a small Robinson R-22 for spotting real estate opportunities while doing aerial evaluations of timber and land. I found it really convenient and way cheaper than having a flight-service dispatched to pick me up in a turbine helicopter with pilot. At least that's how I justified it to myself. And, of course, I had it registered as farm equipment since timber is a designated crop. As my comfort level increased, I'd gotten used to using it as a three-dimensional four-wheel drive rapid transit service.

Talon got a touch sensitive, then continued with his youthful observations on his personal state of affairs, "My friends have been talking about how rich we are."

"Rich is only about having money. Wealth is having the riches of heaven. Wealth is when you have the freedom to do as you please, the time to do it, and the people around you who love you during the process." I smiled, trying to do my best to turn the situation into a learning moment. "As a family, we're always to aspire to being wealthy and never just being rich. An 'Overflowing Cup' - if you will - just like the *23rd Psalm* so clearly states."

He looked at me and shook his head. He'd heard that bit of wisdom preached many times before. "*Please*, Dad?"

"OK. I'll make sure that we'll drive you to practice - *only* - from now on." I assured him. He smiled with a touch of relief, and all was returned to a semblance of balance in his universe once again.

* * * * * * *

"Let me fly..." I was actually spooked by what I saw out of my side of the cockpit. Willy, Kenzo's older brother, looked, ignored me with pure intent and went right back to the conversation he was having with the work crew he was communicating with concerning swing-load logistics for the upcoming week of work. We were in the back of the Seven Valleys of the Kings, a massive interlocking system of huge sea cliffs and thousand-foot waterfalls, blackish grey sand beaches and forbidding treacherous terrain on the northeastern shoreline of the Big Island. Many of the lush green vertical walls were over 2,000 feet in height.

Willy had one skid firmly ground into the three-foot wide flume right-of-way, built by Chinese workers back at the turn of the century for the sugar cane fields along the coasts. His knees were running the cyclic and his attention was on figuring out the coming week's schedule. My attention was straight down. I was looking into the oblivion of a thousand-foot-plus void that would end in disaster if one of the rotors clipped the vegetation or the wall or...anything at all would set into motion a cascading event of destruction. I was more than concerned. I was outright on the edge of panic.

"Come on man. Let me have the controls. Then you can talk as long as your heart desires..." I tried my best to sound calm, pretty sure it wasn't working. Hoping he'd allow me to protect us from what I saw as a profoundly imminent threat, I looked at him.

"OK then, see you first thing in the morning." Willy finished his work schedule, looked at me, pulled some power, and yanked hard left on the cyclic of the chopper, doing a rotary version of a wingover as we fell off the cliff into a Zero G wildly inappropriate straight down dive directly into the awaiting doom of the green abyss so far below...

With him laughing outrageously into my headset, he hit somewhere around 125 knots then he pulled straight back on the cyclic. We got a full 3 G's and climbed with the skids buried deep into the ferns that were dripping off the opposing valley wall across the wickedly deep ravine! As we slowed in our full vertical ascent, he allowed the helicopter to come to an almost complete stop, pushed hard right pedal, and performed a perfect rotorcraft version of a hammerhead stall! Then he dove straight down that hidden valley wall, skids still inches from the rock outcroppings and continued on down the chute looking for the beach far below.

I was impressed to the max and simultaneously wanted to punch him hard in the face with everything I had. I hadn't been that scared since riding with my brothers on the back roads when I was ten years old.

Willy was a Hollywood Stunt Pilot, a real-life card-carrying member of the Screen Actors Guild, and loved to spook every single passenger that ever had the audacity to ride with him. Today obviously was no exception to that simple rule.

With my attitude completely modified, I yelled with wild abandon into the mic, "Man, I gotta' get me one of these!"

He just smiled and blew along the Hamakua Coast's towering sea cliffs back towards Hilo International Airport. We'd both given up a lot of our danger zone hobbies to fly. Surfing and diving had now taken a backseat to all things flight.

Somehow, we thought it was normal. For most of those around us, they probably thought that our sanity had departed our *Earthen Vessels* long ago...

* * * * * * *

Commercials and TV shoots, ferrying tourists over the ongoing eruptions, movies and commercials for corporate clientele, all were on Falcon Aviation's daily schedule for all of the Big Island's helicopter's needs.

When you are having too much fun, things often start going sideways.

First hint of what was on Willy's near horizon was when he did a flight for one of *National Geographic*'s film crews. While out over the lava barrens of the ongoing East Rift

Zone eruption that had not stopped since Faith and I were lamenting our loss of Paradise to the adventure of growing up, things started to break down.

Such a simple thing, one member of the film crew had a small cloth get ripped out of his hands by the wind whistling past his door-less side of the open cockpit. He tried to snag it, but it escaped him.

"What was that!" Willy barked into the open mic. He immediately pushed the collective down and started a steep descent towards the lava field below

"Lost a cloth out the window..." answered the photographer forlornly.

"Something's not right." Willy put his brand-new MD 500E into a full autorotation, an emergency landing procedure, while looking for a level spot to sit it down.

"Look at that, it must have hit the top forward rotating edge of the tail rotor. Had to hit dead center. Twisted the shear pin, to almost its breaking point... Man are we all lucky." Willy declared directly at the two-man film crew. He was flat-out ticked off. His bird had sustained thousands of dollars-worth of damage and now was going into the hangar for repairs. Down time equaled zero income, which was even more expensive in the helicopter business world.

A few weeks later, on a beautiful blue-sky day, with soft winds aloft and a full schedule of tourists seeking adventure, Falcon Aviation had every seat booked for the day. Fat wallets and smiling faces were always welcome customers. First flight left with a full load, paying passengers and the pilot on a chartered flight: volcano, waterfalls, Mauna Loa's upper slopes with an off-site landing on a very special ledge to get the ultimate panoramic images of the western coastline. Some wine and cheese, unlimited views from 6,000 feet above sea level were on the schedule. Such an awesome route, from jungle to lava, from waterfalls to stunning view plane, the route allowed for everyone on board to see the majestic beauty of all things Big Island.

"I'm having a hard time getting enough juice from the battery for my bird to start," came the pilot's call into the main office.

"We'll dispatch Falcon Two to your position. See you there in twenty minutes or so," Dispatch responded. So, the pilot of Falcon One sat and waited for Falcon Two to show up, give them a jump start chopper-to-chopper and get the show back on the road for the tourists who were getting a bit antsy from being stranded on the mountain, no matter how great the view was.

It was extremely tight having the second bird land on the ledge. But with the view being awesome, the pilots keeping everything lighthearted, and the day's weather remaining gentle and cooperating, things were looking good.

Yet, a tiny gust of wind, at the worst possible moment, pushed Falcon Two just slightly, which now had all aboard, back against the lava rubble wall behind it. One touch with the tail-rotor and all went into chaos!

Nowhere to hover-auto and the bird skipped right off the small ledge into some rough brush-covered terrain directly in front of it! Doing a half-roll onto its side to a stop as all four blades blew off and the turbine wound to a grinding halt! Screeching mayhem, then dead silence as the dust settled, it was apparent that one passenger needed medical attention for a broken arm and that everyone else were shaken to the bones. With the disaster, Falcon One powered down its turbine, the pilot got out to assist. But Flacon One wouldn't start again just as it was so critical to have it as rapid evacuation transit for the injured tourist.

One bird down and one bird destroyed.

Everyone was left completely stranded, in the absolute middle of Mauna Loa's mountain wilderness and miles from any type of help, except, of course, by emergency helicopter.

With the events having cascaded out of everyone's control, the pilot of Falcon One made the dreaded call: Mayday! Mayday! Chopper down. Northwest slope. Mauna Loa. Six thousand feet elevation. Send immediate assistance. One injured...Mayday! Mayday! Chopper down...

* * * * * * *

"And that is how Falcon Aviation died." I completed the story as I tucked in the kids for another night's sleep.

"Why didn't Uncle Willy just get new choppers, Daddy?" Asked our oldest, Domino, wanting to know *the rest of the story.*

"Because insurance only covers certain things, seems that they had five passengers instead of only four which was the legal maximum. One of the parents had their little child sitting on their lap for the tour. Unfortunately, that voided the insurance contract - being a technicality and all - and Uncle Willy couldn't afford to replace his lost craft on his own. Since they were leased it turned out to be a really big deal, which unfortunately for everyone, cost him his company. He's now flying in Nevada doing some type of morning traffic report for a local radio station and running tourists up the Grand Canyon, probably scaring the heck out of them!"

"That's so sad, Daddy. Who are we going to fly with when we're out there visiting Grandma and Granddad?"

"Oh, honey, we'll simply have to worry about that next time we're out there. It's just nice to know that nobody got too hurt. That's the most important thing. Goodnight. Love you. Sleep well and pleasant dreams..." I softly said as I turned off the lights.

Escaping back down the steps to Faith and a glass of wine before looking for any more adventures, sometimes normal was all a parent could ever hope for.

* * * * * * *

Obtaining the joy of getting my helicopter license was one of the greatest accomplishments of my life! With the purchase of my first helicopter, I became an aviator with my own craft, joining one of the world's most elite clubs. We flew all around Western Pennsylvania and deep into the heart of West Virginia's broken mountain ranges. I gave many rides to people of all ages --never charged a penny to any of them. For many it was the very first time they'd ever flown. It was my absolute joy to do it as time and finances allowed. I really hope that vivid experience sparked a spirit of adventure for them to embrace a future void of normalcy and fear.

I found some "runs" up various creek systems that were free from the local human population and didn't have any obstacles like overhead power lines or bridges. One such run was from the confluence of Little Sandy Creek and the Redbank Creek. Starting the run by doing a wing over from Little Sandy, as I turned upstream into the Redbank, the helicopter skids blasting inches off the water, always seemed to freak out my passengers -- making them wide-eyed and speechless.

For some, it was way too much. For others, they couldn't get enough and screamed for more.

Eventually I came up with a system of asking how "dynamic" of a flight they wanted on a sliding scale of One to Ten; one being a powder-puff flight where you couldn't feel any motion at all, ten being a wild flight worthy of the Hollywood stunt pilots I'd been blessed to be around now-and-again. Most people would ask for a Six to an Eight. I'd give them a Three or Four, which often gave them an adrenaline rush like never before!

I never told them I'd softened the ride for them; some things are best left unsaid. By being quiet it allowed the flight to linger in their imagination as a death-defying experience for all time.

Yet, mostly the helicopter was for doing quick appraisals of timberlands we were considering for acquisition. But, now and again, we'd take a look around and then stop at some random restaurant - with enough open space to put the bird down - for lunch. Seemed to always cause a stir -- often it would get us a free piece of pie from the owner since it drew in customers to see what on earth was happening!

As for business strategy, being able to cruise 1,000 acres of timber while being back in time for breakfast was extraordinary. It gave us an edge over the competition, which for most of them made it very difficult to compete against us. We'd have our offer prepared long before they had boots on the ground to even start their appraisal process.

Balloons, paraplanes, ultralights, gliders, fixed wing or helicopters - no matter the craft - we all loved aviation. And, whenever I see something flying overhead, I look up and dream of younger years, and recalling the joys of flying on a pure sky day.

By obtaining my pilot's license, I completed Dad's dream of having all of his sons becoming pilots. Four for four -- it was one thing we did that made him beam from ear-to-ear. Dad was always such a positive influence on us by allowing us to chase our dreams and then encouraging us all along the way. Succeed or fail, he'd smile, dust us off, and send us back into the fray until we'd reach the goal of our deepest desires.

Mum, naturally much more conservative, but still very brave, would often say, "When other mothers are asked, 'where are your children?' they go outside and look around. For me, I go outside, and then, I have to look up!"

* * * * * * *

I have to admit that I am still unsure of what exactly happened up on that rocky ledge of Mauna Loa on that fateful day. The first "incident" might have been a tail-rotor strike. The second "incident" - the one that tore the second helicopter apart - might have been what is called a dynamic rollover (using the appropriate helicopter jargon). No matter what exactly occurred, it put the death nail firmly into the heart of Falcon Aviation and that was so sad. Willy was so stricken by the turn of events, that getting factual information was obviously way too painful to talk about, so I'd simply buy him an ice-cold beverage, change the subject, and turn his attention to better memories of days far gone.

No more flights-of-fancy. No more screaming aerobatics in one of the finest pieces of aviation equipment ever devised by man. Even sadder, Willy moved to the high-altitude desert country of Nevada. As far as I know, he's lived there ever since.

I certainly hope he is scaring the crap out of the locals.

20

Buying Eden

"Buying Paradise can be mighty expensive..."

AJG & FKG / 1999 - ongoing

* * * * * * *

"Thanks, Wade, I'll give him a call and set it up." He'd just given me a contact to set up a helicopter charter flight to look at properties on the Big Island. I was hoping to find a mountain property with enough koa timber on it to alleviate the pain of the purchase. Maybe not completely, but at least lesson the initial cost of the purchase by a significant amount. "Are you sure you don't want to come along? Got room if you'd like to join us."

"Not on this flight. Some of us have to work you know." He laughed. He was the acting Superintendent at a local high school.

"I've got Matt with me. Who knows, maybe we'll find something worthy of our efforts?" I relayed back. Matt was a long-time friend from the backwoods of Pennsylvania and a third-generation forester. He knew what he was talking about when it came to all things' trees.

"Let me know. Too bad about that estate down south -- I was hoping you'd buy that one." Wade lamented. I knew he wanted it for the hunting. For me the economics were way out of kilter to make it anything but a burden and a drain.

"I gave them my internal memos and timber cruise valuation. Hope they find a way out of their cash flow crunch." I was impressed with the quality of the owners. They were real people trying their best to hold onto a way of life virtually unknown in the modern world. When you have over 11,000 acres, you inhabit a realm few can comprehend or fathom. And, they had the world's best view to enjoy homemade blueberry muffins and Kona coffee.

Too bad they had a limited amount of the world's most expensive hardwood known as koa left on their ranchlands. Such an awesome wood; highly figured, perfectly colored, sought after by the world's elite for ultra-expensive items. Koa makes the finest musical instruments and is used by guitar aficionados, cello makers, violin artisans and others for world-class first chair virtuosos and orchestras around the globe. Koa was what I was hoping to find on the flight I was arranging to look along Mauna Loa and Mauna Kea's eastern flanks. The windward side with jungles and waterfalls and astounding Pacific Ocean views and a golden opportunity for koa to be amongst the cloud forest few ever see.

I thought that maybe I could find ten acres tucked in somewhere that time had forgotten, a place to build a small mountain cabin. We wanted something a bit more permanent and a place we could leave our boards, and dive gear and other things that were rarely needed in Pennsylvania -- somewhere Faith and I could bring the kids and linger awhile without paying the exorbitant hotel bills that often curtailed our stays.

So, I grabbed my friend and confidant, our trusted forester, hopped on a jet, and proceeded to look for a jungle property that had hidden value.

Wade asked me during the course of one of our late-night conversations, "So what are you *really* after?"

I smiled, laughed and answered, "Didn't you get the memo? Have you not heard that Pennsylvania is taking over the world?"

"Exactly how are you going to do that!" He was more than a bit incredulous.

"We're buying it..." I smiled and added, "...one property at a time."

* * * * * * *

"I'm Boss. I'll be your pilot today. We've got a couple hours blocked out for you. Do you boys have anything specific in mind?" Boss, of Mauna Kea Helicopters reached out to shake Matt's and mine hands. Boss was a fabulous person with a huge heart filled with joy; quick to laugh, talented beyond description. One of his previous jobs had been flying off the deck of a fishing trawler spotting for tuna in the Deep South Pacific. That job had been horrendously dangerous, as the consequences of 'screwing up' would have been horrific.

"We're hoping to stay along the forest line above the old cane fields. Let's start right here in Waimea and work our way south to Volcano. That should do it for today." I smiled and climbed in beside our pilot for the morning. Boss was a huge man - probably close to 300+ pounds on a 6' 2" frame. When he got in, he stuck out of the open cockpit. Doors-off was the only way he flew; the bird couldn't accommodate him any other way. Matt climbed in behind me to counterbalance the craft. He didn't need to be told; we'd been at this timber game for years by this point in time, and both of us had lots of time in helicopters together.

An hour later, with the bulk of our objectives observed and filed away, we were doing a final swing past the lush green cinder cones overlooking the Seven Valleys of the Kings. Within one of the ancient calderas, lush with grasses and hidden from the world, were a group of massive hogs. We buzzed them as we came up quick over their domain. Startled, the mother hog reared up, protecting her realm. Offhand, I breathed into my mic, "Look! That one's ready to attack the helicopter!"

After the briefest of pauses, Matt came back with, "When pigs fly."

We were all still laughing when we exited the bird. I couldn't believe how I'd set myself up for such a witty response to our day's extensive journey.

That flight accomplished two things: we got to know Boss, and we found out that the koa had been brutalized as far as historical harvests were concerned. There was way less koa cloud forest remaining along the slopes than any of us anticipated. For it was obvious that most of its native habitat had been, not just poorly managed, but stripped to the point where only non-native species - those dreaded invasive species like strawberry guava and non-native grasses - had completely taken over.

Koa wasn't just rare. It was on the brink of going the way of the dodo bird.

* * * * * * *

Monday morning, 7 am, summertime Western Pennsylvania. As I walked into our office, our comptroller immediately pointed to a fax sitting on my desk. "Somebody was burning the midnight oil. That must have been sent in the wee hours of the night Hawaiian time."

So I called the sender, my dear friend who I knew since Bitty League Basketball days, Clarence. He'd moved out to Hawaii a few years after I did. Got him out of bed, and I didn't give a rip about doing it. Friends are like that. At this point in time he was living on Oahu and doing his own thing. The article he'd sent was from the *Honolulu Advertiser* announcing the plans to liquidate a portion of the Kung Estate on the Big Island. Being in the form of a very sophisticated press release, it clearly stated that three parcels, totaling in excess of 25 square miles was now on the market. It sat above and to the north of Hilo and was -- as they so quaintly described -- "densely forested".

I knew the area well from our round-the-island over-flights with Boss. So, I pulled out my maps and notes, got a smile on my face, and proceeded to make flight arrangements to get on out to the Big Island as fast as possible

If Pennsylvania was actually going to take over the world, this would be an excellent time to start.

By Tuesday, I was on Oahu getting picked up by Clarence and ready for the first jet leaving the next morning to Hilo. I had a helicopter scheduled for an immediate aerial viewing of the property for sale upon my arrival.

This time, Wade decided to join me. We had a new pilot - the owner of a small company flying out of Hilo. He came highly recommended and our anticipation was rising as the sun lit a perfect Hawaiian morning. Breaks in the clouds allowed wild rays of light to ricochet off the mirrored glass of Hilo Bay. Everything freshly rained upon from the night before -- so clean and fresh, effervescent and pristine. Big Island is such a glorious place upon God's green earth to greet the dawn.

Maps in hand, morning lighting the way, all backlit by the sun illuminating the slopes of Mauna Kea, four minutes to target, doors off and air traffic releasing us for an expedited exit from the airport complex. "How do you wish to proceed, Mr. Gourley?" asked the pilot.

"Please call me Allen. Let's go to Honoli'i Stream. Go straight to the surfers and then follow it up to the forest line...that point should be this southeast corner of the property." I looked across at my pilot, saw his comfortable intent and his one-piece jumpsuit, and asked, "What branch of the military did you train in?"

"Marines." He smiled and gave a chuckle, "Is it that obvious?"

"Yeppers!" I laughed too. Wade came on the com and said, "Look at those waves. Man, that used to be us..."

"When was the last time you got in the water?" I asked Wade, who had taught me how to blue water hunt, spearfishing up and down the coast, mostly down along the southeastern shoreline, but occasionally in and around Hilo's tidal pools.

"Yesterday. Got two kumus and five lobsters."

"Redneck!" I couldn't believe how much I missed the water, and, more accurately, how jealous I was of not being in the water on a day-to-day basis.

"Coming up on target. Now what?" Our pilot gave us an update as he asked for his next objective.

"Your name is Cal, and you are the owner of this company. Am I correct?"

"Yes. Or in your somewhat-odd-vernacular, yeppers!" He smiled while effortlessly hovering directly over the southeast corner of the property.

"With your military background and your Marine *code of honor*, would you be willing and able to keep a secret, Cal? From this point in time forward, everything you see and hear is proprietary information owned by my family alone. This information we're going to discover and calculate is my property, it can't ever leave the confines of this tiny group of souls. Are you good with that? It will be nice to speak freely while we're here doing our flight in real time. It makes things so much more convenient." I looked at him and waited for his response.

"Not a problem. I'll treat this as a need-to-know mission, and nobody needs to know." He laughed. His response was immediate and honest. I instantly liked the fellow. "What exactly are we looking for?"

I flipped the map over, showed him the outlines of the property and calmly said as I pointed to the north, "All of that...from here to way over there is this section. Then, after we look at this tract, there are two more. One's adjoining on the northern edge and the other is just past Akaka Falls State Park a few miles further north."

"You're kidding me! I thought that was all forest reserve..." He responded in awe.

"Me too." I answered, just as amazed by what lie below us, and what appeared to be stretching towards infinity.

"I think we all did." Wade said reverently into his mic.

"How do you wish to proceed?" Cal, my newest friend asked.

"Let's find the top of this edge of the property, then we'll do slow zig zags to the far catty corner. Then we'll go up, find the top northwestern corner, and come cross-hatched back. Keep my door slightly forward so I can look more-or-less straight down and I'll do an aerial strip cruise. It's what I do." I answered with a smile, getting him started on what I called a "run".

"And that's it?" Cal asked, slightly confused and totally out of his normal day-to-day helicopter duties of shuttling tourists on photo shoots and flights-of-fancy. He looked at me and added, "You know when I went to college it was for my forestry degree."

I looked over at him, nodded and calmly answered, "I didn't." It was readily apparent that Cal had never heard of "forestry" being done like what was about to occur. I laughed and added, "I took a double major; surfing and girls - both gave me scars! I got a 4.0 in the girl department, but the jury is still out on my surfing major."

Wade chimed in. "You'll love his wife, she's awesome! As for his methods of how to look at trees, this is what he does. It's how he gets his forest inventories and valuations. He calls it '*3D Logic*'. Don't ask me how? Because it confuses the heck out of me!"

"Keep it at about 35 knots and 150 feet off the tree tops, if you would be so kind, that way I can get a better look down into the stand as it passes by. Please keep it at a steady forward speed. Closer to exactly 35 knots the better."

We'd achieved finding the top southwestern corner, and we were all ready to make the first turn into the day's true objective of obtaining a precise overview and timber stand analysis. As we got into the third set of sweeping turns, with Cal following the parameters of the mission perfectly, I immediately noticed, *this guy is a real pilot*.

Turning back to the job at hand, I had to ask Wade the question building from my observations of the groves flowing beneath the craft, "Is this what I think it is?"

"If this isn't it, it doesn't exist..." Wade softly answered, and Wade never answered anything softly.

Forty minutes later, after slowly digesting all three tracts, I looked at Cal and said, "I have to admit I'm in a bit of shock. Please go back down to the surfers, and let's do this entire event one more time. I have to be sure that what I think I just saw is exactly what I am seeing."

Wade laughed, then he added with a voice I rarely heard, "I never knew this even existed and I've lived here all my life..." He shook his head in stunned disbelief.

Cal got his bearings, accelerated to 125 knots as he eased it over, dove down the mountain's slope back to the mouth of Honoli'i Stream where the surfers were catching the glassy waves far below us. He did a sweeping teardrop turn, and rather proud of his smooth performance, said "Starting run number two. Gentlemen, please enjoy the ride."

I looked down at the surfers, Left Point was breaking - not too big - but the sets of waves were delivering small tubes on a smooth-as-silk early morning sea. I glanced over at the other edge of the bay. Around the corner was Tombstones where I'd almost met my MAKER so many years prior. I thought to myself *oh how far I've come from that terrifying gremmy experience. Back in the day, back when I was spry and the Big Island was massive and delivered a touch of wonder around every bend in the road*

After we landed, Cal smiled and stayed with his bird. The refueling truck had been called on approach and he wished to be there during the process. He had more flights with his entire day planned before him as the ongoing volcanic activity was keeping him very busy. Wade needed to get back to his normal work routine as well, leaving me sitting on a small bench waiting for the helicopter company's in-house comptroller, flight coordinator and bookkeeper, who was working up a bill for me. She finally came out, looking rather serious, and placed the two hours of flight time obligation into my hands. She proceeded with her pointedly polite request, "How will you be paying for this, sir?"

"Will a corporate check be OK?" I smiled.

"Yes, sir. That will be more than acceptable." You could see a wave of total relief run through her eyes. Must be they'd been experiencing *many a delayed payment* and my willingness to pay on the spot gave her tremendous relief.

"Do you mind if we set you folks up on retainer? I'm under the impression we'll be in need of a fair amount of your flight services in the very near future." As I cut a check for considerably more than the bill in my hands.

The look on her face was priceless.

As Dad always said, "*...paying in cash will do that for you.*"

* * * * * * *

That evening, I sat at the mini-desk in my corner Hilo Hawaiian Hotel room that allowed me to enjoy the sunset exploding amongst multiple layers of clouds, as it collapsed the day over Mauna Kea all while setting Hilo Bay, once again, on fire with a myriad of reds, oranges and electric blues. Crunching numbers on a strip of hotel stationary, I'd always do my aerial timber cruise estimates three different ways: old school math, minimum down-n-dirty math, and my own version of segmented-by-individual-stand-analysis math. All three came up with astounding numbers. All three were within a few percentage points of each other. So, I did them again, running the day's flight back through my mind, laying the topographical map alongside the aerial map so as to keep a clear picture firmly before me of the percentage of forested acreage coupled with my internal koa timber volume expectations.

No matter how I calculated the raw data, no matter the style employed, I was utterly astounded by the final tally laid before me! Now I was "with information" as we liked to refer to having very specific valuation criteria prior to anyone else. It gave us a dynamic business advantage: obtaining a clear picture of a targeted purchase. My data was blunt: this was a true A+ Timber Transaction (on steroids), and it appeared that I was the very first person on the planet to have arrived at that glorious conclusion!

I was so excited I slept like a baby.

* * * * * *

"I really like the real estate broker -- obviously top tier. Also, I just made a full price offer along with an added bonus of paying all closing costs and covering the full commission. They immediately answered, 'Yes.'" I said when I called back to the office and told my brother Bob the good news. He needed to hear this since he was involved in our ongoing quest for world domination, and some of it was his money that I was spending.

"Are you sure?" Bob asked, somewhat shocked by my brazen disregard for negotiating a better deal than asking price.

"Absolutely. To quote Wade, 'if this isn't it, it doesn't exist.' After all of the flights over the past year, this is it. I've got it at valuation numbers too high to ignore." I calmly informed my brother. "Going back to Oahu, meeting up with the real estate broker, and I'm going to find a lawyer - a really good local lawyer. Something tells me that he may just come in handy before this is all over."

"Umi..." Bob replied, not knowing what else to add.

"Gumi." I signed off and hustled to the airport to catch a flight back to Honolulu. No time like the present to put this transaction under firm contract and get everyone onboard so we'd be flying in formation and in the same direction.

I was thinking to myself... *I came over looking for a cabin site and end up with the deal of the millennium. This is oddly surreal...* Only GOD forces such events into our lives because we mere mortals couldn't even imagine of such a thing.

As for me, I was kidding when I told Wade that 'Pennsylvania's taking over the world.' How little I knew of the outrageous series of cascading events waiting to explode into my world.

* * * * * * *

Once, a few years earlier, I was told by the CEO of the largest export company in the Great State of Pennsylvania a very simple ancient adage: *"Big timber. Big problems."*

I pressed him on his blunt Old World saying at the time, "Exactly what do you mean by that statement? Sir, if you would be so kind." His answer was much deeper than I'd anticipated.

"Well, young fellow, with big timber you have a multitude of hurdles placed before you. Finding the money to pay for the exorbitant purchase price, which, of course, is payment in full at signing in the world of hard commodities. Now, with that massive expenditure of funds, you have depleted your cash reserves and have allowed little room for error. Then you have the time element, big volumes equal long and delayed harvests. With time now in the mix, markets change - often not for the better - leaving you struggling to monetize your holdings. And, with the lowering of the market prices while being in a pinch, the need for cash flow can force you to accept lower than market results. The money aspect of the transaction can be manipulated, if you are smart. But, the time element is relentless and has no mercy. Time will always be your biggest foe."

After a long pause, he looked directly at me, with a brutal world of harsh experiences showing as splinters in the back of his eyes, as he repeated the ancient adage earned so harshly by him and those who'd gone before...

"Big timber, big problems..." His words hung as a dangerous warning. Then he receded into a world of deep thoughts, never finishing his sentence.

* * * * * * *

Wade had been gone for years, making a life in Colorado while raising three boys. After he and his family moved back to Hawaii we reconnected. It was nice to have one more of the "original crew" back in the islands, someone who I could share a laugh and a memory with. Someone who had actually been-there-and-done-that. He was astute in all things' biology. And having been born and raised in Hilo, he was a vast wealth of information when it came to local boy contact points and high-level introductions.

So, I traded excitement -- via chopper rides -- for information and specific knowledge concerning access and the current state of the local bamboo politics.

His wit, observations and family ethic were priceless then, as it is still to this very day. Our daughter and his son continue to work together on various mountain projects. It is wonderful to see two extraordinarily competent souls move the next generation into the forefront of all things Big Island.

* * * * * * *

A few years after I'd met him on those original overview flights, Boss had a family of tourists with him, on a doors-off, scenic flight over the ongoing volcanic eruptions along Kilauea's East Rift Zone. It was a normal beautiful sky day and the short flight was progressing exactly as planned...then everything changed in the blink of an eye! The turbine's power no longer made it to the rotors overhead. What had happened, Boss didn't know. But his gifted skills, honed to a fine edge through years of flying, allowed him to do a perfect autorotation emergency landing without power onto the uneven black lava, just off the side of the live glowing red lava flow. Boss performed an emergency 'skids down rotors up' textbook landing...only to find out that the lava he put the bird down on was still 1,000 degrees. The lava was black because lava doesn't glow at that temperature. The MD 500D Helicopter burst into flames and melted into the lava!

Boss was lauded for his skill of being able to put it down in such treacherous terrain. Yet, the end result was instantaneously fatal.

Everyone on board perished. It sent shock waves along with a world of pain into every family member involved.

The family on board, a tight-knit wonderful kind family, was on their dream vacation. A trip they'd bought the tickets for a year in advance. Gone in a single tragic event while on a journey of a lifetime. The family was from Pennsylvania.

It was later determined that the engine had a manufacturer's flaw in the main drive shaft - an undetectable internal spiral defect. When it snapped everything cascaded into the worst possible outcome of lives lost and sadness that couldn't be fathomed.

We used to ask the classic question, mostly when life was expensive, not just in costs of goods and services, but in blood sweat and tears. The question was often delivered by wailing lamentations wrapped within forlorn trauma, "What Price Paradise?"

My heart-wrenching answer, "Sometimes Paradise costs everything."

* * * * * * *

We ended up buying the properties, doing a quick flip of the larger portion while keeping the lone parcel on the northern edge of Akaka Falls State Park. By doing so, we were able to turn a profit at closing and obtain a portion of the Big Island for future enjoyment. It made it an A+ Timber Transaction and I had the joy of discovering three wonderful souls along the way. The realtor, JMW, became an absolute dear friend and treats us like family to this very day. We are happy to do the same for him. He even gave the 'Banzai Toast' at our oldest daughter's wedding years later. That toast was astoundingly epic!

As for the helicopter company owner, Cal, I consider him to be such a trustworthy and awesome soul. It is my absolute joy to count him as my friend. The more I get to know him, the more I am impressed by his incomparable capabilities. Our families have grown together through time. He is our daughter's employer. But, we like to think that she runs the show, while allowing him to look good in the process!

Which brings me to one of the most astute minds I have ever come across, Cliff, the attorney I was recommended by the realtor. He saved our butt as the deal moved forward, not just once or twice, but so many times as to be nearing infinity. Good legal counsel is most difficult to find, a good dear friend that just so happens to be a world-class corporate attorney - well, my friends - that is truly one in a billion.

And, finding three wonderful souls with such marvelous attributes during the course of one transaction truly is rare air and a gift from GOD ALMIGHTY.

* * * * * * *

Which brings us to the Kung Estate. Mr. Kung was the Finance Minister for Chiang Kai-shek, the President of Taiwan. And anyone who knows anything about Asian politics knows that whoever controls the money sits at the right hand of the throne of power because money controls the access.

Mrs. Kung inherited the remnants of the family's American holdings. The parcel we kept was the best-of-the-best of the limited amount of the Koa Cloud Forest left remaining on the upper slopes of the Big Island. It is a majestic parcel with waterfalls tumbling amongst verdant forests lost in time. It is truly magnificent, and words can never describe the wondrous beauty contained within its borders.

Mrs. Kung lived to a ripe old age overlooking New York City's Central Park. I never had the opportunity or profound joy of meeting her, which may be my only regret from the acquisition phase of that profoundly odd transaction.

I was looking for a small ten-acre parcel to build my dream cabin on. Yet, as GOD is often known to do, he turned my dream into an adventure.

Which, to this day, is still ongoing and has led to a wildly strange version of: "Big Timber. Big Problems."

Buying Eden can be extraordinarily expensive.

21

Second Time Dead

"You do not have to be dead to be dead."

AJG & FKG / 2001 - ongoing

* * * * * * *

I am not sure how such negative and bitter thoughts had invaded my world. I had always been the carefree, live-let-live personality-type all of my life. Life was good, that is until the world invaded my space and events transpired that I couldn't anticipate or control. Everything was rapidly spinning into a personal form of the *Twilight Zone* torture chamber, and I couldn't take it anymore.

With the fact that our big purchase on the Big Island had been thrust into a quagmire of legal jeopardy, I felt as if I'd been targeted for destruction by wicked forces I never conceived of. Never even thought could exist. When I negotiated the sale of the larger tracts to an entity based in Honolulu, I never foresaw the nefarious means they would employ to achieve the results they wanted. I'd allowed the overlapping of assets via a Courtesy Mortgage against our interests. It was to allow them the means to obtain financing for their tracts and to move forward with their business plan of harvesting the koa (under extremely tight conditions). They got started immediately on the two square miles of agricultural-zoned land and shipped the logs to their 'partners' in China.

Then everything exploded into a world of pain and suffering.

I felt most of the suffering was laid directly upon my shoulders.

Five states, three countries and a multitude of jurisdictional overlaps made for a lawsuit from hell. Finally, after a multitude of orchestrated delays, everything was bundled into a federal courthouse in Hawaii and promptly came to a grinding halt.

Years of intensive litigation with demands, threats and counter-threats came and went. Our lawyer who specialized in litigation mentioned to me during a long phone conversation, "You do know that at some point in time you will have to testify under oath concerning these matters."

My response was both accurate and prophetic, "I will never have to testify. The last thing in the world they want is for me to point out their obvious theft by deception and the fact that they never brought the monies back on shore." I sighed, "Please pass along to their lead counsel that I have the 'run sheets' on the timber they harvested and that they obviously should never wish to talk to me, or put me on the stand because I guarantee that my truthfulness will explode their case into millions of tiny little splinters." I was adamant. "I will not lie for them."

"Even so, you are a principal in a multi-national federal court case, and you will eventually have to testify via affidavit, at the very least." He responded. He too was most adamant in his prediction.

"Never going to happen. My first question to them will be: where did all of the money go? Then if they press me, I'll choke them with the truth until they wished they'd never dragged me into their world of orchestrated-designer-engineered-mayhem." I got it off of my chest.

"You'll still have to testify." My lawyer said softly one more time.

"Never going to happen." I was still adamant. "Bet you a milkshake?"

"Only if it's chocolate." He accepted with a chuckle.

I was no longer able to laugh. My humor had been stolen from me one legal knife-twist at a time.

* * * * * * *

Angry roots grow deep in bitter soil. I was ticked off all of the time. Even my dreams weren't enough to give me relief from the goings on in my day-to-day life.

Faith knew what I was going through, even though I tried my best to keep her away from the details, but when you get that much certified mail it is nearly impossible to hide the ongoing events from an observant person. We loved each other. Always have, and this twist in the road didn't diminish that. But it did diminish my happiness to an unacceptable level of angst and bitterness.

So my lovely wife devised a plan, she decided (demanded) that we needed to go to Canada, up Toronto way, to find this church she'd heard about and see if we could find a touch of joy in our lives. When she said we, she meant me, but she was kind enough to never quite put it that bluntly.

So off we went, bound for Vineyard Church near the Toronto Airport. A series of supernatural encounters with the HOLY SPIRIT had broken out there. It was ongoing and profound if you believed the reports. Faith did, after all, her name is *Faith* and now-and-again she needs to live up to her GOD given birthright.

We got there on a random weeknight. I didn't expect much of anything to be honest. I was tired, grumpy, ticked-off, distracted, and self-absorbed. My world was in turmoil and my patience for anything, including this 'evening out', was tortured to say the least.

But then...GOD!

GOD intervened and swept into our world. The atmosphere inside the meeting wasn't just electric, it was surreal, fantastically supernatural! As I bathed in the presence, the atmosphere went thick pink. The world I previously knew evaporated far away, and I was given back the dreams of my youth. I was given back my lighthearted joy of being alive. I was given back a life I'd forgotten and mistakenly traded for the bitter root of self-imposed exile from the presence of the Divine -- a presence we are all created for, a presence so few recapture or find anew after their childhood years are long forgotten and the dreams of their youth are stolen by the world's insipid demands.

Demands we all toil with, demands we carry as heavy burdens when we should simply lay them down and refuse to drag them one step further along life's way, replace such joy as we age and fail to recognize our place in the Kingdom.

My burdens had killed me in a way I had never known a person could die. One ounce of worry here and a pound of anxiety there, and somehow, I'd allowed life to beat me morbid and crush me into a grave while I still breathed air and trudged the earthly realm.

My encounter at that Altar of Grace, in a church I'd never been, immediately cast all of those cares off of me. People will often ask me, "What is the wildest experience you've ever had?" It was usually a question that was virtually impossible for me to answer. I've been over 200 feet deep without mixed gases scuba diving in crystal blue waters. I've been over 20,000 feet high in an open-air gondola in skies so clear I could see four states and two countries simultaneously. But, after that short journey to the Altar at that industrial church in Toronto, I have a new answer that is simple yet profound. "My greatest journey eve ..., my wildest event I've ever been captured within ... is to take a few steps, bow down and once again give my life to CHRIST!"

That singular act of submission while finding out that life is given freely to all who will come, saved not just my life, but it saved everything around me at the same time. I left my bitterness - and the accompanying decent into a world of turmoil and pain - on the Altar of Grace. At a place where the CREATOR met me, even a fool like me, and that alone made all of the difference.

I never really realized that just like my physical death in the Philippines so many years earlier, I had once again died. My walking death had been from carrying a myriad of unnecessary burdens, which had accumulated to the point of completely stealing my inner joy and crushing me into the Abyss of Sorrows. You do not have to be dead to be dead. But, if you are willing, you can choose not to be dead in any way, as long as you are breathing air and are still above ground. My suggestion is to find the Altar of Grace and leave your fears and worries, burdens and losses there, before you are crushed and swept into oblivion.

I know. I've been there.

It is said, "Big timber. Big problems." Although that ancient adage is true to the world at large, I have a different take and I must add my personal observation.

"Big GOD. Big answers."

HE trumps everything man is capable of casting upon you. Allowing you to be embraced by the peace of an inner joy while the world marvels at your calmness in the midst of life's raging storms.

* * * * * * *

I never had to testify via affidavit or by any other means, even though the lawsuit dragged on for over six long, disgusting years. What a mess, so many half-truths and agenda driven maneuvers of legal woe. Every time everything seemed in jeopardy... But GOD! HE intervened and somehow everything settled down. Miraculously we were spared to live and fight another day.

And, something I still find that was obviously orchestrated by a higher power than any court upon this earthly realm, the entire event proved to become a learning experience unlike any other. So many lessons can be garnered if you take a step back and once again learn to laugh with your friends. Even when the stakes are high and the odds are thin, allow HIM to determine the outcome.

Sometimes we laughed so hard about the ongoing absurdity that our sides hurt!

My lawyers are still baffled by so many of the outcomes along the way that I am sure they use that peculiar case as an object lesson in their internal strategy meetings.

Of the five (known) entities involved in that gruesome swarm of overlapping lawsuits that spanned over six years and cost a fortune to litigate, we were the only entity that remained standing. It was not by gifted oratory skills, or enlightened jurisprudence, it was by the divine power of the HOLY GOD who orchestrated a righteous outcome for us to comfortably exit into a world that did not include their wicked demands or greed-driven agendas. One mega corporation went Chapter 7 bankrupt when it was flagrantly discovered that they were operating a multi-state insurance scam. They were immediately disbanded and turned over to the Attorneys General of the three states in which they operated. After that we dealt with a court-appointed administrator and his vast array of needs, wants and governmental demands. One of the other 'entities' disappeared. As best as we could ascertain he fled to mainland China (where there is rarely any type of extradition). General consensus was that he absconded to be with his huge sum of monies that he'd pre-positioned there. Can you say... Flight from Prosecution!

I never testified. For some 'strange' reason the opposing counsel didn't want to hear what I had to say...imagine that! And, of supreme importance, my litigation attorney still owes me a chocolate milkshake since I won our very important bet.

I will collect Mr. Y, Esq. (I know where you work)! But, since you and your skills were a gift from GOD, I'll make it a win-win proposition. I'll buy you and your lovely wife a fabulous dinner, with chocolate shakes all around. I'll endeavor to bring Faith with me so you'll both have a reasonable adult to talk to. And perhaps my daughter and your wife can regale us with some football stories -- they ended up playing together as members of their law school alumnae powder puff football team!

I would be especially remiss if I didn't add in one of my true heroes to this sordid tale of woe, the original lawyer given to me by JMW (the real estate broker), for he was instrumental in rescuing us time after time. My hat is off to him. His wonderful calm, sage advice and genius counseling helped to save me from drowning when all seemed lost and the barren reefs of life loomed hungry. I thank you. I thank your team. From the bottom of my heart, Cliff, you are an extraordinary gentleman!

* * * * * * *

Faith obviously knew what I needed long before I could even identify the problem that was attempting to destroy my world, crush my spirit and put me into an early grave. Once again proving why I married 'far above my station'.

Faith, my Sansei Princess - having been born into a Buddhist family and then becoming a born again Christian - knew that I needed a touch of the Divine to rekindle my lost faith in humanity. One touch of HIS divine grace returned me to the land of the living, brought me back from the brink of destruction and allowed me to once again to be worthy of my wife's loving embrace.

22

The Liberators

"Access and power are twins of a feather. One cannot fly without the other."

AJG & FKG / 1964ish - ongoing

* * * * * * *

"What are we going to do when we get there!" It wasn't so much a question as an announcement of wondrous anticipation. Everyone was stuffed into the family car, all seven of us, and we were going on our personalized version of the *Great American Road Trip*. From home to Washington D.C. - we were fully committed to reaching the nation's Capital.

Dad driving, the car headed southeast, and Mum doing her best to keep us occupied while the world flowed past our windows on the hodge-podge of roadways we took in the summer of 1964. Mum had a losing battle on her hands, so she turned to Dad and asked, just like we were, "Jim, what *are* we going to do when we get there?" Her needs were much different than ours since she wanted a hotel and a place to feed the herd.

Dad was free from the hassles of running the meat packing company, and the daily grind associated with that endless task, so he was completely free to declare as he so pleased. "We're going to the White House and we're going to see the President."

Dad laughed. Mum laughed. And, us kids, we thought that was just grand.

"What President?" One of us asked. Since I was only six, it most likely wasn't me.

"Well, the President of the United States! Our President!" Dad answered, sure as could be, still laughing to the point where Mum was laughing along with his wild goal of seeing the President. Oddly enough, we all believed him too.

That memory remains one of the coolest experiences of my childhood: windows down, wind whistling through the car, all of us together. We made the journey complete by miraculously finding the White House and parking on the street with it all aglow as the day had given into the night hours. It is a long journey from home to D.C.

"OK! Everybody out!" Everyone was all-too-ready to get some space from each other, all five of us totally happy to comply. Mum and Dad brought up the rear, keeping an eye on us as we made our way around the 'People's House'. Everything was so strange to me, bright lights with a host of tall trees throwing shadows in a multitude of grays. Military Honor Guard personnel manning the gates of a huge gleaming building. It was more than impressive; it was truly magnificent.

Really very overwhelming for me to take in, but we were free to run a bit and frolic about. As we jostled each other, two rather tall people approached Mum and Dad. I didn't have a clue of what was happening, but all of a sudden Dad got very quiet - speechless to be accurate. Mum was the only one properly conversing with the two tall formally dressed folks who'd taken the initiative to stop our parents on this beautiful summer night and engage them in polite conversation.

Somehow all five of us got lined up, stood up straight and proper, and we each got to shake their hands, one at a time.

I really only remember shaking the nice tall lady's hand. She was dressed so elegant and took the time to bend down, look me in the eye and smile. Then they said, with some light banter, "We're waiting for a foreign delegation, so we'd better get back in there so the guards don't have to find us." They turned to go back past the Honor Guards manning the gate, who were extraordinarily alert and hadn't missed a beat.

Obviously, our small country family - even though there were seven of us - must not have been identified as a national threat when it came to having a brief conversation - a wonderful encounter - with Lyndon and Lady Bird Johnson, the President and First Lady of the United States of America!

Just like Dad declared, a few hundred miles prior, we went to Washington D.C. and met the President. Dad always had a way with calling into existence things that appeared to be impossible

Since that exact point in time, all of my life I have enjoyed tremendous access, well above and beyond my pay grade. It is liberating.

* * * * * * *

Turning in a slip for an Educational Field Trip, I was off to skip school to go down to D.C with Dad and Mum for a day's journey into all things politics. Dad was in the Republican National Committee and they'd have meetings with all of the 'big wigs' planning how to best run the nation. It was a pure win-win situation for me since I was perpetually the youngest of five. I could care less, but the journey got me out of school. I'd get to spend some time with my parents without any of the other siblings clamoring for their attention, very rare in my world.

Dad would always ask if I wanted to stay for the meeting. I'd always politely decline. Lunch was more than enough for me. Everybody appeared to be purely agenda driven, and Dad was one of the few authentic souls swimming in a sea of power and politics gone rogue. To me, I couldn't vacate the premises quick enough.

Dad would go back inside, and I'd hang out in the hallway making time with the really hot interns that staffed the front door. They were all ten years older, but a young man could dream a bit...even if he was from the wayward backwoods of *The Valley*.

"So, young Mr. Gourley, what are you going to do for the next few hours? This meeting won't be over until four or a little later," one of the famously pretty interns would eventually ask.

"Think I'll go to the Smithsonian and look around. I can get lost in there looking at stuff famous people have invented, painted, chiseled or found. Who knows? Might learn something."

"Would you like one of us to escort you?" I could tell they were not authentically thrilled with the prospect of *babysitting* one of the attendee's kids. But they would do it if that were needed. It seemed they were as caught up into the halls of power as the bulk of the people at the meeting. However, they'd been trained to be perfectly polite, perfectly attentive, and perfectly cultured. Each and every one of them had been hand selected from all across America for this exact task and for this very moment in time.

"No. I'll be more than fine. I'll be back before this ends if anybody asks." I knew they had no desire to hang out with an underling still in high school. I'd give them an out and leave them chasing the older men, who held the keys to power. It was the least I could do. And even I, a mere high school kid, knew why they were really there. All that I could think of was *these girls need to liberate themselves from this wicked trajectory*.

So, I'd flee down the long, marbled hallways and find the Air & Space Museum, my personal favorite, and waste away the afternoon looking at things that were awesome. Gazing at machines that had pushed the boundaries of all things human, vehicles that had actually done something truly amazing with heroic men at their controls who were crazy authentic in every possible way.

Just like my Dad, who I thought of as my hero and touched by the divine, they were truly remarkable.

* * * * * * *

My times alone with Dad were limited. Rarely did I ever have him to myself. But sometimes, when everything was just right, I'd get an opportunity to speak with him directly one on one and when that occurred it was liberating for me. Most times it went very well, other times were a bit more memorable.

Now and again I would do something or ask something that made my Dad stop, focus and correct me before I breathed one more breath of stupidity. I had just asked such a question, "Dad, how did you know the difference between the good and the bad Nazis?"

I was still very young and hopelessly naive.

He looked directly at me with his answer. He desired to make sure I knew the gravity of what he was firmly telling me and that the liberation of the European Theater from the horrors of Nazism involved young men, just like he was at the time. They risked all in ways that changed their lives forever. Many never came home, nor ever had the simple joy of speaking with their children while liberating their minds from failed perceptions. Turning them towards better tomorrows. The entire universe stopped, and Dad answered, as serious as I'd ever seen him, "There were no good Nazis."

* * * * * * *

Decades later, I got to meet a gentleman who had been caught up in the same generation's warfare with the Third Reich. His name was Max Goldberger, and he was a Holocaust survivor from Romania. Max was a young Jewish boy caught violently behind the lines of the Nazi death grip, thrown into a small internment camp and given *starvation rations* as he was separated from everything and everyone he knew. Max was quick in his means of survival, by his intrepid ability to learn multiple languages he became the Commandant's errand boy since he was fluent in Romanian, German and various other localized dialects needed to get things accomplished on a day-to-day basis. Because Max had become essential in the Commandant's world, he was upgraded to *subsistence rations* and allowed to survive. During the famously brutal winter that descended on the European Continent as the Battle of the Bulge raged, Max developed frostbite, but yet, somehow, he made it through it all.

Max used to cheer with screams of joy as the Allies bombed the power lines and tracks leading to the small concentration camp he was forlornly captured within. With a mind of a true genius, he'd encourage the souls around him to run in a perpendicular fashion towards the direction of the American bombers overhead, knowing it was the safest place to be once their released payloads of deadly bombs found landfall. In doing so, he placed himself, and those who would listen, out of danger as best as possible under the horrific conditions they endured. Max inherently knew that only in the total destruction of everything around them would there be any hope of being liberated. He yearned deeply for WWII to come to an abrupt end.

Finally, at the end of the war, with the Allies liberating Western Europe and Russia claiming half of Berlin and the Eastern European countries, Max once again found himself behind unfriendly lines. What had been the evil of fascism, now had given away to a different type of tyranny known as communism, with all of Max's newly "liberated" world being owned by Stalin and his gang of thugs.

With his genius readily on display, Max rose to the rank of Brigadier General in the Romanian Army. He and his men were under the wicked heel of Stalin, and everything round about him was simply an extension of the Russian Empire. Finally, after realizing that he'd simply been traded by one evil tyrant for another - Hitler for Stalin - Max couldn't take it anymore and determined that he was no longer going to suffer the fate dealt to him by evil men. After all, they'd destroyed his world. They'd burned his home to the ground and snuffed out his entire family by sending them to Buchenwald, becoming dust within the furnaces of death located there. He had grown to know one simple truth; something he shared with me years later, *"You must never service evil."*

Max knew exactly what he was talking about and was never hesitant to share his experiences with those he allowed into his inner circle.

Once Max determined he was done with being a pawn for Stalin, he simply took the train into Berlin, got off on the American side, and turned himself over to the American soldiers stationed there. Due to his rank, a Brigadier General in the enemy's army, he was immediately whisked away and taken to the O.S.S. Office, the precursor to the C.I.A. Once Max was safely in American controlled Western Berlin, his self-defection became a godsend for the Military Intelligence sector of the U.S. Army.

He was a true genius, which extended into a multitude of disciplines and fields. That fact became obvious to anyone who ever spent any time with him. The American officers assigned to his case found out that reality in short order. They quickly determined that not only was he not a threat, but that his disgust with all things tyrant was pure and genuine.

In short order, Max Goldberger, child translator, favored gofer, Romanian General - and willing defector with a multitude of secrets - became a valued member of Wernher von Braun's aerospace team of rocket engineers tasked with creating an American Space Program to put astronauts into space while returning them safely home.

* * * * * * *

Tiffany and I met Max through a dear friend's introduction. We were looking at properties along the Hamakua Coast north out of Hilo. My friend, Steve, picked us up late one morning in his pickup truck to look around. Tiffany climbed into the back with this diminutive unassuming Jewish man, small in stature and quietly focused with his words. I really didn't even know he was back there until Tiffany and Max got into this wildly animated conversation in French! When I turned to look into the back seat I could tell, even though I didn't speak French, that he was totally enthralled with being around a young beauty and was greatly enjoying the interaction at many levels. Max was fluent in French and at least a half-dozen other languages. French, being the international language of love, forced me to quickly ascertain that he was hitting on my daughter. That was simply fine. Tiffany was used to such shenanigans and had been taught well by her mother how best to accommodate an older man and his desire to be in the presence of her joyful beauty, all while keeping him at arm's length. Max soon became a wonderful soul thrust directly into our world. He became family as far as we were concerned, for his presence was like a brilliant spirit throwing a valiant beam of light, linking the past with the present while chasing a better future. The world needed to know that such man as himself actually exists and walks amongst us.

"I am immortal!" Max smiled when he said it to our daughter one evening. They'd started going on what they referred to as "date nights". Max would take Tiffany to the newly restored Palace Theatre in Hilo to watch foreign films and get a bit of culture. They'd speak French as best as possible and nibble on some exotic delicacies in the local cafes prior to the movie's start.

"O? And how is that?" She smiled at him, knowing he was leading her towards something profound.

"I am in the Smithsonian Institute! They have my story and my work there." He was obviously very proud of this particular portion of his past.

"Really! What's there? I'm really impressed!" Our daughter was delighted with the tidbit of awesome information and was equally goading him on.

"I invented rocket fuel."

"What? Really? Cool."

"Yes, and the Smithsonian wanted to document it."

Max let her in on one of his deepest successes. He had, indeed, invented the means to use hydrazine rocket fuel on a three-dimensional axis in the vacuum of space. He offered it to her as a form of allowing her a glimpse of his personal world. A fact that few knew about his profound genius, a trait that he tried his best to hide from those around him, she was allowed to listen and learn. Max eventually introduced Tiffany to his best friend, Earl Bakken, who invented the pacemaker and lived in a palatial estate on the Kona Coast affectionately known as The Blue Lagoon. Formally called Kiholo Bay, an idyllic setting with turquoise waters and its own semblance of a coastal Garden of Eden. Worthy of national park status, he owned it all, much to the consternation of the powers that be. Invitations were rare.

Max had been asked to help with the University of Hawaii - Hilo's science incubator where students and faculty worked on advanced post-grad level projects. Theory and applications, Max helped them navigate to a place in their work they'd have never attained on their own. How they found him I will never know. But why they found him was obvious to everyone around him, for the light of his brilliance was as profound as the day is to night.

Max was adopted by our two beautiful and loving daughters. Our oldest, Domino, was doing some work for us while yearning to figure out what she really wanted to do. Tiffany was at Richardson School of Law at U.H. Manoa on Oahu. It was there that she decided that her class needed to hear Max's story. Together they devised a plan to sweep Max away from his day-to-day affairs and have him present his life story to her fellow students. Domino escorted him from Hilo to Honolulu, and Tiffany hustled him to U.H. Manoa's campus to give his presentation.

Max told how the international community saved his life by forcing the Geneva Convention's agreed upon mandates into the Nazi Regime's world. How the American Red Cross delivered life-giving essentials when nothing else could get through, and if those things would not have occurred when they did, he and many like him wouldn't be alive to tell anybody anything. For just like the millions of others who were destroyed in the *death camps*, he too would have perished, turned to dust, eventually to be forgotten by time.

Max was given a profound and gracious thank you by everyone for his ability to put a human face to a horrific slice of history.

* * * * * * *

"So, what are you working on now, Max? Am I allowed to know?" I'd tracked him down just to check in on him.

"Some wealthy man from Idaho has me helping him design a new GTL process for turning bio-waste into a shelf-stable usable fuel." Max smiled. "We have applied for a patent."

"And, anything local?" I asked, knowing the man rarely put his vast knowledge and unlimited brainpower on hold.

"I've cracked one of the mysteries surrounding the efficiency factor concerning solar conversion to electric. We're building the prototype now. Once it's built, we'll have a working model on display in Kona for everyone to study and see. I even have it tracking the movement of the sun as the day progresses to maximize output."

"That's nice. Any travels coming up? Do you have a schedule or are you open for a meal with Faith and I?" He agreed, and we settled on a bit of home cooking to help him get through the week.

"Also, I'll be traveling to Germany to work with a group of scientists there on the GTL project later this month. I am really looking forward to getting back to Europe."

"What is exactly this GTL thing?" I wasn't up on the science world's latest batch of acronyms.

"Gas To Liquid. It is when you take a hydrocarbon in its gaseous state and turn it into a shelf stable liquid for commercial purposes and domestic usage." He smiled quietly, but looked like a fox chasing dinner.

I immediately realized the possibilities were endless. So, I asked, "Max, would you be kind enough to stop in Pennsylvania on the way back? We have a place for you, and I do think you'll like our family. It will be our honor to put you and whomever you're with up for a few nights. If you would be so kind." Then I had a really deep thought, "I do believe that you'll like my Dad, you know he was in Germany during the war."

Max smiled, had a rather deep thought, and answered, "That will be nice, is the rest of your family as kind as your daughters? They are my angels." Max loved to be fawned over by our gorgeous daughters (what red-blooded man still above ground and alive wouldn't?).

* * * * * * *

There are times in life to be really observant and perfectly quiet. When we got Max and Dad together at my parent's dinner table in Western Pennsylvania it was most certainly one of those times.

Like Dad, Max had endured the most brutal of assaults of World War II. And, like Dad - somehow - he had survived to live an outrageous story of a life.

Through the adventures of serendipity, I was able to be the person who got them together. I was blessed to hear their interaction, their bond of being survivors, and their banter firsthand. It was awesome, historical and, at times, profoundly touching to the extreme. For example, when Dad and Max switched to speaking German, things got really animated and fun to watch since understanding what was being said was impossible.

So much in common: both were octogenarians, survivors of WWII, both had seen the front lines of that war - one as a death camp prisoner, one as a liberator of the same. But it wasn't until they were both taking off their shoes and socks, that something astoundingly profound happened. They were both putting their bare feet up on the dining room table, the formal table, to compare frostbite remnants from that brutal cold winter when the Battle of the Bulge raged, and bodies were being stacked like cord wood all throughout the theater of war.

To this day, it may be the most flagrant display of how close my father actually came to dying on the fringes of the Adrienne Forest while serving in Patton's Army.

He'd been dispatched with a platoon of his fellow warriors to take out a fixed position of 88's, the German version of a Howitzer, and everything went sideways on them. From what I've been told, the Germans dropped one of the artillery pieces and shot directly into the platoon at point blank range. Most were killed instantly, some were captured, but it appeared that Dad was one of the few that remained in neither group. The massive concussion wave had blown him into some tangled brush and suspended him there, unconscious and out of sight of enemy forces who had swept the blast site looking for survivors.

Dad limped back to behind friendly lines and received immediate medical attention for his frostbite. For this encounter with the enemy and the wounds he'd garnered, he got his second Purple Heart. The first Purple Heart he earned was on the first night he was on the front lines after walking across Utah Beach in the ongoing Normandy Invasion. Germany's battle-hardened frontline soldiers quietly released a railroad car of explosives to roll undetected down a small hill into Dad's group of soldiers, known as K Company. They were dug in for the night as battles raged all around. When that train car exploded, Dad became one of the 94th Infantry's first soldiers wounded in action. They sent him to England to be patched up, then sent him right back to the frontlines to rejoin his brothers in action.

When asked about that event, he'd solemnly answer, "That was the longest walk of my life because I knew exactly what to expect."

Once Patton's Army broke out and started their long march into Germany, Dad and his fellow warriors liberated concentration camps all along the way. Many were very small, others considerably larger, but all were filled with despair and people wearing a death glaze in their eyes who had shrunk to nothing but bones and fear. Upon taking Frankfurt, they were told to stand down. Stalin would take Berlin, and the Allied Command was happy to leave the Russian military to absorb the casualties.

After *Victory in Europe Day* (VE Day), Dad was given the only job he ever liked when it came to his military service. For some unknown reason he was chosen to preside over the Four Seasons Hotel in Frankfurt, Germany. As a private, Dad got a real kick out of having delegations of dignitaries, senior officers and Heads of State ask him for permission to get a room. It appeared that some U.S. officer sensed a need to have others of much higher rank be forced to ask a lowly American private for permission to be allowed to stay in a room that was beside Patton's Command Center (which was right next door).

Dad got tipped heavily for room upgrades and special attention. He shared the wealth since everything was paid for in Marlboro and Lucky Strike cigarettes. Half of a cigarette paid for a haircut - Dad would give his German barber two whole cigarettes - big tipper us Pennsylvanians! Since Dad never smoked, and his ration was a couple cartons of cigarettes a week, he had plenty of smokes to barter with. He often claimed, *"...that was the richest I've ever been!"*

My oldest brother once bought an Opal car, manufactured in Germany. Dad about had a heart attack when he found out! Mum's observation concerning that episode was, "Sometimes I think he's still fighting the war..."

* * * * * * *

As for Max's visit with my father, they compared notes well into the evening. Their bonds were much more than a newly discovered friendship, for they truly were long lost brothers. After what they'd both endured, where they'd been, what they'd seen and how they both miraculously survived, their meeting brought them as close together as long-lost blood brothers. Two souls bound by the righteous sorrows of loved ones lost, days of their youth being far gone, and memories of war burned directly into their souls.

That was the only time that Dad and Max ever met.

Max passed away while staying near his son in the mountains of California. His kind heart finally gave out, but his spirit still soars anytime someone has a deep thought and an epiphany of inspiration.

Dad passed away on a Tuesday at 7:15 in the morning, just shy of his 91st birthday. He was loved by all of us. Dad is so dearly missed. Hardly a day goes by that I don't think about him and what kind of counseling he'd give me if he were still here amongst us. Yet no matter the advice, I am sure it would be delivered with wit, humor, and a loving smile!

In our small town of 1,100 people, well over 2,000 souls showed up to pay their heartfelt respects.

He was buried with full military honors.

* * * * * * *

Dad and Mum -- hard for me think of them as anything but together.

Mum smiles and often reminisces about the time that we met the President of the United States and his wife on that summer's evening outside the White House. Mum declares that was the only time she's ever seen Dad completely speechless! As for me, I wish I'd have been aware enough to know what the heck was going on.

Dad showed me how to get things done. He taught me to always go to the top first. So, following his advice, when I call a company or office, I always ask to speak with the owner first. If he isn't in, I will reluctantly speak with the CEO or president of the company. I've found that if they in turn inform the proper person in charge of that particular project or division, that things tend to get done so much faster, and, always with a whole lot less layers of unneeded corporate delay.

Having direct access is one of the major keys to being successful in many walks of life. Start at the top and work your way down.

* * * * * * *

One of the items that has confused me all of my life, is how so many young intelligent beautiful women will do almost anything to be part of the inner circles of the halls of power. The interns that lingered outside of the meetings I attended in D.C. were drawn to men twice their age with half their intelligence. They could do so much better, but yet, they willingly chose not to be liberated from that false illusion and how it so flagrantly diminished their essence.

I found that as unappealing then as much as I find it unacceptable today. Yet, nothing changes - as the same type of people still linger-in-waiting as they lust for power and access - two things that will elude them all of their lives if they make power and access their sole endeavor and criteria for who they align themselves with.

Poor souls.

* * * * * * *

Max liberated the hidden secrets of the universe by simply being himself. For he was a true savant when it came to applying the laws of physics coupled with conceptual mathematics and dynamic chemical interactions. Device design and ingenuity were gifts from GOD that allowed him to see beyond current reality into a realm of a better future for all of mankind.

Max Goldberger has a bronze plaque with his name upon it located at the extreme western point of the Big Island. He is forever immortalized on the Big Island for all to see if you know where to look. Just to make it a wee bit easier, simply look for the advanced solar array that tracks the sun from its rising to its setting on the distant horizon far across the sea.

It, just like Max's genius, faithfully points us towards the brilliance of innovation and imagination that shines bright, calling us to far distant shores previously undiscovered.

* * * * * * *

Dad routinely helped liberate souls that were fortunate enough to come into his daily life with joy, laughter and the wisdom of kindness by softly speaking life into them with the Gospel of CHRIST. During that first night on the frontlines, bleeding and tortured by the massive explosions going off all around, Dad had promised GOD to forever proclaim how he'd been saved from that night's rain of terror being cast down upon him. But, much more importantly, how he'd not only been saved from destruction, but that his immortal soul had been forever liberated by the very hand of GOD ALMIGHTY at that same moment in time.

After VE Day, Dad was given leave to come home for a brief time. Since he'd only been in the Army for less than half of his enlistment obligation, he was being staged for the imminent Invasion of Japan. It was going to be a bloody mess, estimates ran as high as hundreds of thousand of Americans being killed or wounded. Estimates for Japanese fatalities were projected to be in the millions.

Meanwhile, in Hawaii, my wife's father, Sakae Tanaka, was up for immediate enlistment in the 42nd Infantry. They had the horrific distinction of having obtained the highest casualty rates in all of WWII for any infantry outfit. Since they were of Japanese descent, they would be used in various roles - some expected to be outright nefarious - that would give rise to horrific losses once again.

With both of our fathers being readied for such an event, being staged for the pending invasion of the Japanese homeland, the odds that Faith and I would have ever been born were nearly zero. But then, Truman dropped the first nuclear bomb on Hiroshima. A few days later, he ordered the second one dropped on Nagasaki. With those earth shattering violent blasts, WWII came to an abrupt end.

Dad saw no more frontline action. In fact, he was allowed an early discharge due to having spent so much time on the frontlines while earning two Purple Hearts. As for Faith's Dad, he too got a reprieve enlisting at a later date. He remained on the Big Island working as a military liaison to build the new road between the mountains, known as Saddle Road. Sakae was fortunate enough to have never been deployed into an active war zone.

Yet, as fate would have it, that first atomic bomb, known as Little Boy, completely wiped out Hiroshima where the Japanese homeland portion of my wife's family resided! By the destruction of almost the entirety of her Japanese based extended family, two precious souls lived. James Parks Gourley and Sakae Tanaka, being from two vastly different worlds, miraculously survived the global tragedy known as WWII, allowing an unknown future to unfold before them.

And, in that unfolding, they became our Dads.

Life can be so strange as to be cosmically ironic.

23

Spirit of Adventure

"Good morning, please enjoy the flight."

AJG & FKG / 2001 - ongoing

* * * * * * *

Sunrise hinting to appear just over the eastern horizon, strange glossy white ice crystals formed as frost covered my brother Keith's backyard. No sound. No wind. Pure. Clean. High pressure Canadian air mass had formed directly above us. Dead calm before the storm of activity.

Keith did a big loop and dropped the envelope of the balloon at my feet. The tracks from the yard tractor and trailer left a perfect teardrop pattern in splintered frost allowing a pure dark crushed green to emerge from under its grasp. Bob and I immediately started tearing into the project at hand, launching a hot air balloon into the atmosphere. We had a 'window'. Being particularly rare phenomena, with perfectly calm air on the surface and ever-increasing winds aloft. Every few thousand feet of altitude allowed for another ten knots of wind. By ten thousand feet, we expected to accumulate over sixty knots of ground speed. Within 100 minutes, we'd be over 100 miles from this launch site.

Having pulled the envelope out flat, I couldn't help but notice the frost was virtually destroyed all around the work area. From starting on a frozen crackling surface, all things had crushed to a soft deep velvety green.

Keith peeked out from behind his very focused job of attaching the basket to the balloon's envelope. Four main cable hookups. A small menagerie of instruments and sensors with high-pressure propane hoses and related valves. All critical. Each singular item of profound importance. Together helping us with our desire to obtain our window of freedom, our aerial conveyor to points unknown. Keith looked, we nodded, and the inflation process went into tightly orchestrated high gear.

I held the long rope off the top of the balloon's envelope, not so much as to hold it down, but to perform the task of keeping it somewhat under control. I was a human anchor to keep the oscillations in check. Keith had pulled the starter cord on the portable fan unit, it choked and coughed like an old WWI era biplane being hand cranked to life. Sputter, sputter, cough... catching its fire and then blasting to life. With it roaring, a massive amount of cold air sucked off the frosty ground and blew into the rapidly inflating envelope now forming the classic hot air balloon shape. Staggered rainbow markings on a flat black background; the balloon was a custom masterpiece of quilted art.

Nobody talked. We'd all been here many times and simply did what we knew to do. Bob and Keith both were certified balloon instructors, I a mere helicopter pilot. As such I became their slave and did as I was assigned, nothing new here, as the youngest I'd become used to being "'assigned".

Frozen mist appeared softly as the day came on. You could smell the cold; it bit deep into our nostrils one inhale at a time. Exhales hung limpid, then fell down and joined the ice fog now starting to form. As the sun cracked the dawn, the entire atmosphere turned a strange golden-pink. It felt like we were working in a movie set lost in the arena of some foreign world's forested plateau.

I firmly allowed the envelope to pull me one way. Then I'd force it to succumb to my leverage and edge it back to being in line with the basket. Suddenly the fan stopped, and I knew that what had been a task was about to get serious. I kept an even hundredweight tension on the rope, added to the long lever of its location off the tip of the top of the balloon. The force counteracted the oscillating tons of air within the envelope that was half-moon full and ready for the next phase of the launch operations to bring it to a full inflation.

Keith hunkered into the wicker basket, checked the hoses on the four propane tanks one last time, struck a striker to ignite the pilot lights - smiled with the knowledge that this was getting very real and all was ready - and hit the burners with all they had! Two burners, configured to super-heat the fuel prior to burning, making everything into a controlled flamethrower of massive directed blue flames roaring. With the super-heated hot air being directed into the envelope, the balloon wanted to find a new balance, so I kept even more weight on it as it slowly filled. Then the balloon started to stand into the classic pose of being exactly what it had been created to be, a flight-of-fancy to dance along the pathways of currents far above the souls tethered on the ground and doing their daily tasks of mundane endeavors and vapid tasks assigned.

I glanced over at Bob, who was gathering some much-needed gear for the flight at hand. One cooler with who-knows-what? Two handfuls of winter wear, sorely needed as we'd gain altitude and lose even more of the surface temperature far below us. Carhartts and North Face jackets, odd colored snowmobile gloves and pastel extra-thick knit wool hats. Somebody was gearing up for a ferocious bout of cold, and it appeared that included me, judging from the large stack Bob was stuffing in beside Keith as he climbed in to join the fray. It was flagrantly apparent someone(s) had considerably more knowledge about the flight plan than I did. In the back of my mind I was starting to form a deep thought of *maybe we're to expect a longer, higher and wilder journey than I've been led to believe.*

I got a really big smile as I brought the header line to the basket, clipped it into the awaiting quick-snap, and asked the age-old question, "Captain, permission to climb aboard?"

My two older brothers just smiled, a smile I'd come to know, and I climbed in as the burners raged. The ground slowly disappeared below us, which was still enveloped by the ice fog's embrace. Just tips of Pennsylvania's finest hardwood timber still could be seen, thrust upwards grasping at the sky. The tree tops shown below us - proudly glowing in their fall colors of vibrancy above the thick layer of fog - giving everything a supernatural appearance in the coming dawn. As the ground continued to fall away, all around us turned to a deep clear blue, an effervescent ice blue, with the eastern horizon on fire. The burners announced to anyone keen enough to hear: *Freedom is flying above you! It is being declared to all you mere mortals so far below!*

* * * * * * *

"Is that Lake Erie?" I asked, seeing the earth's terrain to the north give way to a silver-white patch of mirrored glass. "If so, that would be Canada on the far side."

I stood with a hodgepodge of over-layered clothing struggled into in the cramp space allotted by the wicker basket. Bob and Keith had donned multiple layers like myself. For being pilots in a rather expensive toy, we all looked like Elmer Fudd on a really bad hair day! If we'd been seen on any street in America, some dear soul would have stopped us then given us each a buck or two to get a decent breakfast.

"Yeppers! Gotta' be Lake Erie. If we had a good set of binoculars, we'd probably be able to see the CNN Tower in Toronto. Look south. Follow the power plants' rising plumes of steam from their cooling towers. That must be deep into West Virginia. From this vantage point to our west has got to be Ohio...I've got it at four states and two countries!" Bob answered, taking a full turn to see all that could be seen. "Pennsylvania, New York, Ohio and West Virginia...add in Canada - our fifty-first state - and we just may have set a new record!" Bob confirmed what we all were gazing at.

Each of us lost in our own worlds, we looked off to different corners of the basket while snuggled in on the freight train known as the Jet Stream. We were going fast to the south-southeast, although within the confines of the basket, we had zero discernable wind. You could hold a match up and it wouldn't blow out.

"Where do you think we are?" I asked, not really caring.

"Three miles up plus, everything else is of no matter." Keith laughed, hit the burners while looking to gain even more altitude. By this time the ice fog had been swept clean off the ridgelines and hilltops, exposing a myriad of fall colors as the day came on and lit the world into a fall fire of leaves blazing. Every valley still clung tightly to their blankets of fog, allowing the terrain below to look like a huge wax rendition of a maker's seal having been thrust into an immense forest of confetti.

Softly at first, then obvious if you focused your attention between burns, the noise of an approaching jet became readily apparent. We all started to scan to see what was coming our direction... First a dot of black, then it became bigger and sported the vestiges of visible wings. We had a jet coming out of the east, a "sun-riser" most likely out of LaGuardia or Kennedy. And that early morning flight, a transcontinental commute, was headed directly at us.

"Exactly where does that altimeter claim we're at?" I looked past Keith, the designated Pilot In Command for our flight, and tried to see for myself.

"Just coming past eighteen five, still climbing..." Keith looked up as he hit the burners once again, making sure not to fry the Ripstop Nylon of the envelope while in the process of gaining more altitude.

"Did you set that thing at sea level or is that dialed into your yard?" I needed to know while feeling a bit weak in the knees. Knowledge has a way of doing that to a human. My internal math was declaring one more record was being set, and it had nothing to do with the number of states (or countries) within view.

"Dialed into my yard, we all know sea level is inappropriate for Appalachia. Why would you ever want to do constant mental math to find the obvious?" Keith laughed, and hit the burners once again.

All as the earth continued to get more oblique, the jet continued to find its own course, a course coming straight at us. In my helicopter training, the only way to spot a pending mid-air collision was to notice that the apparent motion of the aerial traffic in your space only got bigger. It never wavered on its relative position. When that occurred, the opposing traffic was coming directly at you! And someone better take evasive action immediately and without hesitation. Easy to do in a fixed wing or a helicopter, nose over and dive away from danger. Balloons didn't enjoy that quick response, one of the many reasons why they often refer to lighter-than-air machines as *The Ships of the Sky*.

Quickly that black dot got wings, then became an obvious jumbo jet rapidly increasing in size. Still coming out of the rising sun, it was aimed directly at our frail craft sitting majestic amongst the rays of the dawn. I simply allowed the reality to overcome all my trepidations. After all, should they ever discover our bodies amongst the wicker and Ripstop Nylon debris field strewn amongst the forests beneath, I believe that I probably would have earned a completely different epitaph on my future tombstone, one much less flattering:

+++ HE SCREAMED ALL THE WAY DOWN +++

I suppose that revelation was a bit of an absurd oddity to be had, as my morbid run-away thought process cascaded through my stunned frozen cortex.

Then, suddenly, a slight shift in the jet's flight path gave way to a new reality. It veered to the north the tiniest bit - and blew past us at over 500 miles per hour! One very vivid sight burned into my mind was a whole group of passengers, everyone who could find a window to press against, of a glorious 747 backlit by the sun! They were all gazing in awe at us, and our audacious maneuver of drifting along the Jet Stream without a care in the world. That 747 Jumbo Jet, framed for a split second's moment in time, appeared like a TV commercial staged by Hollywood's finest production teams.

They'd diverted just to give their passengers a glimpse of what freedom actually looked like. Sailing high above America, we exemplified the very essence of the *Spirit of Adventure*, which all souls yearn to discover at least once in their lifetimes.

Yet, until they'd diverted, we stood in amazement and prayed for the best. To this day I hope they didn't notice how much we looked like a rambling batch of hobos who'd hijacked a balloon while wearing Salvation Army mismatched outerwear. I preferred to think that they only saw our joyous smiles of flagrant confidence. And they didn't much notice our total sighs of relief as we waved at them. We were most appreciative of their observant pilots, and the wonderful choice they'd made not to tear our fragile craft to smithereens by sucking the hot air out of our envelope. Plummeting us to our doom so far below. All of us on board, forever would be lost, somewhere in the densest reaches of Western "by GOD" Pennsylvania's expansive hardwood forests.

What would they have told our parents!

* * * * * * *

Since it is distinctly frowned upon by the FAA to ever be above 10,000 feet - let alone 20,000 feet (plus) - in an open-air wicker basket without filing some formal type of flight plan, and, much more importantly, having oxygen onboard for at least the pilot, it is probably best not to admit to any such thing. It's probably best not to put the pilot in a position where he'd have to defend himself against such an obscure observation, specially an intrepid balloon pilot - looking like a frozen homeless man in hand-me-down clothing, sporting the grin of a daredevil in mid-leap while calmly searching for a soft landing far below the clouds - who was last observed by a 747's herd of gawking passengers going coast-to-coast at nearly the speed of sound.

Obviously, I must have been very mistaken in my reading of that "somewhat obscured" altimeter. Who Knows? Maybe it was defective? I would hate to get anyone in trouble; it's simply not in my DNA. I shall endeavor to be much less observant if the opportunity should ever present itself again.

* * * * * * *

Anyone who dares to believe that the Spirit of Adventure is still alive, and that it is available to all those valiant souls who seek to grasp its wonderful embrace. Those who are unwavering in their pursuit of the same, each one of them shall be rewarded by a hidden realm of wonder, amazement and overwhelming awe that only the chosen few - the bravest of souls amongst us - shall ever be permitted to discover.

24

Distant Shores

"Back in the day, we too were young."

AJG & FKG / 2010 - ongoing

* * * * * * *

"Nice truck, Frank! I do believe this is *Top Gear's* all-time award winning, pedestal worthy - preferred by terrorist networks worldwide - best pickup truck of all time!" I was admiring his classic Toyota pick-up as I climbed in beside him. He smiled, as we headed up to the high road, taking an early afternoon jaunt along the slopes of Hualalai Mountain then along Mauna Kea's western edge and over to the base of the Kohala Mountains and perfectly quaint Waimea Town where Kenzo lived.

"So what's the latest with Kenzo?" Frank glanced over and asked while we sauntered at old man speed, going 45 miles per hour in a 55 miles per hour zone. "What really happened that day you guys went skiing in Montana? Sounds like he took a brutal hard hit up on that mountain."

I looked over at him, one of the original crew, from days long gone, and asked, "Long version or short?"

"Long. We've got the better part of an hour ahead of us." He answered.

I looked at the road crawling by, and figured we had the better part of an hour *and then some...* so I started in on the long version of the day that changed more than one life.

"Kenzo flew in to meet us at Big Sky, Montana. Keith, Bob, Tim, and a few of our other ski buddies were getting together to spend a week on the slopes. Got a condo, bought some beer, got passes to the resort, and picked up Kenzo on the way to the mountain early the second morning. He'd come in on an overnight out of Honolulu. He got his pass for the week, and we all went skiing for the day. Such a strange sky day..."

I got really melancholy at this stage, trying to be bluntly accurate, as the day needed zero embellishment.

"When we got to the top of the lift, it was pure silver-grey. I mean everything was, so bizarre. Never quite saw anything like. It was like being inside of a dull grey cloud with nothing really in focus.

"Case in point, we were standing there trying to figure out a trail map... then suddenly Phil dropped, Kenzo dropped, then I landed on top of them! Here we were moving the entire time, even though we thought we were all stopped with our skis sideways on the slope. Being suspended in the ground fog and having these little pellets of snow dancing across our skis, we all lost perspective since we couldn't see a darned thing. One by one we fell off a tiny ledge and landed on each other."

I looked over at Frank to make my point clear, "We were caught in pure flat light conditions *on steroids*. I'm telling you, to this day it was one of the strangest atmospheric conditions I've ever encountered. And, to make it even wickeder, it would come and go as we changed altitude; one moment crystal clear, with huge blue sky above us, then a few hundred feet on down-slope, we'd get this granular snow waft across our slope, often dancing uphill. Sometimes only a few inches thick, covering our skis, making our feet invisible. Hard to judge speed any type of relative motion. Then, out of nowhere, it would thicken to the point where you could only see the heads and shoulders of those closest to you."

I shook my head, looked at Frank, looked at his Toyota's speedometer, and thought *obviously I should have driven.*

Frank really got what I was trying my best to describe. "You know, we used to get similar conditions raging off the coast of Alaska. When the winds howled and the waves went berserk, we'd have such poor visibility from the salt spray and gloom that we couldn't see the lobster pots we were holding in our own hands! Treacherous to say the least; lost a few good men while we were out there... So, this is your first day of skiing at Big Sky? Had any of you ever been there before? Hear that it's radically pristine, still virtually untouched."

"Right on all points: first time there, first day skiing, awesome gorgeous with views forever. From the top of Lone Peak, you can see the Grand Tetons one direction and well into Canada to the north. What a spooky place. One step out of the gondola, and you are directly perched on the very top of Lone Peak. Two sides are pure death with thousand-foot shear drops. One side's a triple black diamond on steroids - that way has a nasty chute - rock outcroppings lining the first thousand-plus feet of vertical drop. None of us dared that choice.

"Then you have the only really survivable route - the double black diamond run. Burnt our legs off while getting back to more normalized terrain. Took at least twenty minutes to get back down to oxygen levels where we could actually breath."

I was starting to get to the point in the tale where I got very sullen in my conversation, for the day quickly had taken a turn no one ever wished to endure.

"So anyways, there's Kenzo after we'd done a half dozen or so runs. One of them being off of Lone Peak and the borderline terror it provided us. He was huffing and trying to get his bearings. Seemed so fatigued. After all, he'd just landed a few hours earlier. We'd just had lunch, if you can call it that. Ten-dollar hotdogs and seven-dollar beers. For the seven of us, we spent well over a hundred bucks for next-to-nothing. Typical resort pricing." everything in the story was some type of lament.

I was shaking my head, not just at the price of the lunch, but also at our slow-pace as we continued along our journey of getting across the western slopes of the Big Island. Frank's driving always sucked, much like his guitar playing. Zero touch wrapped into tone-deaf skills.

"So, what happened to Kenzo?" Frank wanted me to pick up the pace, even if he wasn't.

"Getting there. After lunch, most of the guys were gearing up for round two of getting some more runs in. Cold as anywhere I'd ever skied, frozen snot-nosed-death-chill cold. Highest temperature I saw all week was plus five. Middle of the day, and it was still twenty to thirty below the freeze point, add a bit of wind and it was brutal Arctic nasty."

Frank nodded, he knew Arctic cold conditions. He lived them for the better part of ten years running.

"So, one of my Pennsylvanian friends looked at me, and said 'Let's call it a day. Find the hot tub and relax. There's only a few more hours of daylight and these conditions suck.' So, I agreed, and we turned to go. But then, I saw Kenzo there. He was looking abnormally ragged-around-the-edges, so I asked him to join us. He declined and went to go with some of the guys back towards the lift. I asked him again, but this time I got right in his face. 'Come on, man! Let's call it a day.' We'd be right back out there the next day. Hopefully those crazy flat light conditions - all of this wicked haze - would disappear and we'd have deep blue skies like they put in their advertising posters."

I stopped, not wishing to continue with the next phase of my story, for it was very hard for me to tell. Frank glanced over at me, giving me a minute to get a grip and continue at my own pace. Much like I was trying my best with his old fart driving - ten miles under the speed limit - which was on rampant display.

"Well Kenzo laughed, you know how he is, and went with the guys to get a few more runs in. I saw him go, and that was the last time the Kenzo you and I knew so well -- the laughing, happy, brilliant, witty, capable fellow we both grew up with surfing, diving, running around with in all types of adventures from the mountains to the sea... -- well, that was the last time I ever saw that version of Kenzo..."

I had to turn away and look out the window at the magnificent peak of Mauna Kea coming into view far above us, trying my best to find a bit of fortitude to continue on with my version of that day's events.

"I got a call on the house phone in the condo. They'd rushed Kenzo to the Aid Station and they were asking me, his closest known friend, to meet him there. First, I thought that he'd broken a leg or some other stupid thing. But when I got there, it was so far worse than I could have ever imagined! I almost passed out at how mortal he looked as they switched him from the slope-side gurney to the table in the de-facto trauma room. He was quivering all over, blood all down his ski suit - which was being removed with a huge pair of shears. Cut right off of him without hesitation by the trauma team at the directions of the doctor. He was coughing and spitting up blood. It was so gruesome... I asked the trauma doctor if he was going to live?"

I got so sullen that I could barely continue, for that day's imagery was so difficult for me to wish to recall. I was only doing it so Frank knew the true details, the sordid facts of that moment-in-time's tragic unfolding. After all, Frank was one of us and deserved to know.

"Well the doctor looked right at me, and gave me his expert analysis, 'Maybe. The next three hours are crucial. Are you family?' I answered, no, 'but I'm the closest he has here and now.'

"The entire world stopped, he looked directly at me and forced a promise out of me, 'I am counting on you to call his family immediately. They absolutely need to know their son is in critical condition and is going to be airlifted to Montana's only Trauma Center. His ETA should be within the hour. They'll most likely operate on him without permission the instant he arrives. His life is in a perilous state and he needs the best in surgical care we can get him to. He needs it NOW! Are you going to call them? I need to know I can count on you. YES? Or NO?' I answered, knowing how important his question was. 'I will take care of it. I know his parents very well.'"

I looked down at my feet as the Big Island flowed by. I could hardly believe how many internal emotions were cascading through my brain.

"So what bit him up there? How exactly did he crash and burn?" Frank asked, not caring about my internal batch of raging emotions.

Seemed that driving at wrap factor zero was taking all of his efforts.

"I'll get there in a moment... You know I had to call his parents. That was the single hardest phone call I've ever had to make. Tell them one of their favorite sons was being transported via life flight to Montana's only Trauma Center in critical condition. No one knew if he'd live through the day. When I told his Dad over the phone, he broke down and cried... I did too." I became fully downcast, but then I pressed into the story, "You know Kenzo's parents treated me like their fourth son. I stayed at their place and ate many-a-meal with them."

Yet, I got a grip and answered Frank's lingering question. "What bit him? It appears that one of the Snow Cat operators cut a small wall across the middle of a run, for no apparent reason, and didn't mark it in any way. Flat light conditions being prevalent, Kenzo skied right off of it, caught his tips and slapped face first onto hard-packed groomed snow! He must have never seen it coming. Full force faceplant! Cracked his upper vertebrate, almost bit his tongue off and got multiple subdural hematomas. Three to be exact, front, side and rear - bruises deep into his brain - three was three too many. When he got to the Trauma Center, they immediately relieved the pressure on his brain from the massive swelling by performing emergency surgery. Then as per protocol, they put him into an induced coma. They kept him in it for over three weeks. About a month later they discharged him. Kenzo didn't know his name, could barely speak any words or form sentences.

"Frank, to make it clear how dire his 'change' was, he didn't even know what a fork was! Let alone how to use it." I got my bravery back and continued with the facts of Kenzo's injuries as best as I knew them. "To put this into context and using the proper medical terminology, Kenzo suffered three extreme Traumatic Brain Injuries, known as TBIs. He's never been the same since."

Then I got real serious with the next bit of what happened during the course of my experience following Kenzo's crash on the mountain. "You know, when his brothers flew in, they sat me down and informed me of *the question* that the doctors bluntly asked them."

"What was that?" Frank was in shock from what all I was describing. Suddenly he knew what I did, and it really spooked him.

"Well the three of us sat there and discussed whether to *pull the plug* or not. It was that bad. It was blatantly obvious to each of us that the Kenzo we loved would never walk amongst us again. Doctors used phrases like: *'Life altering event.' 'Questionable quality of life.' 'Unknown recovery timeline.' 'Might never speak again.' 'Might never walk again…'* By the time they got to that flagrantly horrific version of his future - a prognosis given to us by surgeons who were tops in their field - we all hung our heads in exasperation and retreated into our own worlds." I quietly offered as the ride turned flagrantly solemn.

"Finally, we convinced ourselves that we had to give Kenzo a fighting chance. We all knew that he certainly deserved it. But we also knew he would never wish to be an invalid or worse… Like being a vegetable and left to rot in some nursing home, simply being warehoused and waiting to die. We really did not know what to do. It was the worst decision I've ever been part of…"

"It was that nasty? Wow! I never knew. He seems sorta' OK to me, at least on the phone." Frank tried his best to sort out this new batch of information he'd never heard before.

"I give tremendous credit to his parents. They nursed him back from the land-of-the-almost-dead to the land-of-the-living. With their help, Kenzo became fairly normalized. But you and I both know, the Kenzo we loved is far-gone. His memories are like a deck of cards shuffled, re-shuffled, then shuffled again. He gets some of the facts right, but they're all intermingled by timeline and who was actually there." I just laughed since I had learned that correcting him would be overwhelmingly futile. "Frankly we just have to adjust, laugh, and enjoy this version, our New Kenzo. He's far better than I'd originally hoped for, especially after what the doctors had told us while he laid there being kept alive by that myriad of machines."

We rode in silence for miles before the conversation picked back up.

"So Frank, how are you doing? Figure out what's bugging you yet?" I asked about his most recent trip to the doctor in Kona. He'd moved back to the islands after his elderly mother passed away. He too was searching for a past we'd all seen evaporate decades earlier.

"From the tests, I've got a lump at the bottom of my esophagus. I'm heading to Honolulu later in the week to find out what's going on."

"It was impossible not to notice at Thanksgiving that you actually took time to chew. Here I thought you'd given up your Neolithic ways. Maybe got a touch of class, even became a bit refined. But it simply turns out you just can't inhale food like you used to." I laughed, "Think of the benefits, now you'll actually be able to taste what you're eating! And, you can at long last act civilized in polite society." Trying to make the best of what appeared to be dire news.

"First time ever..." Frank offered as we turned left at the main intersection in Waimea Town. On our way to track down Kenzo -- the New Kenzo -- while trying our best to reconnect with the youth each of us had obviously left so far behind. Somehow the three of us had gone from *The Incredible Quest for Surf* to being the old geezers we used to make fun of. Time chews into even the toughest amongst us.

Back in the day we used to watch Roberts Tour Company's buses unload elderly tourists at the beach parks, people from all across America's heartland, having come to find paradise five decades too late. On a discounted Hawaiian Tour Package -- much like my very first exposure to Hawaii via Your Man Tours -- older folks on that proverbial *trip of a lifetime*. Yet, they were so far past their prime that the tour guides' first duty when they disembarked was to hand out walkers, canes, and oxygen bottles. Crutches and a helping hand to the folks were provided to those who'd waited too long to discover even the tiniest sliver of Paradise they could only view through the bus's glass windows and never participate in.

I can remember seeing some of them cry -- overwrought with emotions and tears flowing down their cheeks -- as they finally became aware of what they had put off for oh-too-long. What they had made tepid decisions to never find. They had chosen the easy path, the gentle slope. They'd never once get to swim in crystal blue waters or climb amongst the raging waterfalls and linger long enough to find their inner solace of experiencing the true joy that the islands could deliver, being an amazing inner-peace to even the most stoic of souls.

Sometimes you would see one sobbing profusely, not for what they saw, but for how they'd chosen to live their lives, which had folded behind them. How at each and every fork along life's uncertain byways they had never risked, dared or chosen even one single touch of adventure. They were sobbing for all that they'd missed, how they'd so willingly embraced shallow dreams frozen against a horizon never found.

Frank, Kenzo, and I had never suffered from their chosen fate of being trapped in a vapid world called: Normal. Tepid. Tiny. Small.

Yet - much like them - we too were yearning to recover something we could no longer grasp: a faded reality we often dreamed about as our days waxed fallow and our nights afforded us enough quiet to fully visualize the memories of yesteryear's journeys and adventures, joys and loves. All were evaporating into the mists of time. We truly were those outrageous souls who had packed our own personal histories full of a myriad of wild adventures.

Stories too true to be believed.

But now, all was obscured by time and our own versions of what had really transpired. Each of us had our own perspective of those fabled events, which had shaped our lives. What each of us had lost, and more importantly, what each of us had gained along the journey's way.

We had grabbed the reins of life with unfettered passion, as the world raged vibrant all around us. For that reason alone, we had no remorse.

You see, back in the day, we too were young.

* * * * * * *

Kenzo's wipeout on that fateful ski slope of Big Sky, Montana rocked my world. It changed him forever. It took the ability of being who he'd become, a brilliant man overseeing hundreds of realtors while helping to orchestrate one of the biggest growth cycles of real estate going on in the nation. From that peak in his life, he became somewhat of a recluse. Who was once vibrant and outgoing amongst men, became tucked away and quietly awkward. His speech abilities, which were par excellence, never came back, although, to his credit, he never lost his trademark smile or his ability to join the day with kindness. Kenzo became a fixture in Waimea, riding his bike to the local shops and restaurants, living in the moment -- literally one day at a time since any type of planning was impossible. With his diminished abilities, he embraced every single day as if it were his last walk upon the face of GOD's green earth. There is something profoundly elegant about that.

The last time I spoke with him, his health had deteriorated to such a degree that he couldn't hold a thought or complete a conversation without getting totally lost along the way. Now he has gotten to the point where interaction of any kind that takes him to either new ground or into past worlds is not only impossible but is outright painful. Case in point, his last words to me were, "As soon as we hang up, I won't even know I've been on the phone... let alone who you are..."

The Kenzo I knew and loved, my fellow surf ninja, dive partner, shark encounter guru, and very best friend, perished in flat light conditions in a place known for its clear skies and tamed wilderness experience. That civilized wilderness claimed a life that day, for unfortunate but true, you do not have to be dead to be dead.

* * * * * * *

Frank Lee actually did give a damn. He too enjoyed the status of having worked his way into many people's hearts. Upon arrival from our sojourn to rediscover Kenzo -- our New Kenzo -- we got back to his bungalow (man cave) overlooking the lava flats of North Kona. He traded tech work for a place to stay with a fishing buddy of his from back in the day.

When we got there, he picked up his Les Paul -- now a classic guitar worth tens of thousands of dollars -- plugged it in to his Peavey Amplifier. He proceeded to rip into a rocking Van Halen song, "Aint Talkin' Bout Love." It was one of his favorite heart-pumping tunes we used to blast while crisscrossing Maui searching for perfect waves. Frank tore into his rendition with passion, flare, and skills I'd never seen him display before.

It was truly awesome to behold! Somehow, Frank had developed rhythm. I just felt blessed he didn't try to sing. I presume working on a vessel in some of the world's most treacherous waters - while doing the "World's Most Dangerous Catch" on raging seas - can allow a fellow to discover musical skills in his downtime. Who would have ever known?

I was pretty glad that I'd never launched his Les Paul off the cliff at South Point after all.

Frank's diagnosis concerning the lump in the base of his throat came back dire, extremely unfortunate. Frank had esophageal cancer in an advanced stage. Most people only last a few weeks to months after receiving such blatantly horrific news. Frank lived for nineteen months. Beating all of the odds. During all that time he still managed to catch a massive Pacific blue marlin off the western edge of Oahu near Ka'ena Point in the Kauai Channel. Once again, Frank went fishing in some of the most formidable waters in the world. His spirit of adventure never once diminished, even as his days grew short.

Frank Lee - master student, astrophysicist, huge wave surfer, gorilla diver, enjoiner of all things dangerous - died on a Sunday morning overlooking the waters of a clear blue sea.

Frankly I did give a damn. His passing was extraordinarily hard to take. My only solace is that he is now discovering the Distant Shores of GOD's limitless creation.

I had the profound honor of writing his eulogy. Flaws and all, here it is:

Frank Lee (1955 - 2012)

It was very hard for me to learn that Frank had passed away a few Sundays ago. The complications from his cancer and surgery had proven to be too much of a burden to live with, and he is now no longer with us.

He truly was "The Man, The Myth, The Legend" in so many ways. I'll remember him as the roommate who was brilliant, witty, very observant and always prepared to do something - virtually anything really! From diving to surfing to skiing to doing all three in one single day - he was always ready to go. And I do believe that he was the living example of "sleep is highly overrated!" Most guys had an impossible time keeping up; most girls tended to give him a lot of "space." After all, back in the day, one of his nicknames was "Neanderthal"!

Frank was absolutely fearless, but not stupid in his executions and pursuits. He taught me how to dive in Hot Springs at Pohoiki. After a short five-minute "course" in three feet of warm water, I dove with him for the next two years on Maui in wild conditions, in Superman Currents and under Cloud Breaks that would make the most rugged souls shudder, always in pursuit of the every elusive lobsters for dinner. It was finally determined that I needed to get certified so I could pick up the tanks. I still have a sneaking suspicion that it was really so that I could PAY for the tanks for a change!

With Frank I surfed "Caves" at Honolua. We looked at the planets in the U. H. observatory on top of the mountain while listening to ear splitting rock and roll and drinking white wine, stayed in Kapalua, drank beers at The Blue Max in Lahaina Town listening to George Harrison and George Benson in their pick-up group and chatting with them between sets, chased girls, watched him get way better on guitar, went on the six month odyssey known as the "Incredible Quest For Surf." Later in life it got more mundane as we talked about investment strategies. The list goes on and on...

But above all, we grew up together in a far away land, known as Hawaii Nei.

We will all miss Frank Lee, friend, sailor, poet, warrior. He made my life such a more interesting place to live in. I am sure that there are people scattered all around the planet, that we don't have a clue about, whom will miss him greatly also.

God's speed dear friend. May our journeys cross paths again. May God Almighty embrace you by showing you the physics of the universe and the chemistry of His Divine Love.

Aloha Oi,

Allen and Family

25

Earthen Vessels

"The best is yet to be."

AJG & FKG / 2019 - ongoing

* * * * * * *

Steel grey skies all around, prancing lightly on frozen ground, whistling winds from the far north. Everything nasty, frozen and bored... It feels like it's been ten winters in a row without something divergent or new. I tracked down Faith - in her sewing room of course - and asked the age-old question, "How long is a Pennsylvanian winter?"

"Until your tan freeze-dries right off of you. And then... Like... Forever!" She gently smiled. Flipped over the quilt she was working on, and asked with a simple nod whether I liked it?

"Best quilt ever!" I answered her silent question, trying to keep things positive, even on a wicked-cold winter's day. "I love having that off-pink highlighted by a soft-brown. Who would have ever known they'd go together that well?" Then I got a deep thought, "Sort of like when your parents met me, they never believed that their lovely daughter -- their very own *Sansei Princess* -- would go together so well with some *Pennsyltuckey* farmer from half-a-world-away."

Faith smiled, laughed, and added, "See what love can do."

"And frozen winters," I added, not yet past my melancholy stage.

"And three kids... three wonderful kids." She offered, not really speaking to me, but to life at large.

"We should go see them. All of them." I had a deep anti-winter thought and with wild abandon threw it into the conversation.

"OK." She put the quilt down and immediately went downstairs to make arrangements for multiple flights to multiple cities.

"You know, I saw an article in the *USA Today,* and it listed the ten most expensive cities in America to live in," I mentioned in between phone calls.

"And..." Faith knew I had some type of point, even if I didn't always get to it very directly.

"Our children just happen to be living in three of them. Each managed to find somewhere that has Hawaiian pricing without ever having to leave the Mainland!" I had a bit of exasperation in my voice.

"We are so fortunate." Faith smiled and continued to wait on hold as the airline's representative played on their network to figure out the best legs from Pittsburgh to Boston to Daytona to Denver. Then, while we were at it, on out to Hilo to get away from the dull grey and find a touch of natural Vitamin D for our frozen un-tanned winter existence. "We might as well keep going, once we're packed and all..." She had made an executive decision.

I nodded. Nothing more needed saying, so it wasn't.

We surprised the heck out of our oldest daughter Domino by showing up out of the blue for no apparent reason. We bought her some food, took her shopping, and enjoyed Boston for a bit of time. If we hadn't asked where Talon was one-too-many times, we'd have surprised him completely. But since we were there, it was surprise enough. We didn't surprise Tiffany at all. Apparently, brothers and sisters actually know how to communicate without parental guidance. She surprised us at the airport, waiting when we walked off the escalator, and welcomed us to Denver. It was wonderful.

Two out of three ain't too bad...

We were a bit off of our game, and as the years sauntered past, they had gotten considerably better at theirs. All of our kids, each of them, were becoming their own *force-of-nature* and finding their own calling into a future that beckoned them to enjoin the fray.

To discover their own journeys and to make their own choices while embracing the future's unknowable pathways called life.

All so uncertain, but yet, all they really desired was to be on life's ultimate pathway called the *Spirit of Adventure,* for they intrinsically knew the best is yet to be!

Faith and I used to be in charge of everything. We controlled every aspect of their worlds. Drive here. Go there. Approve this. Deny that. Find them a way to succeed and find them a way back home. At one time, we were integral in all aspects of their little worlds. Then, as time flowed by, we became less involved. Yet, still many decisions were ours to nod "yes" or shake our heads "no". Either way, our decisions still kept importance in their day-to-day worlds of motion and intent.

Now, we've gone from being completely absorbed and involved to being merely observers. Such a strange divergence from whom we'd been into a place where we currently are... I'm not even sure when the change occurred or exactly how it happened? But, it is well upon us and it has now become our new normal.

As they all finished college, challenges for them diverted from getting good grades to embracing the joy of bravely blazing a trail into an unknowable future.

"Do you think that I'd be selling out if I moved to Hawaii?" Domino asked me one evening after she'd gotten her degree from Boston University. We were sitting on the "Foyer Couch" where we often found ourselves when deep thoughts intersected with deeper questions. Every home needs a Foyer Couch.

"Not at all. You were born in Hawaii. You know that when you were a newborn in the nursery -- less than a day old -- your two grandpas were gazing through the glass, both had the same question rolling around in their heads: *Does she look more Japanese? Or more haole? Who's side will she take after?* Both of your granddads were thinking the exact same thing."

Domino looked at me and asked, "Are you making some type of point? Or is this some sidetrack so you can think something else through?" She smiled in her oh-too-observant cute way. I had my arm around her. I was in my *Daddy* element and there was no place I'd rather be.

"Hawaii is yours for the taking. But you will have to claim it as your very own domain without remorse or trepidation. Friends will come easy. Really good dynamic awesome friends -- the kind I found after many a misstep -- are much harder to grasp hold of and keep. You must *earn* their love. They've known many who came and went, interlopers are so common that they've got a sixth sense of who's for real and in it for the long run. And, likewise, who isn't."

I really enjoyed our Foyer Couch conversations. They tended to bring out everyone's deepest longings and desires. "Hawaii is your absolute birthright. But to truly own it you'll have to grasp it with both hands, beat it into submission, and make it your personal kingdom. It can by your Eden if you let it."

"I can be a princess...a *Princess in Paradise*..." She laughed with her revelation that going to Hawaii wasn't a sellout or escape from reality. But that it was a challenge of Biblical proportions and could involve a most excellent future with many possibilities unfounded, with stories yet to be told.

"Honey, my loving daughter, you have always been my Princess! But, in this case you will be a *Yonsai Princess*. Fourth generation." I told the truth, as all good Foyer Couch conversations demanded. "You will have so much to live up to...one item being finding the right man worthy of your reclaimed *royal* bloodline!"

She hit me - more than a swat. I probably deserved it.

Within a year, she not only had most excellent friends, but they too had embraced the *Spirit of Adventure* like generations before their time had. She called home on a Pennsylvanian winter's night. Wind blowing. Frozen world all around. She couldn't wait to tell me about her latest adventure with her friends off the coast of Kona and what she'd discovered.

"I went Black Water Diving last night!" Domino offered with a real intense joy in her voice.

"Night diving?" I asked, not too impressed but trying not to allow my lack of enthusiasm to be noticed through the phone lines.

"No, Dad -- *Black Water Diving*!" she said with emphasis. "We took a boat out off the coast to where it is 8,000 feet deep under a new moon with only stars above us. Then we dropped a halo of lights over the side, let them down to about 60 feet, put our gear on and dove down to hang out with the creatures of the abyss that came up to check on the lights!" She was so excited it made the phone tingle.

"You did that willingly?!" I was shocked.

"We saw so many things: invertebrates, angler fish, bioluminescent creatures with names too long to pronounce or remember. We were completely engulfed by glowing critters. IT WAS AWESOME!"

She couldn't have been happier. She was in her new world, her personal sliver of a New Eden. She'd become a Kona Girl with an adventuresome pack of adrenaline warriors. She couldn't have been more ecstatic than if she had been granted superpowers.

I couldn't have been prouder. "That's great! Here's your mother, I'm sure she'll want to hear this firsthand. Love you. Please don't forget to have some fun while you're at it!" I handed the phone to Faith so she too could embrace the joy of having our daughter diving deep into the blackest-ink of a moonless-sea. All while coaxing some of the most bizarre creatures out of one of the world's deepest abysses to enjoy the evening with her and her batch of adventuresome souls she'd discovered along her journey's way.

What mother wouldn't want to hear that!

* * * * * * *

So many stories, so many adventures, but most of them are now being found and enjoyed by our children and those around them. I am sure that we are only hearing the "tamer versions" and that many of the details of their exploits are kept from our knowledge.

That's OK. We were the same way with our parents. Although, I suspect, that our parents knew way more than we ever imagined.

Parents are like that.

I can't in good conscience or good form tell their tales - their intrepid journeys of life - for it is not my place to do so. Should they ever wish to put some ink on paper, to cast their own life's pathways out to the world at large, then they will have to choose to do that on their very own. After all, they have earned their own stories and adventures as a very personal walk along life's byways.

Faith and I have been so blessed, not only are we together, but we truly have become one.

One mission. One joy. One life. One future...

*Our wondrous gift of a life, from a magnificent G*OD*, who called us forward onto a path rarely taken, far beyond anything we could have ever imagined while orchestrating a future for us to fully embrace. Complete with the divine joy of being constantly amazed by such truths... we've come to realize that we are wondrously wrought. Simple* **Earthen Vessels** *molded by H*IS *loving hands, glazed in the fire of creation and then lovingly tossed into an outrageous world of -*

Friends that became like family...

Family that became like best of friends...

Joys too many to remember...

Adventures too wild to imagine...

Sorrows too painful to ever forget...

Love is like that. For it truly is the adventure - this adventure called Life.

Sometimes all I can remember of those days gone by is my innocent childhood, back when life was amazing and wild adventures abounded all around me.

*Often, in the midst of the night, when my world is quiet and my mind finally rests, H*IS *voice calls me to never forget those simpler times and that long forgotten vision of having...*

Black sand on my outstretched hands...

Epilogue

* * * * * * *

"Searching for Paradise can be such an adventure..."

* * * * * * *

"I'm thinking of starting a new club. A rather exclusive club to be joined by only the bravest of souls." I offered to my lovely daughter Tiffany.

"Oh?" She allowed me to continue with my deep thought.

"I'm thinking that it could be formed as a modern day tight-knit group of friends and family that searches out the very best of life to embrace."

"Like food and stuff?" She played along.

I hadn't thought of the food aspect, but it intrigued me. "Finding epicurean delights along the way might make an excellent component of our theoretical club's ongoing quest to span the globe with joy and love. All while chasing dreams and exploits as we spread a tiny bit of light into the world at large. Excellent food is always welcome, Tiffany Esq., but I'm thinking more like the 'stuff' portion of the equation."

"OK then, Dad. What kind of stuff?" She asked, slightly more involved by this point in our ongoing banter. She appeared glad that I'd so readily included one of her favorite things, food. She always liked it when I included her suggestions.

"Well... I'm thinking like surfing, skiing, climbing, scuba diving, blue water hunting, flying all kinds of craft across the skies and whatever-it-is that you younger folks think qualifies as being categorized as "brave" in a world without limits." I had my answer somewhat rehearsed.

"Maybe like heli-skiing in the Swiss Alps?" She offered as an inspired example, really embracing my vision. "So, who all might join such an elite gathering of souls?"

"Well, if you are a direct descendent of Grandpa G., that alone should qualify." I once again was ready with an answer. "And, if you submit a true story in writing for review by the members. Should it be grand enough, wild enough, kind enough - or simply great enough - they too could join our illustrious band of intrepid action warriors."

"What about Mom?" She threw at me, the lawyer in her needed to adapt for every eventuality.

"Well of course your Mother. She is already a member. After all, she married me! She is perfectly fearless, as you well know. With me as her husband, what could be more of an adventure than that?" I saw where she was headed and immediately adapted.

"Ahhhh... touché," She enjoyed the banter. "So, what might a small gathering of 'invited souls' call such an epic club?"

"I've been thinking about that, I am planning on calling it...

+++ The Paradise Lost Adventure Society +++

"I do believe it has a nice ring to it. Surely it exemplifies the goal of the quests we'd all be embarking upon, searching for life's adventuresome journey's way."

"I like that. I can expect to be a charter member?"

"Absolutely!" I was more than enthusiastic.

"Sign me up!" She laughed, "and Dad, when does our next adventure begin?"

"Well Talon wishes to be the first in the family to step foot upon the Continent of Antarctica... you know... he just might need a few chaperones...

*All that raced through Tiffany's mind was...***FIELD TRIP!***

The Epic Series:

Rain Falling On Bells

Book 1:

Fragments Of Truths

Rain Falling On Bells

Book 2:

Deep Blue Secrets

Rain Falling On Bells

Book 3:

Joy Dawn

Rain Falling On Bells

Book 4:

Courageous Dragonflies

Rain Falling On Bells

Book 5:

Brave Love

Also by Author:

THE GOLD ILLUSION

"SUMMER RAINS"

*

THE LEATHERWOOD

A HISTORICALLY INACURRATE NOVEL GONE WONDEROUSLY ASTRAY

*

EARTHEN VESSELS

--- TRUE ADVENTURES OBSCURED BY TIME ---

ALL BOOKS ARE

AVAILABLE AT:

* * * * * *

* * * * * *

AMAZON

BOOKS

* * * * * *

* * * * * *

PAPERBACK

E-BOOK

Made in the USA
Columbia, SC
29 June 2021